THE
Yukon Fact
BOOK

THE Yukon Fact BOOK

Everything YOU Ever Wanted
To Know About The Yukon

Mark Zuehlke

Whitecap Books
Vancouver/Toronto

Edited by Elizabeth McLean
Proofread by Lisa Collins
Cover design and illustrations by Rose Cowles
Interior design by Warren Clark

Printed and bound in Canada

Canadian Cataloguing in Publication Data

Zuehlke, Mark
    The Yukon fact book

    ISBN 1-55110-716-3

    1. Yukon Territory. I. Title.
FC4007.Z83 1998   971.9'1   C98-910658-6
F1091.Z83 1998

The publisher acknowledges the support of the Canada Council and the Cultural Services
Branch of the Government of British Columbia in making this publication possible. We
acknowledge the financial support of the Government of Canada through the Book Publishing
Industry Development Program for our publishing activities.

Contents

T

V

W

Y

Acknowledgements

Completion of this book would have been impossible without the assistance of literally dozens of people in federal departments, the territorial government, national parks, territorial parks, federal and territorial historic sites, territorial museums, territorial and community tourist information centres, and many other information outlets too numerous to mention.

Patricia Acton provided extraordinary assistance in searching out information and bringing me back voluminous bundles of research material from Whitehorse. Rob and Syd Cannings also provided some excellent information.

Frances Backhouse was endlessly supportive throughout the research and writing of this book. Her companionship was especially welcome during a research trip to the Yukon.

Introduction

In any given year several hundred thousand travellers come to the Yukon. When asked their reason for visiting the territory, the most common answer is to experience wilderness. This is not surprising. There are precious few places in the world where it remains possible to wander for trackless days through truly untrammelled wilderness. On a global scale, the world's wilderness is so reduced today that, excluding Antarctica but including the Arctic, scientists estimate only 26 percent of the planet can still be classified as wilderness. In the north and central Americas it totals 41 percent. Europe has just 3 percent of its land mass classified as wilderness. Yukon? Approximately 80 percent.

Admittedly, most visitors experience the Yukon through the windshield of a vehicle while trundling along the Alaska and Klondike highways, rather than from a ridgeline of the Tombstone Range or a canoe on the Yukon River. This is unfortunate because there are few places in the world where it is possible to walk for kilometre after kilometre through lush forests and along mountain ridges without seeing a trail left by humans or another person for days at a stretch.

While this book is about much more than the Yukon's wilderness expanses, I think their reality informs almost every page and sets the geography, the history of its peoples, and the challenges they face today in preserving the land within a perspective necessary for understanding this vast landscape, more populated by wildlife than by humanity.

This book attempts to encapsulate as much factual information about the Yukon as possible—to give a sense of the territory's rich soul and unique heritage. This process, of course, could be endless so the limiting constraint was that it must all fit into one easily used and read volume. That's the big-picture purpose behind this book, but it's also hoped the facts contained here will make some enjoyable and informative reading on a subject-by-subject level that will enhance both residents' and visitors' understanding of Canada's most accessible northern region.

It should be noted that, while most Yukon communities are listed herein, there was no attempt to include them all. The decision to include one community and not another was, however, not completely arbitrary. Communities listed and the details in their descriptions were selected on the basis of what that information contributed to the sense of who Yukoners are and how they live now, or have lived in the past.

This is also not a book of biography. So, while many people are mentioned, far more who played, or continue to play, an important role in the territory's life and development will not be found in these pages.

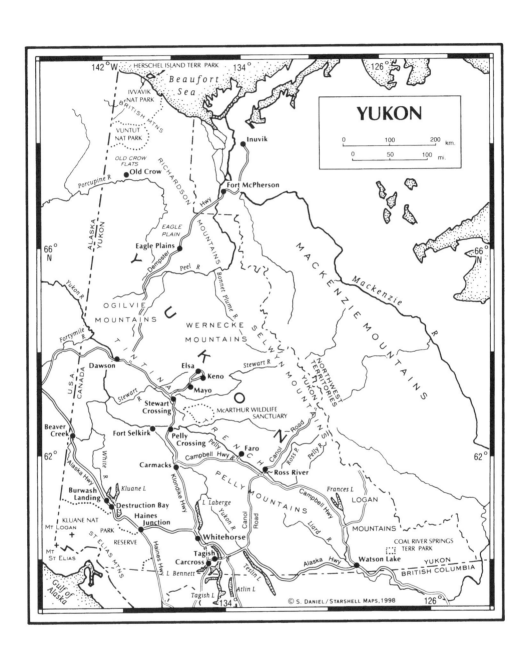

Yukon Facts at a Glance

The Yukon has a total area of 483,450 square kilometres, including 4,480 square kilometres of freshwater area. The majority of the land is forested—281,030 square kilometres. Eighty percent of the Yukon is wilderness, compared to a North and Central American average of 41 percent. The territory encompasses about 4.8 percent of Canada's total land area. This makes the Yukon the ninth largest of the ten provinces and three territories. Only the four Atlantic provinces of New Brunswick, Nova Scotia, Prince Edward Island, and Newfoundland are smaller.

The province's boundaries are: southern boundary 60^0 north latitude bordering British Columbia; western boundary 141^0 west longitude shared with Alaska; northern boundary the shoreline of the Beaufort Sea; and eastern boundary a ragged line shared with Northwest Territory that roughly follows the height of land from about 136^0 30' west longitude in the north to about 124^0 in the south.

Maximum altitude is 5,959-metre Mount Logan in the St. Elias Mountains in Kluane National Park; the lowest point is sea level along the Beaufort Sea shoreline.

Time zone is Pacific Standard Time (noon Greenwich Mean Time = 4:00 a.m. PST). The province changes to Daylight Saving Time in the spring (noon Greenwich Mean Time = 5:00 a.m. PST).

Total population is 33,580 with 24,000 (70 percent) living in Whitehorse.

The capital city is Whitehorse.

The Yukon became a separate territory within the Dominion of Canada on June 13, 1898.

Agriculture

In 1887, the assistant director of the Royal Canadian Geographic Society, George Mercer Dawson, surveyed the Alaska boundary at the **Yukon River**. During this survey, Dawson speculated that parts of what was to become the Yukon Territory could support hardy crops. However, Dawson could see no market for agricultural enterprises located so far north.

With the 1896 beginning of the **Klondike Gold Rush**, the lack of mouths to feed ceased to be a problem. Various small farm operations, based largely on production of vegetable crops, were soon busy suppliers—especially around **Dawson**. When the **gold** rush ended, most of these operations were abandoned.

But the high costs of importing food to the Yukon ensured continuing interest in developing a viable agricultural industry that could reduce the dependence of Yukoners on the outside world for vegetables, fruits, grains, and other agricultural products. Wherever a community developed in the Yukon, some farming operations were usually established.

By 1990, the Yukon territorial government began to look seriously at agriculture as a vital economic pursuit. Studies were conducted to determine how much of the Yukon had agricultural potential and what portion of this land was being utilized.

Of the Yukon's total land base, less than 2 percent is suitable for agriculture. Mountainous terrain, glaciers, icefields, and harsh winters combine with generally deficient soil-nutrient levels to render most land unsuitable. Wherever **permafrost** is present, the soil cannot support agriculture. The Yukon, Takhini, Pelly, Stewart, and Liard valleys contain virtually all the territory's agriculturally viable land. While weather, soil, and terrain conditions render most of the territory unsuitable to agriculture, the summer's long periods of daily sunshine help to offset the effects of a short frost-free season.

Most Yukon agricultural operations are clustered near the major communities. About 70 percent of farms in the territory are within 160 kilometres of **Whitehorse**, with the largest agricultural area located west of the city in the Takhini valley.

Yukoners have made intensive use of the arable land they have. In 1991, for example, of a total 7,355 hectares designated agricultural, 40 percent (2,942 hectares) was in production, another 23 percent was under development, and the remaining 37 percent was unutilized. Of this land, 1,395 hectares was being used for agricultural crops, rather than for grazing land or livestock production. The total number of farms was 137 and gross farm receipts totalled $1.7 million on an average capital investment per farm of $175,000. Total value of agriculture production was calculated at $2.3 million.

The largest sector in the industry was livestock, providing total sales of $914,945, with egg production constituting the fastest growing subsector. Livestock was followed in order of importance by game farming, forage crop production, cereal production, and vegetable growing.

Agricultural trends established by 1991 continue today, but the size of the industry has been expanding rapidly. In 1996, the value of agricultural production increased to $3.5 million, an 80 percent increase over 1991. Capital investment in farms, over the same period, rose to just under $45 million, a 94 percent increase. Total area farmed increased to 2,297 hectares from 1,395 in 1991.

Air Travel

The Yukon has two major airports at **Whitehorse** and **Watson Lake**, with most commercial traffic passing through Whitehorse. Direct daily passenger service to Whitehorse is provided by Canadian Airlines from Vancouver, British Columbia, or by Air North from Juneau and Fairbanks, Alaska. For part of the year, Air Transat provides scheduled round-trip flights from Frankfurt, Germany to Whitehorse.

Additionally, most Yukon communities are serviced by landing strips and strips constructed for emergency or access purposes are located in some isolated regions, including Ivvavik, Vuntut, and Kluane national parks.

Aircraft movement through Whitehorse far outnumbers air traffic through all other Yukon communities. In 1996, for example, 42,575 flights landed at Whitehorse. This compared to a total number of flights landing in other Yukon communities of about 26,000.

Alaska Highway

Stretching from Dawson Creek, British Columbia to Fairbanks, Alaska, the Alaska Highway is 2,451 kilometres in length. About 925 kilometres of this highway lie within the boundaries of Yukon Territory.

Construction of the highway is considered one of the most spectacular engineering feats of the 20th century, primarily due to the speed with which the long road running through incredibly rugged terrain was constructed. The decision to build the Alaska Highway was made by the United States after the Japanese bombing of Pearl Harbor in December 1941 and subsequent Japanese capture of two Aleutian islands led to fear that Alaska was vulnerable to invasion by Axis forces. A land link was deemed essential to sustain the military garrisons established to defend Alaska.

Work on the highway began in February 1942 with work crews pushing overland from both Dawson Creek and Fairbanks. In 8 months and 12 days a mostly one-lane dirt track barely wide enough in places for a military truck was completed. The United States Army 97th Engineers and 18th Engineers met each other at Mile 1202 just outside **Beaver Creek** on October 28, 1942, formally completing the continuous link.

Construction of the Alaska Highway was complicated by deep muskeg and the need to erect 133 bridges to provide Alaska and the Yukon's first road link to the rest of North America. (Yukon Archives, Macbride Museum Collection, #3553)

In addition to 11,000 U.S. soldiers working on the highway, 16,000 civilians were involved. Of these, 3,700 were Canadians. The influx of all these people into the formerly scantily populated northern regions of British Columbia and the Yukon transformed some communities into boomtowns and created others from scratch.

Building the highway required crossing eight mountain ranges, countless streams, and cutting a road through seemingly endless forests. More than 8,000 culverts and 133 bridges had to be installed or constructed. At various points during the construction, **permafrost** hampered the engineering effort. One of the worst sections encountered was near Beaver Creek, where a large expanse of permafrost was transformed into an ice-bottomed mud bog when the top layer was scraped away. Equipment became hopelessly mired and new construction techniques had to be developed to enable completion of the road. The American government bore the complete highway construction cost of $147.8 million, and Canada provided right of way.

At the end of World War II, the Canadian government took over the 1,954-kilometre Canadian section on April 1, 1946. It paid the United States $108 million for adjacent airfields, flight strips, buildings, telephone systems, and other assets, but not highway construction costs. It was opened to unrestricted civilian traffic in 1947, but continued to be maintained by Canadian army engineers until 1964 when the federal department of public works took over maintenance.

Today, the highway serves as the major link for the majority of Yukon communities. Maintenance of the Yukon highway portion is now the responsibility of the Yukon **government**. About $40 million is spent annually to maintain and reconstruct the highway. Permafrost continues to plague construction crews and travellers. Massive potholes are common after the winter thaw is over, and washouts can occur during spring and summer rain storms.

Amphibians

Four species of amphibians are known to live in the Yukon: the boreal toad, wood frog, spotted frog, and boreal chorus frog. The northern wood frog is widely distributed throughout the territory, whereas the other three species reach the northern limits of their range in the southern regions of the Yukon.

Because amphibians are cold-blooded and obtain their warmth from the environment rather than internally, the Yukon is not a hospitable home.

The range of the four amphibians in the territory is limited by the extreme cold of winters, cool short summers, scarcity of hibernation sites, and thin winter snow cover.

In winter, amphibians survive in the north by hibernating underground, under ponds, or under leaf litter beneath a thick blanket of insulating snow. Most amphibians will freeze to death if cooled below $-1°$ or $-2°$ Celsius for more than a brief period. A few northern species, however, have a form of naturally occurring antifreeze in their cells that enables them to survive temperatures as low as $-5°$ to $-7°$ Celsius. Both boreal chorus frogs and wood frogs are able to utilize glucose to prevent their cells from bursting in subfreezing temperatures. This enables these frogs to be frozen solid during hibernation and still emerge alive in the spring.

During spring and summer, northern amphibians take full advantage of the warmth and sunshine. To increase heat absorption, their eggs are large and dark. The eggs are also laid in warmer shallow **water**, well submerged to protect against the possibility of nighttime freezing on the surface. All the amphibians, from tadpoles to adult frogs and toads, spend much time basking in the sun in shallows. Some amphibians that are nocturnal in warmer climates are active in the north during the warmest and brightest parts of the day.

The wood frog is the most common and widespread amphibian species in the Yukon. It is also the most northerly living amphibian in North America, occurring at least as far north as **Old Crow**. Wood frogs inhabit forests, meadows, muskegs, and **tundra**. The colour of the wood frog is highly variable, ranging from brown, tan, or grey to pinkish, with a dark eye mask, white jaw stripe, and creamy white underside. A light stripe may run down the centre of the back. Adults can be up to 50 millimetres in length. This species congregates to breed in clear, shallow ponds in late April and continues mating and breeding through June. During this period, the frogs tend to chorus with a distinctive, ducklike quacking sound.

The great abundance of wood frogs in the north results from the species' ability to tolerate cold as well as its accelerated development. In any climate, the wood frog has the fastest rate of development from egg to tadpole of any North American frog. From the moment it is hatched, a young wood frog can grow to full 50-millimetre length in 7 to 12 weeks, winning the race for adulthood before freeze-up.

The other three amphibian species present in the Yukon have quite limited ranges. The boreal chorus frog is known to exist only along the La Biche River in the territory's extreme southeast corner, probably having spread north to here out of the Liard River basin of British Columbia. It inhabits damp, grassy, or wooded areas, but is seldom seen as even in summer it opts to largely remain underground. In winter, it hibernates underground.

The boreal chorus frog is small, with a long body and short legs. It is grey, brown, or green with three irregular stripes down the back and dark stripes on the sides that extend from the nose to the groin. The belly is white, yellow, or olive, with a few dark markings. In early spring, before the winter melt is complete, the boreal chorus frog begins mating and continues the process into June. Breeding takes place in almost any body of water, shallow or deep. Eggs are laid in small clumps attached to submerged plants and hatch within two weeks. Two months later the tadpoles will have transformed into young frogs of up to 12 millimetres in length.

Also occurring only in the Yukon's Liard Basin region is the boreal toad. Preferring damp conditions, it is found in meadows and forests that are sometimes quite removed from any direct source of water. While further south the boreal toad is nocturnal, in the Yukon it is active during daylight hours. The adult boreal toad is quite large—up to 125 millimetres in length—with a chunky body, short legs, and numerous warts. Back colour varies between green, grey, and brown. The warts are generally reddish and surrounded by dark blotches. A white stripe usually runs down the middle of the back. The warts and the toad's parotid glands at the back of the head serve a defensive function, both emanating a foul-tasting poison that results in the toad being disdained by potential predators. The poison is also irritating to the skin of many humans.

In winter, boreal toads often hibernate in communal burrows that are as deep as 1.3 metres underground. Heavy snowfall provides vital insulating cover over the burrows because, unlike the boreal chorus frog and the wood frog, the boreal toad has no protective antifreeze function in its cellular makeup.

Male boreal toads in the Yukon and British Columbia do not emit a call during breeding season, although they do in Alberta. In all locations, however, the toads breed in spring in shallow areas of ponds or in stream backwaters with sandy bottoms. Eggs are laid in clutches that can number up to 16,500. The tadpoles that emerge from these egg clutches are capable of distinguishing their siblings from other tadpoles feeding in the same waters. By July or August the tadpoles have transformed into "toadlets" of about 10 millimetres length.

In the southwest Yukon the spotted frog has been identified. The first discovery of this species in the Yukon was made on the west shore of Bennett Lake in 1994. More aquatic than the wood frog, the spotted frog prefers permanent ponds. Although it may forage on land, it will usually remain close to shore. The spotted frog is much larger and sturdier than the wood frog—growing up to 100 millimetres in length. Its olive, tan, light brown, or dark brown skin is varied by small bumps and dark irregular spots. In northern climates, spotted frogs have shorter legs than in more southerly climes. This may help conserve heat and moisture.

Breeding is undertaken communally in the spring. Males call from underwater in a short series of quiet, low-pitched grunts. Although eggs hatch in a week, many tadpoles are unable to complete the transformation to young frogs by freeze-up, forcing the tadpoles to overwinter. Both tadpoles and frogs hibernate underwater. Lacking the antifreeze function of the boreal chorus frog and wood frog, the spotted frog relies on the shallow ponds in which it lives being covered by a thick layer of ice and snow.

Anatum Peregrine Falcon. *See* **Peregrine Falcon.**

Ancient Yukon

The Yukon—in fact, all the land west of the Rocky Mountains—is a relatively recent addition to North America. Only 75 million years ago, where the Yukon now stretches, lay a narrow neck of mountainous land that extended along the present-day eastern border of the territory across the northern reaches and into Alaska. Scientists have theorized that a link, similar to that of **Beringia** during the last Ice Age, may have joined western North America to Asia and been travelled by dinosaurs. West of that lay a great sea.

The formation of present-day Yukon began long before that time, however, between about 1.2 billion and 760 million years ago. The territory is believed to have been formed from a series of "exotic crustal fragments," known as terranes, that originated at different times and in different places around the globe.

While these crustal fragments were beginning their journey northward from points as far away as present-day Australia, another process was causing underwater sedimentary plains to be created off the coast of what was then North

America. Inland, vast amounts of sedimentary strata were carried out of the interior of the continent by rivers that were larger than the present-day Mackenzie, Mississippi, Amazon, or Nile. These rivers drained inland seas covering much of the North American interior. In the area of the modern **Mackenzie Mountains** a wide, gently sloping shelf grew as shallow-water sediments accumulated. Eventually the depth of this sedimentary layer would reach four kilometres. Today, this platform is known as the Mackenzie Mountains Supergroup. Iron oxide constituted a major ingredient in this platform's construction and many localities of the Mackenzie Mountains region are consequently rich in iron ore.

The shelf off the Mackenzie Mountains extended as far as today's Wernecke Mountains, which form the western flank of the Bonnet Plume River. Here, deep basins bordered the shelf's edges. Over the submarine cliffs flowed rivers laden with debris. In a process that began about 570 million years ago and continued for 430 million years, to the end of the Jurassic Period, the waters eroded the cliff edge, causing massive blocks of rock to break free and tumble down into the basins. Marine sediments, including dying and decaying organisms, also accumulated on this vast underwater shelf. These carbonate and limy shale formations would eventually be upthrust as part of the Ogilvie, Wernecke, and Richardson mountain ranges.

At the same time these mountains were being built, northern and eastern Yukon was being buried under great quantities of sand, mud, and chert coming in from the west as some still unknown offshore disturbance pushed these sediments eastward. Throughout this period reefs formed on the shelves lying off the shore of North America. These shallow, warm-water reefs provided the nutrients and environment essential for a great profusion of new life formation, constituting what is known as the Cambrian explosion from about 570 to 500 million years ago.

Darting in and around the reefs was an ever growing and diversifying array of creatures. While some were soft-bodied and vulnerable, most developed an armoured mix of shells, claws, shields, and lancelike spines as weapons and protection. Some forms of these creatures survive today. Brachiopods, which look like clams and have calcite shells, still live in the oceans. More than 100,000 species of molluscs, including snails, slugs, mussels, oysters, and octopuses, emerged. So, too, did some arthropods, which today constitute 80 percent of all visible life. These have hard, external, jointed skeletons and jointed legs. Crabs, lobsters, spiders, beetles, and ants are arthropods. Another life form dating to the Cambrian explosion was chordates. These possessed segmented muscles, a tail fin, and a flexible backbone. **Fish**, **amphibians**, reptiles, and **mammals** (including humans) are chordates. While many forms of life which emerged during the Cambrian explosion survive today, a greater number disappeared in a mass global extinction about 250 million years ago.

Eventually marine plants crept from the edge of the oceans onto the more hostile beachfront. The oldest known vascular land plant fossils date to 415 million years ago. This plant had neither leaves nor roots. It consisted of simple stalks ending in spore-filled sacs and stood only a few centimetres tall.

About 160 million years ago, an immense block of the Earth's crust crunched up against the western coast of North America. With the same kind of force that crumples the fronts of two vehicles inward and upward during a slow-speed head-on collision, both the coast of North America and the crustal plate started to fold upward. The birth of the Rocky Mountains and the Mackenzie Mountains had begun.

The first terranes to arrive formed the Foreland Belt, which comprises most of the modern-day Mackenzie, Richardson, and Ogilvie mountains. The mountains of this belt are primarily composed of sedimentary strata. Approximately 140 million years ago other terranes started crashing into North America. As some of these terranes crumpled back on themselves, they were rear-ended by following terranes, shoved up over the edge of the continent, and stacked on top of each other. In the Pelly Mountains three such sheets, each featuring distinctly different rock construction, were piled in layers that are visible today.

Over many millions of years four belts of terranes were added to the North American coast to ultimately form the rest of the Yukon. The Omineca Belt followed the Foreland Belt. This belt forms a large bladder-shaped band stretching from **Watson Lake** to **Dawson**. It encompasses the Logan, Pelly, and Wernecke mountains and is cut by the **Tintina Trench**. This belt is composed mostly of sedimentary strata, and igneous and high-grade metamorphic rock.

Following on the heels of this belt came the Intermontane Belt, which intruded quite narrowly into the Yukon from the south, extending as an ever narrowing wedge to a point northeast of **Whitehorse**. This region has a plateau topography underlain by volcanic and sedimentary strata. Then came the Coast Belt, which encompasses the Dawson Range and is composed largely of granitic structures. Finally, there arrived the Insular Belt, which formed the **St. Elias Mountains**.

Not all these belts are composed of terranes. Some of the land was built in place through folding, subduction, and the lifting of the Earth's crust. The St. Elias region, for example, has a roughly 450-million-year history. But most of that time it was probably under water, except for periods of glacial activity due to ice ages. By about 15 million years ago the St. Elias region had become the coast of North America. It was intensely volcanic with large volumes of lava and ash extruding onto low-lying coal swamps and coastal sand bars. As this volcanic activity heated up, the earth began rising, and the St. Elias Mountains were born. Meanwhile, near Vancouver Island and Puget Sound far to the south, a terrane 600 kilometres long, 200 kilometres wide, and more than 13 kilometres thick began drifting northward at a rate of about 6 centimetres per year. About 10 million years ago this terrane, known as the Pacific Plate, ground its way over another plate immediately to its north called the Yakutat Terrane—essentially trying to shove the Yakutat underneath itself. This put incredible upward pressure on the St. Elias coastal area, which continues today; the St. Elias Mountains are still lifting at a rate of about four centimetres a year.

Virtually all of the Yukon is part of what is known as the Cordillera, the mountainous skeletal spine that runs down the western flank of North and South America from the northern reaches of the British and **Richardson Mountains** overlooking the **Beaufort Sea** to Cape Horn near Antarctica. Cordillera is Spanish for "little string." In northern Canada, the eastern edge of the Cordillera follows the broad arc of the Mackenzie Mountains in the Northwest Territory, links to the eastern edge of the Richardson Mountains and then bends northwest along the British Mountains to meet the Beaufort Sea in Alaska. All of the Yukon's many mountain ranges are part of the Cordillera and are still subject to the endless process of mountain building and mountain erosion that results from plate tectonics in action.

Soon after the first terranes pushed up against the edge of North America they were populated by wildlife, most notably dinosaurs, which reigned supreme over animal life throughout the Mesozoic Era from about 245 million to 65 million years ago. During this period Yukon experienced, as it does today, long periods of polar night during the winter months, but high global temperatures meant there was no frost. The mean annual temperature would have remained about 10° Celsius and the humidity would have been similar to that in present-day Vancouver, British Columbia. **Plant** growth was vigorous during the season when almost continuous daylight persisted. Most trees in the Yukon had large, broad leaves that would be shed with the onset of winter. Deciduous conifers, like the bald cypress, also lost their fronds. Few trees would retain their leaves throughout the year.

During the winter months, the dinosaurs likely migrated south to escape the long polar night and the reduced feeding opportunity. With the spring, hadrosaurs and other herbivores would again migrate north to tap into the broad-leaved forests that provided ideal nutrition. Following them would be the long-legged carnivores, such as tyrannosaurs, which preyed on the herbivores. About 65 million years ago the age of the dinosaurs ended abruptly, probably due to an extraterrestrial cause such as the Earth's collision with a large meteorite.

With the dinosaurs and other large reptiles no longer a threat, the age of large mammals began. **Woolly mammoths**, lions, horses, camels, giant bears, and other great creatures roamed across a vast savannah-like landscape.

(*See also* **Glaciation.**)

Archaeology

The oldest archaeological site in North America is found in a set of small caves overlooking the Bluefish River, near **Old Crow** in the northern Yukon. Known as the Bluefish Caves, this site is found on a ridgeline that features a jagged limestone outcropping.

In 1975, archaeologists William Irving and Jacques Cinq-Mars of the University of Toronto were investigating artifacts unearthed by the erosion of the Old Crow River's banks. They soon expanded their exploration, searching overlooking ridges by helicopter for optimal locations where early humans would have enjoyed unimpeded views of the hunting plains in the Bluefish Valley. Although the caves were discovered during this trip, serious excavation was not begun until 1977. During these diggings no stone tools or other recognizable signs of human activity were identified. The site was consequently abandoned.

That winter, however, a palaeontologist at the University of Toronto identified some bones taken from the cave as those of a horse, an animal that became extinct in North America at the end of the last ice age some 10,000 years ago. It seemed likely their presence in the cave resulted from humans having killed the horses as game and carried their carcasses to the shelter of the caves. In 1978, excavation was renewed at the Bluefish Caves.

Since then tools dated to between approximately 10,000 and 13,000 years ago have been unearthed in the caves. Also discovered were tiny flakes of flint, the by-products of stone-tool manufacture, dated to between 15,000 and 20,000 years ago. The Bluefish Caves were obviously used by generations of early **First Nations peoples**, for more than 10,000 animal bones, including those of **woolly mammoths**, have been found here.

The artifacts unearthed at the Bluefish Caves present the most convincing evidence to support the presence of human habitation during the last ice age in the northern part of the continent, but much of the evidence remains somewhat tentative because of the failure to discover true tools and other artifacts from the 15,000- to 20,000-year period.

Many Yukoners and others believe that evidence found at Old Crow proves human habitation between 27,000 and 30,000 years ago. A caribou leg bone shaped by human hand for use as a scraper was found in 1966 in the exposed banks of the eroding Old Crow River. When subjected to radiocarbon testing it was dated at about 27,000 years old. Unfortunately, radiocarbon dating techniques in the 1960s were relatively unsophisticated and later developments in this field proved many datings from this period to be highly inaccurate. Such was the case for the Old Crow caribou scraper. In 1986, using more accurate radiocarbon dating techniques, scientists determined that the tool had been made only about 1,350 years ago.

There is, however, an archaeological school of thought that maintains humans arrived in North America about 50,000 years ago. Its belief is based on the findings of a series of bone fragments at Old Crow and other sites that appears to have been flaked by humans to form tools. Radiocarbon dating from these fragments and from soil levels associated with them do yield ages ranging from 50,000 to 10,000 years ago.

Another group of archaeologists disagrees that the markings on these animal bones were made by humans. They argue that the markings were made by natural processes, such as the bones being crushed by other animals walking on them, pressure from overlying soil layers gouging or scratching them, and soil erosion and water washing leaving impressions on the fossilized bones.

If better evidence exists in the soil of the Yukon, however, to place humans in the north prior to about 20,000 years ago, most experts believe it is likely to be found in the Old Crow region.

Another major archaeological site is found near **Carmacks**, where digs have yielded fossils and tools related to the "Microblade Peoples" who lived in the Yukon between 8,000 and 4,000 years ago.

In southwestern Yukon a number of archaeological sites suggest that about 1,250 years ago the region was subjected to extensive volcanic activity that left thick beds of white volcanic ash over the landscape of much of southern Yukon and nearby portions of British Columbia and the Northwest Territories. This ash appears today as a white band running between layers of the normal brownish Yukon soil, exposed in the banks of rivers and road cuts. Known to geologists as White River Ash, these deposits can be traced to a massive volcanic eruption in the **St. Elias Mountains**. The ash drifted approximately 1,000 kilometres eastward across southern Yukon, covering an area of some 250,000 square kilometres to a maximum depth of about 1.5 metres.

Archaeologists and anthropologists believe that the people living in this area at the time were the ancestors of today's Déné or Athapaskan peoples. They survived primarily by hunting, fishing, and trapping and practised a migratory existence related to the movement of **caribou** and other large **mammals**, and the return of salmon to spawning rivers. In winter, the larger camps would break into smaller groups to more easily subsist from hunting. Archaeological evidence gathered by William Workman of the University of Alaska in Anchorage reveals that the massive volcanic eruption occurred during the winter months.

With spring breakup the heavily polluted snows melted, saturating rivers with chemicals and fine ash from the eruption. **Fish** populations were likely devastated and the salmon spawn blocked. Caribou and other animals would have died from eating ash-covered foliage. Evidence suggests that, by summer, the people began to flee this vast area of the southern Yukon, some heading south and others north, but all seeking land outside the ash-contaminated zone. In the northern Yukon, archaeological digs have unearthed the arrival during this period of Athapaskan-speaking Kutchin peoples who used the same tools as those found in the volcanic region to the south. Similar discoveries have been made in the Interior plains of British Columbia, suggesting that some of the Athapaskan refugees moved down the province's valleys into this region. There are further indications that some of these peoples might have continued migrating down the interior valleys as far as Utah and Colorado.

The traditional **languages** of the Navaho and the related Apache are unlike any other languages spoken by First Nations in Utah, Arizona, and Colorado. Rather they are closely related to Athapaskan languages. Mounting evidence creates a convincing argument that the Navaho and Apache came to the southwest United States as refugees from a volcanic ash–devastated southern Yukon.

Not all archaeology in the Yukon focuses on prehistory First Nations peoples. A significant degree of archaeological research is also dedicated to unearthing artifacts dating to the period after the arrival of the first Europeans. At Fort Reliance near **Dawson**, for example, archaeologists have been studying the history of this fur-trade and prospecting-supply settlement since the 1970s. Located on the east bank of the **Yukon River**, 11 kilometres below the mouth of the Klondike River, Fort Reliance was founded by François Mercier as a small, semi-independent fur-trading post. It went on to play a significant role in opening up the Yukon to prospecting and mining, which eventually led to the **Klondike Gold Rush**. Prior to the arrival of Europeans, who displaced them, the site was also a village of the Han people.

(*See also* **Beringia.**)

Arctic Circle

The northern parallel of latitude at 66° 33' north forms a boundary known as the Arctic Circle. South of this line of latitude the sun rises and sets daily. North of the line, the sun remains above the horizon at midnight at midsummer and never rises during midwinter.

As light rays are bent by the Earth's atmosphere, however, the sun can be seen even when it is slightly below the horizon. This means that at points slightly north of the circle the sun can be seen during midwinter. As the distance north from the Arctic Circle increases, the number of days the sun is visible in winter decreases until, at the North Pole, the sun fails to shine for six months. Alternatively, in the summer season, the sun never sets. This phenomenon happens because the Earth's axis of rotation tilts relative to the plane of its orbit around the sun. During the Yukon's winter, when the northern hemisphere tilts away from the sun, the Earth's curvature creates a permanent shadow centred on the North Pole. This area starts forming with the fall equinox, grows to its maximum at winter solstice, then decreases until it completely vanishes by the spring equinox. During the spring and summer, the northern hemisphere tilts toward the sun, resulting in continuous sunlight centring on the North Pole.

Although the Arctic Circle does not constitute a climatic boundary, human habitation north of this line is scanty. The only community of notable size north of the Arctic Circle in Yukon Territory is **Old Crow**, which lies about 115 kilometres due north of the circle. There are, however, large forested portions of the Yukon north of the Arctic Circle and much of the wildlife found in the territory's more southerly regions is also present here.

Atlin Lake

Atlin Lake's 774 square kilometres are surrounded by mountains that make it one of North America's most scenic bodies of water. The narrow lake is about 113 kilometres in length. The Tlingit knew the lake as *aht-lah,* which meant "big water" or "stormy water." George Mercer Dawson of the Geological Survey of Canada adopted this name for the lake in 1887.

Atlin Lake is accessible from the Yukon by Highway 7, a largely unpaved road south of **Whitehorse**. The area is extensively utilized for outdoor recreation, as well as mining.

During the 1898–99 phase of the **Klondike Gold Rush**, the Atlin area was the site of another **gold** discovery. This resulted in a smaller gold rush siphoning off goldseekers who had been en route to the **Dawson** area. About 10,000 to 15,000 prospectors travelling the White and Chilkoot passes opted to chase gold along Atlin Lake. The rumours of easy pickings near the lake so captured the local imagination that almost overnight some 80 percent of the workers engaged in construction of the **White Pass & Yukon Railway** abandoned their tools to try their hand at mining.

Aurora Borealis. *See* **Northern Lights.**

Bears

All three of North America's bear species are found in the Yukon—polar bear, grizzly bear, and black bear. The polar bear's range is limited to the northern flanks of the British and Richardson mountains and concentrated primarily along the shores of the **Beaufort Sea**. Grizzly and black bears are found throughout the territory, even close to urban centres. While grizzlies and black bears are numerous in the Yukon, the polar bear is less so, probably numbering no more than a few hundred animals. This compares to about 10,000 black bears and 6,000 to 7,000 grizzly bears.

Male black bears range in weight from 80 to 250 kilograms, with females considerably lighter. They range in colour from black to brown to cinnamon. During most of the year black bears are solitary, pairing up only briefly for mating. Cubs remain with their mother for about a year. Although most active at night, they do feed and travel during the day. Black bears maintain an average foraging range of about 200 square kilometres, but these can overlap with the ranges of others of their kind. Black bear density in Yukon forests is usually quite high, about one every 14 square kilometres.

Black bears have superb senses of smell and hearing, so rely on these more than on their eyes; however, their eyesight is as good as that of humans. Their usual gait is a lumbering walk, which can quickly turn into a bounding gallop. Black bears prefer vegetable matter to meat. They favour berries of virtually any variety, but will also eat fresh sprouts of grasses and sedges, tree buds, roots, and tubers. Additionally they eat insects, small **mammals**, and **fish**.

Bears do not truly hibernate; rather they go into a deep sleep from about the end of October to mid-April—less in areas with milder winters. By late summer they have packed themselves with a huge mattress of fat by gorging on everything available. They then seek the heaviest snowbelt of their range and dig a shallow hole, usually under a tree, tall shrub, or overhanging bank. The heavier snow cover helps provide insulation so the hole need seldom be more than a metre or two deep. By the spring, the grossly overweight bear of the autumn will have become thin, possibly even emaciated. But it will have survived another winter.

Black bears are forest animals; in the Yukon this means that the mountainous terrain tends to concentrate the species into river valleys and related strips of boreal forest habitat. The high numbers of black bears in the valleys, where humans also congregate, and their relative boldness lead to frequent encounters with people in the Yukon. One reason black bears are less afraid of humans than are most mammal species is that they have no natural enemies other than the grizzly bear. Where a grizzly's territory and that of a black bear overlap, the black bear is constantly on guard against sudden attacks.

Grizzly bears are much larger than black bears. Males weigh about 250 to 320 kilograms, females about 200 kilograms. They have prominent shoulder humps and long claws that protrude beyond the fur on their front feet. The name grizzly derives from the white tips commonly found on the ends of the hair of older males, which gives them a grizzled look. They can range in colour from black to light brown and individual bears usually have a variety of shades in their coat. There is little chance of confusing a grizzly with a black bear because of the distinctive shoulder hump, significantly larger size, and flatter, more dishlike shape of the face.

The habits of grizzlies are very similar to those of black bears, although they are more active during the day. They eat tubers and roots, and will dig marmots and ground squirrels out of their holes. Berries are the food that most packs on the fat required to make it through their deep winter sleep, so they devour all of these they can. Experts calculate that a grizzly bear can consume 200,000 berries a day. Grizzlies are also fairly good hunters and will kill weak cloven-hoofed animals, and sometimes cattle and horses. During spawning season, grizzlies are often seen at the edges of streams feeding on salmon.

Grizzly bears are extremely solitary, except for females with cubs. Their home ranges are large, at least 200 square kilometres. They travel vast distances that, over a lifetime, can add up to more than 4,000 square kilometres. Grizzly sows are highly protective of their young, in part because the boar will kill the cubs if possible. A sow will stay with her cubs for up to two years before leaving them to mate again. Grizzlies bed down for their winter sleep in a manner similar to that of black bears.

In the Yukon, grizzlies live throughout the territory from its border with British Columbia to **Herschel Island Territorial Park** off the Arctic coast. They are, however, spread fairly thinly, with higher concentrations in the southern and coastal environments.

Contrary to some accounts, grizzly bears will almost always try to avoid confrontations with humans, taking flight if that option is possible and there are no cubs threatened. People in the woods can usually avoid a meeting with either black bears or grizzly bears by making noise to warn of their approach. Most attacks in the wild occur at, or near, campsites where food and cooking utensils have been improperly cached or cleaned up so that bears are attracted by the scent.

Polar bears are often larger than grizzly bears, with adult males measuring two to three metres in length and usually weighing between 420 and 500 kilograms. The heaviest male recorded was 950 kilograms. The males are normally a fourth to a third larger than the females.

The shape of polar bears is unique compared to that of grizzly and black bears. They have longer necks and legs, with a long, narrow head and very small ears. The foot pads are entirely covered with fur. Their winter coat is coarse, thick, and shaggy, and coloured creamy white; in summer the coat is thinner and takes on a yellowish-white hue. Older males often have a mane.

Polar bears are almost entirely carnivorous. Favoured foods are seals, both young and old, fish, mussels, crabs, starfish, eggs and nestling young waterfowl, and occasionally walrus and whale meat (usually these last two will not have been killed by the bear but will be discovered as carrion on the seashore or ice floes).

Solitary creatures, polar bears are most common on the Yukon coast in August after the ice floes on which they have been carried south break up, forcing them ashore. During this time, polar bears may travel inland as far as 120 kilometres.

On land, their walk is a shuffle, although they can move quickly when necessary. At sea, they can swim at a speed of about 6.5 kilometres an hour and remain submerged for as long as two minutes at a time. They swim by paddling only with their partially webbed forefeet, their back feet trailing behind.

Polar bears have differing winter sleep habits based on gender. Females excavate dens in snowbanks or on the sides of pressure ridges of ice in late autumn. With her young, the female will remain in the den from mid-November to late March with few excursions outside. Adult males, however, usually only deep sleep from late November to late January.

Beaufort Sea

The Yukon is bordered on the north by the Beaufort Sea, part of the Arctic Ocean. The Beaufort Sea is generally calculated as covering 450,000 square kilometres and lying south and east of a line connecting Point Barrow, Alaska and Lands End, Prince Patrick Island in the Northwest Territory. The **water** of the Peel River and all other Yukon rivers that flow into the Mackenzie River discharges into the Beaufort at the vast Mackenzie Delta just east of the Yukon's eastern border.

The Beaufort Sea is home to **Herschel Island Territorial Park** and also borders the shoreline of **Ivvavik National Park**. The coastline is low lying, with many barrier islands and sandspits. Scouring by ice and erosion by powerful storm surges contribute to this low profile. Inshore waters are shallow, with depths of only about 200 metres ranging out as far as 80 to 200 kilometres from shore. The width of this shallow shelf is greater in the Yukon and Mackenzie Delta region than in Alaskan waters. This is partly due to heavy discharges of sediment by the Mackenzie River. Beyond the coastal shelf, the water deepens rapidly to about 3,500 metres, reaching a maximum depth of nearly 4,000 metres in what is known as the Canada Basin.

Tidal fluctuations are minimal, ranging only from 0.3 to 0.5 metres in two daily fluctuations. Currents are also minimal and largely wind driven. The Beaufort Sea's water is characteristic of the rest of the Arctic Ocean—low temperatures and low salinity. There is, however, a flow of Pacific water into the Beaufort Sea that brings with it salmon and herring. This contributes to the coastline's popularity with seabirds, which use it as a vital summer breeding and migration staging area. Seals and whales, including the endangered **bowhead whale**, are also found here.

The Earth's rotation causes an unusual phenomenon in the Beaufort known as the Beaufort Gyre. Water and ice in the Beaufort Sea circulate in a clockwise direction. As the water flows along the Yukon coast it encounters only one major obstacle—Herschel Island. This ocean current, through its effect on prehistoric glaciers and erosional forces, is responsible for the island's separation from the mainland.

Beaver Creek

With a population of about 125, Beaver Creek is Canada's westernmost community. It is located just 22 kilometres south of the Yukon-Alaska border on the **Alaska Highway** and 3.5 kilometres from the Canada Customs and Immigration station northwest of town.

The small community is situated where its namesake, Beaver Creek, crosses the highway. It was founded in 1955, primarily as a service community for the highway. Until 1902 the Beaver Creek waterway was known as Snag Creek. At that time the upper part of the creek was renamed Beaver Creek, while the lower portion remained Snag Creek.

Gold prospecting started in the Beaver Creek area in 1904 and continues today. The closest the area ever came to a gold rush, however, was between 1909 and 1914. In 1913, a rich placer gold field was discovered just over the Alaska border on the Chisana ridge by Peter Nelson and William James, who had been mining at Beaver Creek since 1909.

On October 28, 1942, the southern and northern crews building the Alaska Highway met here. U.S. Army 18th Engineers' Corporal Refines Sim Jr. of Philadelphia and 97th Engineers' Private Alfred Jalufka of Kennedy, Texas were

On October 28, 1942, the southern and northern crews building the Alaska Highway met at Beaver Creek when bulldozer drivers U.S. Army 18th Engineers' Corporal Refines Sim Jr. of Philadelphia and 97th Engineers' Private Alfred Jalufka of Kennedy, Texas came blade to blade. (Yukon Archives, Finnie Collection, #442)

operating the two bulldozers that came blade to blade to complete the highway.

Beaver Creek is also somewhat notorious as the setting for the Yukon short stories and novels of western novelist James B. Hendryx.

Beringia

Most archaeologists believe that the first humans came to North America sometime between 20,000 and 15,000 years ago. They further believe that these first humans came to North America on foot, crossing from present-day Siberia to present-day Alaska via a land bridge that lay across the Bering Sea. Because the land bridge crossed the Bering Sea, the parts of the Yukon and Alaska where they would have initially lived is known as Beringia.

That such a land bridge existed is little disputed today. About 20,000 years ago, during the last phase of the Wisconsinan Ice Age, vast glaciers draped much of the northern hemisphere, including most of present-day Canada. The formation of these huge sheets of glacial ice required immense amounts of water and resulted in ocean levels dropping by up to 100 metres. In the Bering Sea, a lowland that might have measured more than 500 kilometres in width developed to link Asia with North America.

This land was unglaciated because of its extremely dry climate conditions. Sparse grasslands supported herds of large grazing species such as bison, giant horses, and **woolly mammoths**. Preying on these animals were lions, short-faced bears, and **wolves**. Also present, but not as prevalent as they are today, were black **bears** and **caribou**.

Most of these animals travelled in an east–west migration that carried them out of Siberia and into Alaska. In their wake came humans, pursuing the herds of grazing animals that provided their primary source of food. These people did not cross the land bridge in one massive wave; rather they probably came in small groups that were organized as tribes or clans. The process of human migration took place over many millennia, bringing peoples of different ethnic backgrounds into North America. Some of these peoples settled along the Alaska and Yukon coastlines, while others followed ice-free valley corridors through the Yukon into the heart of North America. From here, some appear to have simply kept going, pushing south all the way to the southern tip of South America in a journey that would have taken thousands of years and many generations to complete. Those who stayed were the ancestors of today's northern **First Nations peoples**.

About 13,500 years ago a rapid onset of global warming brought increased moisture to Beringia. As the glaciers shrank, the level of the sea rose and soon the land bridge was submerged, ending the migration into North America. Grasslands gave way to **tundra**, thickets, and wetlands. The enormous grazing mammal species either became extinct or pressed further south, leaving Beringia home to the present-day species of animals, which were better adapted to survive in the changed conditions. Between about 12,000 and 9,000 years ago, some 40 mammal species disappeared, including the giant horse, dire wolf, woolly mammoth, mastodon, lion, and giant beaver. The cause of this extinction is unknown, but is generally believed to have been due to overhunting by humans or climatic change.

Yukon First Nations' myths and legends may well record the changes that affected Beringia when the sea rose, the climate became wetter, and the large mammals left or became extinct. According to First Nations legend, there was a time when the world was flooded and **Raven** created the world as it is today. In one legend, Beaver Man and Traveller crossed the land, changing the animals from giants and eaters of humans into the smaller **mammals** that now occupy the northern forests. Another legend tells of how Game Mother, reclining in her swing strung between the mountains around Bennett Lake, released moose, caribou, sheep, rabbits, and wolves into the world to provide sustenance for the humans who had been created by Raven from poplar bark.

(*See also* **Archaeology; Glaciation; Woolly Mammoth; Yukon Beringia Interpretive Centre.**)

Biodiversity

The Yukon is often described as Canada's last great wilderness because so little of it has been settled or subjected to disruption from logging, mining, or hydroelectric development. Approximately 80 percent of the Yukon is wilderness, much more than the estimated 3 percent of Europe and 41 percent of all of North and Central America. With 23 **ecosystems**, the territory is also a highly complex geological and biological region. Within these ecosystems are found six general categories of habitat for wildlife:

- still water—comprising such **water** bodies as lakes, ponds, marshes, and even **polygons**;

🪓 flowing water—principally the many creeks and rivers running throughout the Yukon;

🪓 boreal forest—the forest type that dominates the 60 percent of the territory that is forested;

🪓 mountain environment—the habitat above the tree line in Yukon's many mountain regions;

🪓 Arctic **tundra**—the narrow band of land lying between the northerly tree line of the boreal forest and the coast fronting the **Beaufort Sea**;

🪓 marine and coastal habitat—the Beaufort Sea's shoreline and waters.

These general areas are home to 214 bird species, 61 mammal species, 40 **fish** species, thousands of invertebrate species, four amphibian species, no reptiles, and more than 1,300 plant species.

Many scientists think there is currently a global "biodiversity crisis" underway. This crisis is the result of human action, either directly through pollution, forest clearing, tilling agricultural land, and draining wetlands or indirectly through the introduction of exotic species that subsequently crowd out native life forms. Scientists believe that between 1995 and 2020, human interference will destroy more species than the entire process of natural selection has culled in the past 3.5 billion years. Some experts predict that in the next 50 to 100 years, between 20 and 50 percent of all species known to exist in the world will disappear.

In the Yukon, expansion of road networks has led to some fragmentation of wildlife habitat, five hydroelectric dams have affected fish habitat and migration paths, **placer mining** continues to impact fish streams, and increased demand for Yukon timber is negatively affecting **mammals** and other land animals in parts of the territory.

(*See also* **Amphibians; Birds; Ecosystems; Endangered Species; Invertebrates; Vegetation.**)

Birds

There are 214 bird species in the Yukon. These include numerous waterbirds ranging from loons to mergansers; birds of prey such as golden and bald eagles, various hawks, and peregrine falcons; several species of grouse and ptarmigan; concentrations of shorebirds, primarily along the Arctic coastline;

at least seven species of owls; and a profusion of songbirds.

Despite the harshness of Yukon winters, quite a number of species are known to overwinter. Gyrfalcon; goshawk; willow and rock ptarmigan; ruffed, spruce and sharp-tailed grouse; boreal and black-capped chickadee; white-tailed ptarmigan; and golden eagles have all been recorded as overwintering. Ravens, of course, are as common throughout the territory during winter as at any other time of the year.

Most of the Yukon's breeding birds migrate from the south to the territory, arriving as the snows melt. Birds that breed in the territory are capable of extremely fast mating, laying, brooding, and young-raising cycles so that they are strong enough for long migratory flights back to warmer southern climates. The arctic tern, for example, requires only two months in the Yukon to breed and prepare for a migratory journey that takes it 18,000 kilometres from the **Beaufort Sea** coastline to coastal Antarctica.

Yukon's small wetland areas are vital to the world's bird populations as migratory habitat. Approximately 3 percent of the territory's area is classified as wetland. About 48 wetland areas have been identified as being of prime importance to migratory bird breeding. Some of these wetland areas are quite small; others are large, such as **Old Crow Flats**, which has more than 2,000 wetlands pocking a 600,000-hectare plain. These wetlands range in size from about 0.5 hectares to as much as 4,700 hectares. Combined, they provide a breeding and moulting ground for up to 500,000 waterbirds.

(*See also* **Endangered Species; Peregrine Falcon; Raven.**)

Bison. *See* **Wood Bison.**

Bonanza Creek. *See* **Klondike Gold Rush.**

Bonnet Plume Heritage River

In June 1998, the Canadian Heritage Rivers System designated Bonnet Plume River as a Canadian Heritage River. As part of the conservation plan for this river, a management plan was undertaken for the entire watershed, which extends from its headwaters in the Selwyn and Mackenzie mountains at the Yukon–Northwest Territory border some 350 kilometres north to its confluence with the Peel River. Approximately 2.5 percent of Yukon Territory, or 12,000 square kilometres, is included in Bonnet Plume's watershed.

The Nacho Ny'a'k Dun and Tetlit Gwitchin **First Nations peoples** have deep roots in the watershed area, having for centuries used it as a hunting area and the river as a trade and travel corridor. As part of their land claims negotiations, both peoples secured extensive resource management interests in the area.

Bonnet Plume's watershed and the river itself constitute a largely undisturbed ecosystem supporting large, healthy populations of grizzly **bears**, **wolves**, moose, gyrfalcons, and woodland **caribou**. Because of its isolation, however, scientific information on the region is scanty and there has been little effort to date by non–First Nations governments to use traditional and existing local First Nations' knowledge. Controversy exists in the territory over the extent and type of changes that should be allowed in the Bonnet Plume before the wilderness values of the area become permanently impaired.

Currently, three types of land use pose possible threats to the watershed's wilderness aspect: overuse of the river by recreational boaters, mineral exploration that is targeted on the main stem of the river and involves large tracts of land, and existing and new road construction.

The scenery in Bonnet Plume is spectacular, enhanced by the near absence of human activity. Mountain peaks and ridges border the river as it cuts through steep canyons and incised valleys. Small lakes, such as Bonnet Plume, Margaret, and Quartet, provide excellent fishing and camping sites.

First Nations knew the river by the Athapaskan term for "black sand" because of the large amounts of black magnetite sand (a form of iron ore) found in its bed. During the **Klondike Gold Rush** it was renamed by **gold** stampeders after a local First Nations chief, Andrew Flett, who was also known as Bonnet Plume. Flett had worked for years as an interpreter for the Hudson's Bay Company and became highly regarded by gold stampeders using the watershed to reach **Dawson** from Edmonton. Known as the Edmonton route, this was the most difficult way to reach the gold fields. By the time many of these travellers reached the river they were suffering from starvation, sickness, and often on the verge of dying of hypothermia. Flett fed them through the winter and saw them off to Dawson in the spring. Grateful, the stampeders started calling the river Bonnet Plume in his honour.

Bowhead Whale

By far the largest animal in the Yukon, the bowhead whale can reach a length of 20 metres and a weight of 50 tonnes. Its massive mouth contains about 700 bristly baleen plates. Each plate is composed of an elastic horny substance that grows from the roof of the whale's mouth. The plates act as strainers, collecting plankton and other small organisms upon which the bowhead feeds from water and bottom sediment. The bowhead usually has a black body with a partially white, highly bowed lower chin from which its name is derived. It has a rounded back with no dorsal fin. A broad spatulate-shaped flipper is found on each lower flank. A bowhead's skin is smooth and free of barnacles. The blowholes are widely separated, resulting in a distinctive V-shaped blow that can be easily recognized at some distance.

The bowhead is slow-moving and unaggressive. Although not generally deep divers (preferring to skim food near the surface), bowheads can remain submerged for more than 40 minutes. Usually a bowhead prefers to travel alone or in small groups that seldom exceed 6 individuals, although advancing ice in the winter can result in congregations of up to 50 whales.

The bowhead is a migratory species but only in relation to the advance and retreat of winter ice. Its prime feeding ground is at the edge of the Arctic ice, so the whale follows the ice's retreat in summer and flees before its winter advance. This migration takes the bowhead into the Bering Sea off Alaska's west coast in winter and back to the **Beaufort Sea** off the Yukon coast in summer.

Although the bowhead once lived throughout the northern Arctic, only a few hundred survive outside of the Bering and Chukchi seas off Alaska and the Beaufort Sea. Scientists estimate that the western Arctic population of approximately 3,500 to 3,800 bowheads represents about one-quarter of its traditional size. However, this is a remarkable recovery, considering that between 1848 and 1914 commercial whalers hunted the species into near extinction.

During that period the bowhead was known as the Arctic right whale, as were several other northern whale species. Commercial whalers claimed these whales were the "right" whales to kill because of their choice blubber content and the quantity of their natural oil and baleen. Bowhead blubber is up to 70 centimetres thick, which also meant that this species naturally floated on the surface after it was killed.

Bowhead oil was highly prized for use in house, factory, church, and street lamps, as machine lubricant, and an ingredient in soap, paint, and rope. The baleen was among the most valuable taken from whales and was used in the manufacture of buggy whips, fishing rods, umbrella ribs, and the stays of dresses and corsets. In the late 19th century, baleen sold for $5 a pound and the profit from one dead bowhead could finance a year's whaling voyage. An industrial innovation may have saved the bowhead from extinction. In 1906, the invention of spring steel provided a cheap substitute for almost every aspect of baleen use. Overnight, the price of baleen collapsed to 50 cents a pound. Eight years later the bowhead whalery in the western Arctic was largely abandoned.

In 1935, the bowhead whale was protected from commercial harvesting. Today, the bowhead population is carefully monitored during its migrations and a "hands-off" policy of protection has been adopted. The result appears to be a slow, steady increase in the species' numbers. Despite the improving figures, the bowhead remains one of only two animal species in the Yukon categorized as endangered.

Bowhead whales, like most whale species off the North American coast, were traditionally hunted by **First Nations peoples**. Today, the Inuvialuit people, who live in the Mackenzie Delta area of the Northwest Territory, are permitted to hunt in the Beaufort Sea for one adult bowhead per year for subsistence purposes.

(*See also* **Endangered Species.**)

Buffalo. *See* **Wood Bison.**

Burwash Landing

Home to the world's largest **gold** pan, Burwash Landing is situated on Kluane Lake at the 1,759-kilometre point of the **Alaska Highway**. The gold pan measures eight metres in length and is situated next to the Kluane Museum of Natural History, which has excellent displays of First Nations artifacts, wildlife, minerals, and natural history.

Burwash Landing came into existence as the result of a gold discovery in 1903 that sparked the Kluane-area gold rush. On July 4, 1903, a claim was staked on a tributary of the Jarvis River by a First Nations Tagish miner known as Dawson Charlie (sometimes called Tagish Charlie). Dawson Charlie, along with George Carmack and Skookum Jim Mason, had also been responsible for the rich gold strike at Bonanza Creek which sparked the **Klondike Gold Rush** in 1896. The creek was named Fourth of July Creek and yielded the first payable gold discovered in the Kluane region.

The community of Burwash Landing was founded on the northwestern shore of Kluane Lake early in 1904 by Louis and Eugene Jacquot of the Alsace-Lorraine district of Europe. They established it as a supply centre to provide goods and boat service to the miners working the creeks near the lake, and named the community after their friend, Lachlin Taylor Burwash, mining recorder of the short-lived Yukon mining town of Silver City. During the 1913–15 gold rush in Alaska's Chisana River district, Burwash Landing continued to serve the gold miners crossing the border.

Today, Burwash Landing has a population of about 100 and retains its role as a service centre, although more to tourists and truckers travelling the Alaska Highway than to miners.

Canol Road

In April 1942, the U.S. military embarked on a grand scheme to tap a local source for vitally needed oil to support its northern World War II operation. The war effort included construction of the **Alaska Highway**, the deployment of thousands of troops in Alaska to guard against a feared Japanese invasion from the captured Aleutian Islands, and a major airlift of supplies to Siberia to aid a beleaguered Russian army's ultimately successful struggle to turn back a German invasion.

Oil existed along the Mackenzie River in Northwest Territory at Norman Wells—but the oil field was inaccessible. The U.S. military convinced a reluctant Canadian government, worried over the project's feasibility and its incursion into national sovereignty, to allow the construction of an oil pipeline and supporting road from **Whitehorse** to Norman Wells. The distance was about 825 kilometres, which seemed an easily managed distance to U.S. army engineers who were already two months into construction of the 2,451-kilometre-long Alaska Highway. The approved budget for the pipeline and road construction was $24 million. A refinery was also to be constructed in Whitehorse. The line was dubbed the Canol Pipeline, an acronym for Canadian oil.

On paper the plan may have looked simple enough. The reality, however, was that the pipeline had to cross through the heart of both the **Selwyn Mountains** and the huge barrier presented by the **Mackenzie Mountains**. The entire route cut through one of the most isolated regions of the Yukon, with steep valleys gouged by rushing streams and heavily affected by the presence of discontinuous **permafrost**.

The construction effort was plagued from the beginning by shoddy work and unforeseen logistical and supply problems, as well as an absence of any financial controls by the military commanders overseeing the project. Costs escalated and the entire project exceeded its original budget by five times.

Nevertheless the American effort persevered and both oil line and accompanying road were completed in almost exactly two years of frenzied construction. By April 1944 the oil line was pumping 3,000 barrels of oil a day to the Whitehorse refinery and the road officially opened to traffic the following September. When the northern war effort wound down in March 1945, however, the refinery was abruptly closed and the oil line shut down. Total months of operation—13; total cost—$134 million.

By this time few were sorry to see the pipeline abandoned. For the American military, the project had become an expensive embarrassment exposed in vivid detail by a U.S. senate inquiry headed in early 1944 by soon-to-be-president Harry Truman. The Canadian government had belatedly decided that the pipeline constituted a threat to its sovereign claim to the north and would have to become Canadian property after the war. This raised the issue of how to fund the hefty maintenance costs required to fix permafrost damage and construction faults.

Shortly after the end of the war, the pipeline, transmission stations, and the entire refinery were dismantled and shipped to Alberta where they were used in the Leduc oilfield. Maintenance shops along the Canol route were abandoned, bridges quickly stopped being repaired, and the road surface was allowed to deteriorate. Soon the northern section from **Ross River** to Norman Wells became impassable to vehicular traffic and the southern portion could only be travelled by heavy trucks equipped with winches for crossing the river.

The project's epitaph was probably most succinctly described by one critic as a "junkyard monument to military stupidity."

Today, however, the Canol Road has found new life with outdoor adventurers. On August 18, 1990 it was officially designated Canol Road National Historic Site and the 372-kilometre stretch from the Yukon–Northwest Territory border to Norman Wells became the Canol Road Heritage Trail. In the Yukon, from kilometre 0 at Johnsons Crossing to Ross River, the road traverses 234 kilometres of spectacular scenery rich in streams and lakes. There are no services on this stretch of road, requiring travellers to carry extra gas, spare tires, and other supplies. This part of the road is becoming an increasingly popular route for cycling expeditions.

From Ross River 231 kilometres remain to the end of the driveable section of Canol Road, with no option but to backtrack the entire distance. No services exist along this section. The highway is maintained, but washouts are common. Motor vehicle traffic is often extremely light; consequently it is becoming a mecca for adventurous cyclists. With the exception of **water**, which can be collected from the many creeks the road crosses (boiling recommended), all supplies must be carried.

Beyond the Yukon border, Canol Road Heritage Trail can be travelled by cyclists, but the road deteriorates more each year and the feasibility of cycling some sections is questionable and only to be undertaken by the most competent and determined. Hikers and cyclists are urged to travel in groups and to arrange for air drops by small plane or helicopter of resupply caches at intervals along the trail. Many river crossings are extremely dangerous at all times of the year, with some far too deep for wading. Weather in this rugged country can change radically overnight.

Canyon City

In 1897, two entrepreneurs realized there was **gold** to be made in enabling the stampeders rushing toward the **Klondike Gold Rush** to get past the major obstacle presented by **Miles Canyon** and the Whitehorse Rapids—situated about eight kilometres east of present-day downtown **Whitehorse**. Together, these two hazards had claimed the lives of a number of people who tried to pass through them on small boats loaded with passengers and supplies.

In the winter of 1897–98 John Hepburn constructed a 10.5-kilometre-long tramway along the western bank of the river. At the same time, Norman MacAuley erected a tramway on the east side that ran for about 8 kilometres. The two then set the same price for hauling cargo on their respective tramways—three cents per pound and $25 per boat. Because of the boat fee most prospectors preferred to hire professional boatmen, who took the boats through for less. But usually they also opted to unload their supplies and use the tramways to ensure the goods arrived safely at the other end of the canyon and rapids. The tram cars were horse drawn and the boats moved by trams pulled over log rails.

MacAuley soon bought out Hepburn and concentrated the operation on the river's east bank. A tent town sporting a roadhouse and saloon were soon thriving on that shore. Other entrepreneurs added more stores and dwellings to the new Canyon City. In June 1898, **North-West Mounted Police** Superintendent Sam Steele decreed that only experienced pilots registered with the police would be permitted to steer boats through the canyon. This enabled the police to ensure that boats entering the canyon were at least minimally seaworthy. It also added greatly to the congestion at Canyon City because of the additional delay while boats were inspected. Many boats failed the test and had to be moved by land, adding to the wait for MacAuley's tram service.

During 1897 and 1898 it is estimated that 20,000 gold seekers funnelled through this narrow point on their journey to the Klondike, all leaving some money in MacAuley's pockets. In July 1900, however, MacAuley's monopoly on the tram system was rendered worthless. That year, the **White Pass & Yukon Railway** link to Whitehorse was completed, skirting the rapids and canyon. Almost overnight Canyon City was abandoned and the business centre shifted to Whitehorse. Today only a few artifacts remain at the site.

Carcross

Located on the Klondike Highway south of **Whitehorse**, the village of Carcross was originally named Caribou Crossing by miners who had reached this junction point of the Tagish and Bennett lakes en route to the Klondike **gold** fields at **Dawson**. Twice a year large herds of **caribou** migrated across the easily forded Nares Lake shallows east of the townsite, which was no sooner developed to serve Klondike miners than it became an important stopping point for the **White Pass & Yukon Railway** in September 1898. The Caribou Hotel also opened in the same year. Still in operation, it is the Yukon's oldest continuously operating business.

When railway construction through the White Pass was completed, the final gold spike was hammered into the track here on July 29, 1900.

The name Caribou Crossing was changed to Carcross in 1902 due to the lobbying of Bishop Bompas, who had established a school for First Nations children the year before. Bompas was infuriated that mail addressed to the school was being redirected to other Caribou Crossings in British Columbia and Alaska. While the post office adopted the name change, the railway retained the station name of Caribou Crossing until 1916. The community remained an important rail depot until the station's closure in 1982. Today the old station is a visitor's centre. This is not, however, the original station, which burned down during a fire in 1910 that destroyed the station, the Caribou Hotel, a store, and most of the other buildings in downtown Carcross. The station, hotel, and store were rebuilt within a year.

For many years the sternwheeler *Tutshi* stood along the shore of the community, but in July 1990 it was destroyed by fire when someone cast aside a cigarette butt.

In the Carcross cemetery two of the co-discoverers of the Bonanza Creek gold strike that sparked the **Klondike Gold Rush** are buried. These are Skookum Jim Mason and Dawson Charlie (sometimes known as Tagish Charlie), whose First Nations' names were Keish and K̲áa Goox̲ respectively. Also buried in the cemetery is Kate Carmack, whose First Nations' name was Shaaw Tláa. She was Skookum Jim's sister and, at the time of the strike, the wife of the third co-discoverer, George Carmack. In 1900, Carmack deserted Kate for a white woman and refused her any part of the fortune amassed from the gold strike, as well as access to their daughter. In 1920, she died penniless.

One kilometre north of Carcross is reputedly the world's smallest desert— a 260-hectare expanse of sand that once lay on the bottom of a large glacial lake covering the entire valley bottom. Strong winds off Bennett Lake keep the sand here constantly shifting, rendering it difficult for plants other than lodgepole pine and kinnikinnick to grow.

Caribou

Barren-ground and woodland caribou share many characteristics. Both are members of the deer family and are adapted to survive in cold weather and snow. They have warm, hollow-haired coats that protect against extreme temperatures. Their muzzle, tail, and hooves are also furred. Caribou hooves are well suited for travelling across diverse landscapes. On soft snow, the large hooves act as virtual snowshoes. Their sharp edges can also be used to clear snow away to enable the caribou to reach lichen, their favourite winter food. In summer, their diet includes forbs, grasses, sedges, and willows.

While larger than deer, caribou average half the size of moose. The average weight of a bull moose is about 400 kilograms, while a bull caribou averages only 125 to 275 kilograms. Females are smaller yet, averaging 90 to 135 kilograms. Both males and females have antlers. Males' antlers are large and are shed after the rutting season in early winter. Females retain their antlers until after spring calving. Pregnant females use their antlers to help claim and defend feeding areas, ensuring high-quality food sources for themselves and their young.

A caribou follows a ridgeline near the Dempster Highway. (Erik Simanis photo)

Females give birth to a single calf in early June. Newborn calves can walk within hours of birth, but almost half fall prey to **wolves**, grizzly **bears**, and golden eagles, or die of pneumonia, drowning, or abandonment.

There are 22 woodland caribou and 2 barren-ground (Grant's) caribou herds in the Yukon. The territorial population estimate for woodland caribou is 30,000 to 35,000, while the Porcupine barren-ground herd is believed to number about 160,000 and the Fortymile herd about 22,000.

Woodland caribou herds occur in pockets throughout the southern half of the territory, extending north to the Bonnet Plume watershed area. This boundary merges with the southernmost extent of the barren-ground populations, which encompass most of the northern Yukon. The two largest woodland caribou herds are the Bonnet Plume herd, numbering about 5,000 animals, and the Redstone herd ranging across the **Mackenzie Mountains**, which is estimated to number between 5,000 and 10,000.

Several woodland caribou herds are considered vulnerable. These include the small herds in the region of **Carcross**, Aishihik Lake, Chisana Ridge, Moose Lake, and Ethel Lake. Studies show that all the small, isolated herds of woodland caribou tend to migrate only short distances between valley-bottom wintering ranges and alpine summer ranges. They do not move between herds, even when ranges overlap.

Once, the Fortymile herd of barren-ground caribou numbered in the hundreds of thousands and ranged as far west as Fairbanks, Alaska and as far south as **Whitehorse**. The herd formed the centre of an ecological system, feeding a pyramid of other animals, supporting **First Nations peoples**, and later feeding explorers and **gold** miners. During the **Klondike Gold Rush** the population began to decline rapidly as hunters harvested caribou by the thousands to feed the influx of prospectors.

Most of the devastation of this herd resulted from humans hunting for food and sport. Even as recently as the 1960s there were instances of Fortymile caribou being killed and left to rot. By 1975, the population had plummeted to only 5,000 and the herd was in jeopardy of extirpation. The survivors had largely withdrawn from the Yukon, surviving in a small pocket of land on the Alaskan side of the border.

Since then, the population has recovered both in numbers and range, but it remains threatened by hunting. The Canadian hunting harvest is relatively low because the caribou migrate into the Yukon only in late fall when road closures prevent access to the herd. In Alaska, however, year-round road access makes hunting simpler and the government allocates 2 percent of the herd to sport hunting annually. This means that about 400 Fortymile caribou are killed each year by sport hunters and a further 100 by First Nations subsistence hunters. Between 1989 and 1995, roughly 2,500 caribou were lost to the herd through hunting. Researchers believe that this level of hunting could threaten the viability of the herd's recovery, especially when natural predation is factored in.

The habitat of the Fortymile herd remains largely intact, so the 19th-century population level could be supported. Yukon biologists estimate that the herd will only achieve a true recovery when its numbers reach 60,000. Such a recovery is only likely through effective cooperative management between Yukon and Alaska wildlife agencies, especially with regard to hunting practices.

By contrast, the Porcupine herd population is relatively healthy, but could be threatened by natural resource development in its vast migrational territory and by overhunting. The year-round range of this herd includes much of northeastern Alaska, the northern Yukon, and the **Richardson Mountains** portion of the Northwest Territory. From late October to March it dwells in the Ogilvie and Richardson mountains boreal forest, feeding among trees and ranging across the open lake country. In April, pregnant females lead the northern migration to the calving grounds of Yukon's **Ivvavik National Park** and Alaska's adjoining Arctic National Wildlife Refuge. Summer is spent seeking relief from the swarms of **mosquitoes** and other parasitic insects. During this time, the herd can form huge aggregates of up to 70,000 and 80,000 animals, which move across the **tundra** in search of cool windswept areas. In fall, the caribou mate, with bulls sparring through September and October to establish dominance and the right to breed. After mating season, the caribou migrate to their wintering grounds.

Gwitchin, Inuvialuit, Northern Tutchone, and Inupiat from 13 communities in Alaska, the Yukon, and Northwest Territory depend on the herd for food. Non–First Nations people from these villages and from larger communities, such as Fairbanks and Whitehorse, also hunt this herd. For thousands of years the Gwitchin people of **Old Crow** have relied on the herd as their primary food source and caribou are a cornerstone of the Gwitchin culture. Annually, the harvest of Porcupine caribou has ranged from 2,000 to 7,000 animals a year.

Barren-ground caribou require large areas of relatively undisturbed tundra and boreal forest. They are most vulnerable to disturbance while on their calving grounds and while wintering in the lower reaches of watersheds. Both areas have potential for oil and gas exploration and consequent development. Global warming also poses a risk because this phenomenon increases snowfall levels in northern climates. Deep snow adversely impacts caribou calf survival rates.

The effort to ensure the survival of the barren-ground caribou population has resulted in several international agreements and the formation of various parks in both Canadian territories and in Alaska. **Vuntut National Park**, formed in 1993, was created partially to secure the protection of vital caribou range.

Caribou Fences

One of the most important sources of food for Yukon **First Nations peoples** was **caribou**. Hides, bones, and sinews from these bovines were also used to make clothing, shelters, and tools. As both barren-ground and woodland caribou migrated in herds, First Nations hunters developed group strategies for capturing and killing large numbers of caribou to provide for the needs of the tribe or family.

The most common method for achieving a large herd kill involved the construction of a caribou fence. Some of these fences were large, permanent structures; others were relatively small and built in such a manner that they would quickly collapse and cease hindering the free movement of the caribou herds.

Location was vital to the success of a fence. Hunt leaders would devote many hours to situating a fence structure across the width of a narrow valley or along the side of a mountain where a migrating caribou herd was known to pass.

Construction varied depending on whether the fence was being erected in woodland areas or in the open. In forests, the entire hunting group would work together piling up brush to a height of about 1.5 metres to form a wall supported by standing trees or, if there was a gap between trees, posts cut specifically to serve as braces for the fence. Where the fence was constructed in an open area, enough posts to support the entire fence had to be cut and transported to the site.

The fence was usually built in either a zigzag pattern or as a two-sided lane that led straight into a pocket-shaped barrier at the end known as a "snare pocket." The fences were often 1.5 kilometres long and sometimes more than 4 kilometres. The snare pocket was widest at the mouth and narrowed slightly toward its dead-end, with an average width at the mouth of about 35 metres and average length of about 240 metres. Inside the pocket, a series of small brush or hide walls was tied perpendicularly into the outer walls to create a narrow lane down the middle and a series of small three-walled chambers between the outer wall and the open lane. The chambers were about 2.5 metres wide and a snare was set at the opening to each.

Snares were made from braided caribou hide thongs or lacings, known as babiche. Each snare hung down to less than a metre above ground and formed a large loop wide enough for the caribou's antlers to pass inside. A long stick, called a "drag pole," was secured above the fence opening and held the loop.

To drive the caribou herd into the fence, the people would rush along the side of the herd howling like **wolves** and waving their arms to frighten the animals. Panicked, the herd would bolt and fail to recognize the danger of the ever narrowing fence it had entered. The hunters, meanwhile, lay in wait near the snare pocket. When the caribou entered the snare pocket they would become entangled in the mazelike structure of the snare sets. As an animal bolted to the side to try to escape, its head entered one of the snare loops, the drag pole was yanked down, and the noose cinched tight on the caribou's throat. The pole would usually become entangled in the heavy brush forming one of the walls and soon the caribou, exhausted from trying to break free, would either choke to death or collapse. Those that failed to strangle themselves would be stabbed to death or killed with bows and arrows by the hunters.

With the introduction of firearms, the use of caribou fences declined among Yukon First Nations peoples and this hunting method is no longer practised. The remains of several fences can still be found in the territory. The best preserved are several corral-shaped fences near **Old Crow**, where fences were commonly used to capture caribou of the Porcupine herd. There is also a straight-line fence close to the **Alaska Highway** near **Haines Junction** and fragments of several fences can be seen above the Fortymile River when travelling the Top of the World Highway from **Dawson** to Eagle, Alaska.

Carmacks

Named after George Washington Carmack, one of the co-discoverers of the gold that sparked the **Klondike Gold Rush**, Carmacks is located on the shore of the **Yukon River** 175 kilometres north on the Klondike Highway from

Whitehorse. The community got its start when Carmack found two seams of coal nearby—one at **Five Finger Rapids** and the other near Tantalus Butte. He built a cabin and dallied in a little mining and fur trading before quitting the place for the venture that eventually led to the discovery on Bonanza Creek in 1896. The cabin at Carmacks was reportedly equipped with an organ that Carmack was fond of playing, many volumes of classical literature, and back issues of *Scientific American* and other journals.

With the onset of the Klondike Gold Rush, Carmacks prospered as a riverboat fuelling stop because it was roughly midway between Whitehorse and **Dawson**. It also served as a major stopping point on the Overland Trail that linked the two communities.

Carmacks is situated near the ancestral home of the Ts'awlnjik Dan First Nation and the approximate boundary between the Northern and Southern Tutchone First Nations. The history of these peoples stretches back more than 10,000 years. Archaeological sites in the Carmacks area have yielded fossils and tools related to the so-called "Microblade Peoples" who lived here after the last Ice Age ended between 8,000 and 4,000 years ago. Most of the tool implements dating from this era utilized small, replaceable blades called microblades that were inserted into tools made of bone or antler.

Today, the population of Carmacks numbers approximately 500. It is an important service stop and recreational jumping-off point for travellers on the Klondike and Campbell **highways**.

Cheechako. *See* **Sourdough.**

Claim-Staking

Anyone, whether a Canadian citizen or Yukon resident, who is over the age of 18 can stake a claim in the territory. No license is required. All staking is governed by the Yukon Placer Mining Act, the provisions of which must be strictly followed.

Any land in the territory can be subject to a claim unless it is part of a national park, a cemetery or burial ground, already subject to a claim, government appropriated, land prohibited by the territorial government from mining, controlled by the Department of National Defence, within the boundaries of a community, occupied by a building, or excluded due to a **First Nations land**

claims settlement or unsettled claim. If the land is owned by somebody else the person staking the claim must receive permission from the mining recorder before proceeding.

A claim cannot exceed 152 metres in length and if next to a creek must be limited to one side of it, measuring back a distance of 305 metres. If the claim is not next to a creek, it is measured as if it were fronting the nearest creek. Non-creekside claims cannot exceed the depth of 305 metres but can run a length of up to 8 kilometres. Rental paid to the territorial government shall be $25.00 per mile or fraction thereof. The fee is payable on an annual basis. To sustain a lease beyond one year, the stakeholder must prove an expenditure of at least $1,000.00 for each leased mile contained in the claim's boundary.

A stake is physically marked by the driving of two posts into the ground. Post #1 is downstream from post #2 and set at the furthest extents of the claim. Each post should be as close to the base line as possible, so for creekside claims basically at the water's edge. The post must be a minimum of 1.22 metres in height and have a marking sign of at least 30 centimetres high and 10 centimetres wide that clearly announces the claim holder, the date the claim was made, and the dimensions of the claim. Between the posts a straight line of sight should be cleared through all vegetation.

Climate

Nowhere in North America has greater annual temperature range fluctuations than the Yukon, which also has the continent's highest air pressures. The difference between the territory's highest temperature month and lowest temperature month is about 40° Celsius. The greatest absolute range of temperature yet recorded is at **Mayo**—98.3° Celsius. **Dawson** holds the Canadian record for highest sea-level pressure, 107.96 kilopascals (kPa), set on February 2, 1989. Normal Canadian January sea-level pressure is 102.31 kPa.

Yukon's climate is generally referred to as continental, despite the presence of the **Beaufort Sea** on its northern border and the proximity of the Pacific Ocean on the western flank of the **St. Elias Mountains**. The Beaufort Sea is ice-covered too much of the year to moderate air temperatures, while the Pacific Ocean's moderating influence is diminished by the towering St. Elias Mountains, which cause most of the moisture flowing inland to dump on the Alaska Panhandle as rain or as snow. In the winter mild Pacific air does frequently spill over the mountains to moderate the predominant cold Arctic air.

The single most significant factor affecting the Yukon's climate is topography, particularly its mountains. Mountains influence Yukon weather more than any other controls, including latitude, marine effects, and weather systems. Mountain ranges channel winds, block storms, lengthen weather spells, increase precipitation on windward slopes, and reduce precipitation on downwind slopes. The St. Elias Mountains and the Coast Range present an almost impenetrable barrier to Pacific storms and mild weather fronts. To the east, the Mackenzie and Richardson mountains pose a less significant barrier to the large air masses flowing out of the Arctic. Between these two mountain systems lies the Interior Basin—an irregular, rough highland ranging in elevation from 900 to 1,500 metres. This highland, often called a plateau, is fragmented by local mountains, and valleys and deep glacier-fed lakes that are both consistently long and narrow.

Winter weather is generally cold and dry, dominated by cold Arctic air that stalls over the central interior for weeks on end. As the cold air flows in from Alaska on one side and the Northwest Territory on the other, it becomes even colder over the Interior Basin as a result of heat loss to radiation during the long northern nights. Most winters, a nearly continuous low pressure centre in the northern Gulf of Alaska sends a stream of storm into the southern half of the Yukon. During the short spring, this storm track shifts northward, diminishing the intensity of these weather disturbances.

In summer, the Yukon's weather is influenced by a large high pressure cell usually located over the mid-Pacific and by weak low pressure systems over the northern Bering Sea, west of Alaska. This creates a track of weak storms that cause significant cloud and precipitation, especially in the territory's north. Although hours of sunshine are high in the summer, June-to-August rainfall usually is greater than total precipitation during the six-month winter. This is despite the number of rainy days in summer matching the number of snowy days in winter.

Fall sees the contrast between Arctic and Pacific air increasing, with more resulting storm activity. As fall progresses, the major storm tracks slip further southward, causing considerable concentrations of cloud and precipitation in southeastern Yukon. By mid-December, after freeze-up, Arctic highs dominate and the wet weather ends, giving way to dry air and clear skies.

Throughout the Yukon, the degree of northerly latitude greatly affects the length of day and amount of sunshine. In the south during winter, the sun is visible only a few brief hours each day. But north of the **Arctic Circle** (66° 33' N), winter sees no direct sunlight at all. On December 21, **Whitehorse** receives its shortest day—only six hours. Along the Arctic coast, however, polar night persists for seven weeks from November 29 to January 15. Polar night is the period when the sun fails to rise above the horizon, though darkness is seldom complete even then. Starlight is sharp, while moonlight and the **northern lights** are far more intense than they are farther south.

In April, the length of days increases by ten minutes daily. All of the Yukon enjoys a great deal of sunlight in the summer. On the Arctic coast, the sun stays up continuously from about May 19 to July 26, while Whitehorse's longest days extend over 19 hours from about 3:30 a.m. to 10:30 p.m. The length of the Yukon's summer days compensates for the decreased intensity of solar radiation caused by the relatively low angle at which the sun's rays strike the earth at higher latitudes. This means that total incoming solar energy during the Yukon's summer is approximately equal to that of Canadian regions in far more temperate latitudes.

The prolonged light fosters rapid plant growth, enabling many vegetable and grain crops to be successfully grown in the territory (*see* **Agriculture**). Longer days also mean greater heat accumulation, producing warmer temperatures than might otherwise be expected in such northerly regions. Most of the territory experiences fewer than 60 frost-free days a year.

Given the long days of summer it is hardly surprising that May and June are the Yukon's sunniest months. Each averages 280 hours of sunshine. Yukon summer days enjoy about four hours more sunshine than experienced in the southerly portions of Canada. The least sunshine is experienced in December when days are short or nonexistent in the more northerly regions. The monthly total duration of sunshine in December ranges from 0 to 30 hours. Most parts of the Yukon receive about 1,600 to 1,800 hours of sunshine annually.

From late summer to early winter, when waterways remain open, the Yukon is prone to fog in the valley bottoms. This fog peaks in late fall–early winter when ice-crystal fog begins to form. Ice fog, as it is commonly known, forms in frigid air below –30° Celsius, when the air is able to hold little water vapour. As the air cools further, the traces of supercooled water vapour condense into a fog of ice crystals rather than water droplets. Ice fog usually occurs where there is a source of extra water vapour. This source is most often artificial, such as airplane or motor-vehicle exhaust, industrial discharges, or even the vapour expelled during breathing. In settlements, periods of ice fog occur during the coldest spells, when the amount of heating fuel consumed increases, and last longest when winds are calm or light. Increasing industrial activity and motor-vehicle use are causing an upswing in the rate of ice fog generation within the territory.

Precipitation levels in the Yukon vary considerably from north to south and by elevation. In the interior, annual precipitation ranges from 200 millimetres along the Beaufort coastline to 700 millimetres on the south slopes of the **Mackenzie Mountains**. Pacific Ocean storm tracks bring about 2,000 millimetres of precipitation annually into the southwest corner, despite the barrier presented by the St. Elias Mountains. **Teslin**, southeast of Whitehorse, receives only 330 millimetres of precipitation, which is about the territory's average. This is the same average amount experienced in Alberta's dry southeastern corner.

July and August are usually the wettest months, with April the driest. Summer rainfall is heavier in the Yukon than elsewhere in the Canadian north. About 60 percent of yearly precipitation in lowland areas comes as rain or drizzle, while the rest is snow. At elevations over 1,000 metres, rain and snow are usually evenly matched, while above 2,500 metres precipitation is almost entirely snow.

Along the Arctic slope in the north, winter snowfall averages less than 100 centimetres. The lowest snowfall rates are at Komakuk Beach where only 60 centimetres of snow falls annually, but it also remains longer than anywhere else in the territory. In the Liard Basin, the St. Elias Mountains, the higher Cassiar Mountains, and the western slopes of the Mackenzie Mountains, snowfall ranges between 150 and 250 centimetres. During May in all parts of the territory the snow melts, announcing the arrival of the short spring.

Northern coastal sites experience the highest winds in the territory. At Komakuk Beach, for example, the winds are above 30 kilometres per hour 20 percent of the time. In Mayo, Snag, and Teslin, winds exceeding 30 kilometres per hour occur only 1 percent of the time.

Compared to the eastern Arctic, Yukon winters are remarkably mild. At times Pacific air edges into the southwest, bringing mild weather that can last for weeks. Except on the narrow Arctic slope bordering the Beaufort Sea, where February is the coldest month, the rest of the territory experiences its average coldest temperatures in January. The average temperature range in January is from −20⁰ Celsius in the south to −30⁰ Celsius in the north. Interior valleys are generally warmer than elsewhere in the territory.

Yukon winter sees an amazing reversal in the normal pattern of temperatures decreasing as elevation increases. From late October to early March, a shallow, intense inversion layer is present almost continuously over the Yukon, causing temperatures to increase as elevations rise. In extreme circumstances, valley temperatures of −45⁰ Celsius can rise through inversion to −15⁰ Celsius at the 1,000-metre level, and to near 0⁰ Celsius at altitudes of 1,500 to 2,000 metres.

Because of the inversion effect, higher elevation communities often experience less severe winter temperatures and more midwinter mild spells than valley communities. Over a 6-year period, for example, **Faro**, at an elevation of 691 metres, recorded temperatures as low as −55⁰ Celsius. Meanwhile, over a 13-year period, the nearby Anvil mine at 1,158-metre-high Anvil recorded no temperature lower than −46.1⁰ Celsius.

Cold spells are usually of short duration throughout the territory, but are especially so in the south. Over 30 years in Whitehorse, January temperatures dropped below −40⁰ Celsius 60 times. Only one of these occurrences lasted even 10 days. To the north, Mayo experienced 137 such cold spells, with three lasting 15 days or more and the longest spell running for 24 days. Yukon cold periods are seldom accompanied by severe wind chill, as air movement usually ranges from calm to light.

Yukoners usually consider spring to start in May and fall in September. The brief summer begins in early June and is fading fast by late August. Except in the far north and at higher elevations, temperatures throughout the territory during June, July, and August average 10⁰ Celsius. Summer temperatures are only slightly cooler than those experienced elsewhere in most of western Canada. For example, the average Dawson temperature in July is 15.6⁰ Celsius, compared to 15.8⁰ Celsius in Edmonton. Winter temperatures, however, are much colder. Dawson's average temperature in January is −30.7⁰ Celsius, compared to −16.5⁰ Celsius in Edmonton. Whitehorse is also considerably colder than Edmonton, posting a January average of −20.7⁰ Celsius.

The average annual temperature in the Yukon is below 0⁰ Celsius in all areas, generally decreasing as latitude increases. All Yukon weather stations, except **Watson Lake**, near the British Columbia border, post freezing temperatures in every month of the year.

Snag, a weather station northeast of **Beaver Creek** in the territory's west, holds the distinction of having recorded the coldest temperatures in Canadian and North American history. At 7:20 a.m. on February 3, 1947, a reading of −63° Celsius was recorded here. At the time, skies were clear, winds calm, and visibility unlimited. The previous morning, the weather station had posted a new record low of −62° Celsius. Weather staff reported that audibility increased during the cold spell. There was also intense radio static, fog patches hovered over dog teams, and a person's breath hissed as it left the mouth.

It is entirely possible that colder temperatures have since occurred at Snag but if so they have gone unrecorded. In September 1966, the weather station here was closed. It originally opened in 1942 as part of the war effort, providing a weather station and emergency landing strip for flyers taking cargo over the Bering Sea to Russia as part of the massive airlift of supplies to the Russian army.

The following are Yukon weather records:

- The highest temperature recorded in the Yukon is 36.1° Celsius, recorded on June 14, 1969 at Mayo.
- The lowest temperature is −63.0° Celsius, recorded February 3, 1947 at Snag.
- The greatest annual snowfall, of 452 centimetres, was recorded at Tuchitua in the winter of 1971–72.
- The greatest number of foggy days was 86, recorded at Komakuk Beach during 1976.
- The wettest period ever recorded was at Watson Lake, where it rained, drizzled, or snowed for 186 days in 1966.
- For 107 days snow blew constantly at Komakuk Beach in the winter of 1982–83.
- The sun shone at Haines Junction for 2,064 hours in 1972.
- The wind hit 108 kilometres per hour at Shingle Point on December 31, 1973.
- Carcross experienced a 140-day frost-free period in 1946.

Coal River Springs Territorial Park

Situated about 80 kilometres east of **Watson Lake**, Coal River Springs Territorial Park was officially dedicated as the Yukon's second territorial park and first ecological reserve on September 17, 1990. The park was a combined effort

Limestone walls form the Coal River Springs into a series of stepped terraces. (Marten Berkman photo)

of the Yukon **government**, the Liard First Nations, and the Nature Conservancy of Canada.

The springs are a series of pools of icy blue **water** separated by limestone terrace steps that descend through lush **vegetation**. Looming over the springs are mountains composed of limestone outcrops. As groundwater percolates through the cracks in the rock the limestone is dissolved. This calcium-enriched water then emerges at the foot of the mountains. Here, mosses and other vegetation alter the acidity of the water as they absorb carbon dioxide. The resulting pH level change combines with thermal warming to reduce the water's ability to retain the dissolved calcium, which then mixes with the dissolved carbon dioxide and separates from the water as a precipitate.

This precipitate is known as tufa or travertine. It is deposited on the surface of any object contacting the water. Twigs, leaves, and even entire trees can become coated in the rocklike tufa. Living mosses bordering the pools are turned to a stonelike formation. Tufa continually builds up at a rate of two to three centimetres annually and this process has created the terraced formations surrounding the springs.

Over time the edges of the springs' pools grow inward and upward until they are suspended over the water below. Left undisturbed, the pool walls would eventually close over the pool to form a dome, and a new pool would form on the surface of the dome cover. It is believed that several such chambers are hidden below pools that are visible today.

The water flow and resultant buildup of tufa changes due to natural influences. Mosses grow, calcify, and block some drainage channels, causing new channels to be created. Wildlife, such as moose and beavers, also can divert flow by disturbing channels. In 1984, for example, a beaver dam diverted the flow away from the main formation, resulting in some of the pools drying up and losing their colour. Some of these main terraces remain dry today, although the streambed recovered naturally in most places.

An abundance of vegetation is supported by the pools due to the average water temperature of 11° Celsius, which ensures that it remains ice-free year round. Some plants are uncommon to the rest of the region, such as bluegrass, wild sarsaparilla, red and white baneberry, and knotweed. Black and grizzly **bears** are present in the area, as are **wolves**, possibly attracted by the healthy moose populations. The boreal toad and northern wood frog are also found here in the wetlands.

Coal River was established as an ecological reserve to protect the fragile tufa formations. Heavy human traffic is discouraged and no plans exist to improve access routes. Most visitors are whitewater canoeists or rafters travelling the Coal River.

The spring formations are highly vulnerable, so any contact with the water is prohibited. Although the coal springs are thermal springs, their average temperature is insufficient to classify them as true hot springs.

Columbian Disaster

On September 25, 1906, the worst paddlewheeler accident in Yukon history occurred on the **Yukon River** as the steamer *Columbian* rounded a bend below Eagles Nest Bluff adjacent to the present-day Campbell River Highway, about 9 kilometres east of its intersection with the Klondike Highway, north of **Carmacks**. On this day the *Columbian* was carrying about 2,700 kilograms of gunpowder and explosives to the mining camps near **Dawson**.

As the sternwheeler rounded the bend, Phil Murray, a young deckboy,

In 1899, the sternwheeler Columbian *made its first trip up the Yukon River to Whitehorse. Seven years later it would suffer the territory's worst disaster.* (Yukon Archives, Macbride Museum Collection, #4012)

grabbed his rifle and started shooting at what has been described as either a flock of ducks startled into flight by the appearance of the vessel or some squirrels on the shoreline. Another crew member, believed to be a fireman, confronted the boy and demanded he hand over the rifle, as its use was against regulations set by the steamship company. As the boy stepped forward to surrender the weapon he tripped and it went off, discharging directly into the store of explosives. The entire pile exploded, ripping away the front of the ship, demolishing the steering equipment and engine controls, and killing six crewmen, including the boy and fireman.

The captain was able to save the vessel from sinking and the lives of the rest of his 18 crewmen by reversing the paddle against the current. This enabled him to bring the wreck ashore so that he and his crew could escape.

Contact Creek

On September 24, 1942, just 0.8 kilometres south of the Yukon border with British Columbia, road crews working south from **Watson Lake** toward Fort Nelson, B.C. as part of the **Alaska Highway** project bulldozed up to their counterparts working northward. When they met, the Yukon was connected by road to the rest of Canada for the first time. The previously unnamed creek was quickly anointed Contact Creek by the U.S. army engineers.

Crow. *See* **Raven.**

Dawson

On August 17, 1896, on the banks of what was then called Rabbit Creek, Californian George Carmack and his Tagish partners Keish, known by whites as Skookum Jim Mason, and K̲áa Goox̲, or Dawson Charlie (sometimes known as Tagish Charlie), discovered **gold**. They staked their claims, renamed the creek Bonanza, and started history's most famous gold rush. Just a few days earlier, not very far away, at a site on Sixtymile River a somewhat less dramatic event unfolded. Prospector Robert Henderson, who had actually advised Carmack to try panning another creek near Rabbit Creek, visited Joseph Ladue, the owner and operator of a small trading post and sawmill that produced sluice boxes for the dozens of prospectors roaming the area's many streams in search of the elusive gold. Henderson showed Ladue a small amount of gold dust he had discovered on Gold Bottom Creek, a tributary of the Klondike River. A frustrated prospector himself and a shrewd entrepreneur, Ladue recognized the potential for real riches lay perhaps not in gold itself but in creating a townsite to supply the miners that were sure to pour into the region when the inevitable bonanza strike was made.

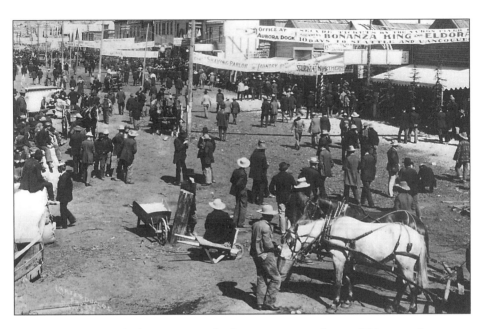

In 1899 Dawson was the largest city north of San Francisco and west of Winnipeg. Its streets thronged with prospectors and those who mined them for profit. (Larrs and Duclos photo, NAC C6648)

Barely five days after the strike on Bonanza Creek, Ladue arrived at the junction of the Yukon and Klondike rivers and staked out a townsite on the swampy lowland fronting the mountain that overlooks the Klondike's mouth. Although the site had long been a traditional seasonal gathering place for **First Nations peoples**, Canadian law did not recognize their right to the land and consequently Ladue was able to claim the entire area for himself. Shortly, Ladue had constructed a rough warehouse and a small cabin for himself that also served as a saloon. He named the new town Dawson, after the famous director of the Geological Survey of Canada, George Mercer Dawson.

By January 1897 the number of houses in Dawson numbered only five, but a small tent city was growing rapidly as prospectors abandoned Circle City, Alaska to make a 400-kilometre trek through winter snows to reach the site of the **Klondike Gold Rush**. By spring the **population** was about 1,400, including at least two women and a Jesuit missionary. All this time, the news of the gold strike had still not reached the outside world. Canadian government surveyor William Ogilvie, based at Fortymile Creek, had yet to find a way to get word back to the federal government in Ottawa. When the news did finally reach Ottawa later that spring nothing more than a small pamphlet was published announcing the gold find. It was so lacklustre in its wording that the announcement failed to generate any interest.

One year after the first strike, Ogilvie estimated that $2.5 million worth of gold had already been extracted from the creeks. Ogilvie duly reported this to Ottawa by hiring two men to carry his dispatch out by birchbark canoe. By the time this message reached Ottawa, however, the news would have spread in a far more dramatic fashion.

Meanwhile, Ladue was raking in gold himself. He and other entrepreneurs who could lay hands on wares to sell the prospectors were able to get tremendous prices. A night in Ladue's saloon cost an average of $50.00, while a single egg sold for $1.00, and a five-minute bath cost $1.50. But supplies of all sorts were in short supply and at times the booming community teetered on the edge of famine.

In June, bartender Harry Ash opened the Northern Saloon in a log building and the first night raked in $30,000 and averaged $3,000 a night after that. He left three months later after making a reported profit of $100,000. Before summer's end 10 saloons were in operation and a few dance-hall girls were ensconced in the community and taking in $100 a night. Ladue was selling town lots for up to $12,000. The price of a log cabin was $200 a square foot. By summer's end some 3,500 people called Dawson home. The community was a hodgepodge of buildings and tents haphazardly erected and linked by muddy lanes and paths. Across the **Yukon River** another community, known officially as Klondike City but nicknamed Lousetown, had also developed, displacing the First Nations people who had used this area for a camp as well.

June also saw the arrival of the first supply steamships from downstream. When they departed the ships took with them about 80 prospectors with a fortune in gold. Soon these miners were steaming south on two ships, the *Portland*, bound for Seattle, and the *Excelsior* en route to San Francisco. The *Excelsior* arrived first on July 14, 1897, so when the *Portland* steamed into Seattle Harbour thousands lined the docks eagerly hoping to catch sight of the wealthy gold prospectors who had been making headlines in newspapers around the world. Even before the prospectors stepped off the ship, however, thousands of Americans and Canadians were already trying to find a way to get to Dawson and join the gold rush.

In Canada, Canadian Pacific Railway passenger trains headed west bulging with stampeders. Steamships sailing for the ports of Alaska likewise overflowed. In all, more than 100,000 people tried to reach the Klondike and some 40,000 managed the trip.

Most arrived in the spring of 1898, via the various routes that became collectively known as the **Trails of '98**. Along with the miners came more entrepreneurs, further bolstering Dawson's commercial district. On May 27, 1898, the town's first newspaper, the *Klondike Nugget,* published its first edition. The next day the town was flooded by spring runoff that only subsided about 10 days later. On June 8, an armada of roughly hewn boats arrived from upstream, the first great onslaught of stampeders who had travelled the Chilkoot Trail.

By now, building lots in Dawson sold for $40,000, a single room rented for $100 a month, and a log cabin's rent was $400. By comparison, a four-bedroom apartment in New York City rented at the time for about $120 a month.

Dawson celebrated Dominion Day on July 1, 1898 with the status of having become overnight the largest Canadian city west of Winnipeg and the largest western community north of San Francisco. It had a telephone service, running water, and steam heat connected to some of its buildings. There were two banks, two newspapers locked in a circulation war, five churches, and many more saloons and dance halls. Among these was the Palace Grand with a seating capacity of 2,200. Twelve sawmills were cranking out millions of boards to be joined with nails that sold for almost $20 a kilogram. For those with money it was becoming possible to buy almost anything desired. "If you have money, spend it; that's what it's there for," one prospector advised his recently arrived nephew.

Approximately 16,000 people lived in Dawson itself, with about another 15,000 working and living on the nearby creeks. Elsewhere in North America, boomtowns linked to gold rushes had become lawless and violent places. But the presence of the **North-West Mounted Police** ensured that the mostly American throngs of prospectors kept the peace. In 1898, there was not a single murder in Dawson and very little theft. No doubt this was the result of a law that forbade the carrying of sidearms. This peacefulness existed despite a great deal of drunkenness, as prospectors and Dawson residents alike consumed more than 545,000 litres of alcohol during 1898.

The consumption of alcohol served particularly to capture the attention of the federal government in Ottawa, which realized it was losing a great deal of revenue in the form of a liquor tax. The Yukon had been a part of the Northwest

Territories at the time and the liquor taxes paid in Dawson flowed into the territorial government coffers. Ottawa, anxious to divert the funds to itself, undertook the creation of a distinct territory that would be subject to federal administrative control. On June 13, 1898 the new territory was declared and Dawson became its first capital.

No sooner was Dawson being called the "Paris of the North" than its fortunes started to decline. By 1898 most of the viable claims on the creeks had been taken up and some of these were already exhausted. For the majority of the 40,000 prospectors who reached the Klondike there was little chance of striking it rich by staking a new claim and the claims already discovered were too expensive to buy up.

By the spring of 1899 word arrived of another great gold find on the beaches by Nome, Alaska. Here, it was said, the sand speckled with flakes of gold. Prospectors started looking westward, even as Dawson rebuilt from two fires that had collectively destroyed the most expensive parts of the community. In the first fire, which broke out near the end of 1898, more than $500,000 in real estate was lost. The second, on April 26, 1899, destroyed 117 buildings valued at more than $1 million. As the town started rebuilding that summer more than 8,000 people departed Dawson, most headed for the new gold rush at Nome.

The town that rose out of the ashes less resembled a boomtown than it did a relatively prosperous and increasingly conservative southern Canadian town. Sewers were installed. Streets were improved. Houses were built of sturdier materials. The number of saloons declined rapidly, while the numbers of formal parlours in homes increased. Dawson continued to prosper as a mining city, but it was a prosperity based on more advanced mining techniques than **placer mining** on creeksides. By 1902, the same year Dawson was incorporated as a city, the population had dropped to fewer than 1,000. Many houses and businesses were boarded up and their owners moved away forever. Yet the community continued to prosper despite its dramatic population decline. In 1903, for example, Andrew Carnegie donated $25,000 to the community for the building of a library.

In 1911, gold mining operations around Dawson yielded an all-time high but the outbreak of the Great War in 1914 resulted in most of the mines closing. They would remain closed until the mid-1930s when higher gold prices caused a minor boom, but the last gold mining dredge closed in 1952. The following year, the territorial capital was shifted to **Whitehorse**.

By the end of the 1950s many of the historic buildings in Dawson were in such bad shape it was feared they would either rot away or collapse. In 1960 Parks Canada rebuilt and reconstructed the Palace Grand Theatre. Since then Parks Canada has restored a number of the buildings as part of its Klondike National Historic Sites project. The restoration is largely responsible for Dawson's emergence as undoubtedly the largest tourist attraction in the Yukon. Approximately 60,000 people, most arriving in the summer, come to Dawson annually to get a taste of the world's most famous gold rush.

The permanent population of Dawson numbers about 2,000 people. It is situated 536 kilometres northwest of Whitehorse on the Klondike Highway. Exhibits of the gold-rush era and Dawson's social history can be found in the Dawson City Museum and Historical Society building. Several of the Klondike National Historic Sites buildings also house displays. On the shore, the steamer *Keno*—one of the last **sternwheelers** to ply the Yukon and Stewart rivers—may be found.

Dempster Highway

The only Canadian highway that crosses the **Arctic Circle**, the Dempster Highway extends from a point 40 kilometres east of **Dawson** to Inuvik 741 kilometres northeast on the shore of the Mackenzie Delta in the Northwest Territory (NWT). Throughout the Yukon section, this highway cuts across a region that is entirely wilderness on both sides of the road except for the tiny service facility at Eagle Plains.

Construction of the highway was conceived in 1957 under the "Road to Resources" program of Conservative Prime Minister John Diefenbaker's government. This program aimed to stimulate northern economies, confirm Canadian sovereignty over the north, and provide access for natural resource development. The first oil well had been drilled in the **Eagle Plain** three years earlier and the petroleum potential of Fort McPherson in NWT had also been recognized. These two developments led the federal government to give priority to construction of a road through the **Ogilvie Mountains** to provide access to both the Eagle Plain and Mackenzie Delta.

Surveying and clearing began in 1958 and by 1961 about 115 kilometres of road had been constructed. The project then foundered as petroleum and mining exploration in the region failed to produce the resource discoveries anticipated. For the next 10 years little was done on the highway and it seemed likely the project would be entirely abandoned. That changed with the discovery of vast oil and gas reserves in Prudhoe Bay, Alaska and a planned northern pipeline. Following the Prudhoe Bay discovery came major Canadian and American oil and gas exploration of the **Beaufort Sea**. The government decided that an all-season road to the Mackenzie Delta was now a vital necessity. Construction began again in 1970 and by 1979 the road was completed, with an upgrade in 1988.

To protect the fragile **tundra** over which much of the road is constructed, engineers built many sections of the highway on a 10-metre bed of crushed rock. The rock provides an insulating layer to prevent the **permafrost** underneath from melting, which would cause the road to sink into a mire of mud.

Driving the Dempster is a considerable challenge and should only be undertaken by the adventurous. The highway snakes a torturous path across the landscape and its gravel surface is alternately either extremely dusty or muddy. From Dawson to Fort McPherson no services exist except in a very limited way at Eagle Plains 369 kilometres from the southern start point. From Eagle Plains to Fort McPherson there are again no services. Spare tires, extra fuel, and other emergency supplies are a must for travelling this highway safely. Travellers should also be familiar with gravel-road driving techniques.

Increasingly the Dempster Highway is becoming popular with cyclists and hikers from around the world. There are few real hiking trails off the roadsides but endless opportunities exist to head off in any direction into the wilderness for hikes ranging from a few hours to weeks at a time. The highway passes through the south and north ranges of the Ogilvies, including the spectacular Tombstone Range, crosses the Eagle Plain, then cuts through the **Richardson Mountains** into NWT.

Wildlife is abundant the entire way, including woodland and barren-ground **caribou**, grizzly and black **bears**, **wolves**, moose, and sheep. Remarkable densities of up to 400 per half hectare of smaller **mammals**, such as mice, voles, and lemmings, have been recorded. At least 158 species of **birds** are also present, including the golden eagle, gyrfalcons, and the endangered anatum **peregrine falcon**. Three species of loons breed along the Dempster, 20 species of shorebirds occur, and snow geese pass by the Arctic Red River en route to Arctic breeding grounds. Of all the birds that migrate through the Dempster country in summer, only about 20 species overwinter.

The Dempster highway was named in tribute to **North-West Mounted Police** corporal W. J. D. Dempster, who participated in more of the exhausting police dog team patrols between Dawson and Fort McPherson than any other Mountie. The trail the police used is crossed by the highway. Dempster was also the leader of the rescue team that sought to save the **Lost Patrol**.

Destruction Bay

Approximately 108 kilometres north of **Haines Junction** at the 1,743-kilometre point of the **Alaska Highway**, Destruction Bay borders the western shore of Kluane Lake. This village has a population of only about 50 people.

The community was created in 1942 by U.S. army engineers working on the highway during World War II. Soon after the engineers erected some barracks and other buildings, high winds swept down the lake and blew down most of the structures. The previously unnamed facility had earned itself a name.

Over the years false tales have been spread that the community's name refers to the many stampeders en route to the **Klondike Gold Rush** who were drowned when storms destroyed their boats on the lake. There is no truth to these tales.

Today, Destruction Bay has a boat ramp that provides access to the excellent trout fishing on Kluane Lake and is a small service centre for tourists travelling the highway.

Diamond Tooth Gertie's

In 1971, Diamond Tooth Gertie's opened as Canada's first and only legal gambling hall, bar, and cancan show palace. Operated as a nonprofit facility by the Klondike Visitor Association, "Gertie's," as it is commonly known, is located in a historic **Dawson** building constructed in 1901 to house the fraternal Arctic Brotherhood. Today, the building is filled from mid-May to mid-September with hundreds of tourists who come to try their luck at the gambling tables—featuring roulette, blackjack, Texas hold-em poker, and the wheel. Dozens of slot machines line the outer walls. Several times a day a floor show overseen by a Diamond Gertie impersonator features a bevy of cancan girls who dance in a style that was seldom, if ever, seen in Dawson during the **Klondike Gold Rush**. Noted for its high kicks that exposed petticoats and stockinged legs, the cancan was popularized in Parisian dance halls in the 1830s but was never as popular in conservative North America, even in the gold-mining town saloons and dance halls.

Indeed, most dance halls in Dawson were relatively formal places. Waltzes, polkas, reels, and schottisches were common dance-hall fare and the women, known as percentage girls, wore typical Victorian attire: long-sleeved, high-collared blouses and long, flared skirts. Some of the more daring might have revealed a bit of ankle, but hems were never shorter than mid-calf. On a typical night, a percentage girl would go through 125 to 150 dances of one to two minutes duration, receiving 25 cents of the dollar the men paid for each dance.

Of slightly higher stature than the percentage girls were the variety girls. These wore fashionable Parisian gowns when mingling with the men and somewhat racier outfits when performing dances on the stage. Above the variety girls were the actresses and singers who rarely mixed with the prospectors. Much of the entertainment offered the prospectors was actually vaudeville theatre, including songs by children, and skits.

For her part, the true Diamond Tooth Gertie, whose real name was Gertie Lovejoy, was known as a demure little woman, who though pretty was rather self-effacing. This was despite the fact that when she worked the dance halls she wore a small diamond between two of her teeth, which gave rise to her moniker. Gertie went on to marry C. W. C. Taber, one of Dawson's most prominent lawyers, but she could never live down having worked the dance halls among the more easily scandalized, genteel members of Dawson's post-goldrush society.

The modern-day Diamond Tooth Gerties strive to rekindle the atmosphere of the Klondike dance halls where women, such as the one pictured, entertained thousands of prospectors.
(NAC PA-13326)

Dog Sledding

The use of dogs for transporting goods in winter was developed by northern **First Nations peoples** many generations before Europeans arrived in North America. European explorers and traders quickly recognized the efficiency of using dogs and adopted the technique, making some significant improvements to sled design. In the Yukon, most pre–European contact sleds were a basic flat-bottomed toboggan dragged by dogs through the heavy snow. This design was modified by the Europeans through the addition of two narrow wooden runners that raised a rectangular-shaped basket up off the snow.

French-speaking dog-sled operators tended to yell *"Marche!"* as a command for their dog teams to set off. This was misinterpreted by English explorers as *"mush."* Out of this confusion developed the tradition of referring to dog-sled drivers as mushers. Today, most mushers call out *"mush"* as the order for the dogs to proceed.

Dog-sled teams usually number 2 to 12 animals. They are commonly hitched in pairs to a single towline, called a gangline. In deeper snow, the dogs might be reconfigured into a single file so the first animal breaks a path for the rest of the team and the going becomes increasingly easier. The lead animal is generally replaced after a short time of breaking trail and allowed to rest in the easier rear position. When snow becomes too deep, mushers sometimes have to don snowshoes and break the snow themselves, leading the dogs behind them.

Free of the natural hazards often found in denser woods, frozen rivers have always served as important dog-sled thoroughfares. (Yukon Archives, Claude B. Tidd Collection, #8383)

The size and type of dog used in dog sledding varied dramatically through-out history. At times a musher just used whatever dogs were available. At other times specific sizes of animals were selected for various types of sled loads and trip duration. For example, smaller, wiry, but muscular dogs were often selected for short trips where speed was of the essence and the load relatively light. For longer trips, or those involving heavy loads, larger dogs were used.

North-West Mounted Police patrols in the Yukon, for example, preferred to use five-dog teams comprised of large malamutes and Mackenzie River breeds of huskies. These dogs ranged between 36 and 68 kilograms. In addition to their strength and stamina, these breeds were noted for being able to endure snow and ice on their feet that would immobilize other breeds.

Mushing across rugged wilderness terrain presents the dogs and driver with a variety of challenges and hazards. Heavy ice on slopes or ridges must be avoid-ed, often requiring long detours. If the ice is overlaid with snow the challenge is to recognize its presence before dog team, sled, and driver are on top of it. Failure to recognize this danger often results in the whole outfit skidding out of control in a tangle down a slope, where serious injury may result.

If the dogs make a sharp turn, and the driver is insufficiently prepared, the sled can be cracked like a whip. The sled and driver may be slammed into trees or thrown over the edge of a bank.

A difficult danger to recognize is slush ice, often indistinguishable from sur-rounding areas of soft snow. Composed of snow, ice, and water, and often over-laid by a covering of snow, slush ice immediately drenches the dogs' paws, requiring the driver to stop immediately on getting clear of the slush to dry the animals. Failure to do so will result in the dogs' paws icing up. Iced paws are prone to being cut and can result in the immobilization of a team. In cases where slush ice and other sources of water are expected, many drivers outfit their ani-mals in leather booties to protect their paws. These are also commonly used in areas where granulated ice crystals are expected because of extreme cold.

Open water also poses a great problem to mushers. At times trails lead across lakes and streams or near bodies of water. Water can also be present on the ice surface. When temperatures are running below −40° Celsius, exposure to water for even a few minutes can result in dogs and driver suffering frostbite.

Most dog-sled teams and drivers that die on the trail are killed when the sled and team break through ice or snow bridges crossing streams and lakes. If the water is deep and escape difficult, both animals and driver can succumb to hypothermia in just a few minutes. Even if the team and driver manage to get out, hypothermia will probably set in and death is extremely likely.

While dog sleds are still used by some northerners as a means of basic winter transportation, the snowmobile has largely replaced the use of dogs. Dog sledding is increasingly confined to sport and recreation. Dog-sled racing is a popular northern sport. In the Yukon, there are various dog-sled races held each year, including what is generally considered the toughest sled race in the world—the 1,600-kilometre **Yukon Quest** between Fairbanks, Alaska and **Whitehorse**.

Eagle Plain

The Eagle Plain is a broad area stretching from approximately the Peel River in the south to the junction of the Porcupine and Driftwood rivers in the north. To the west, the plain is bordered by the **Ogilvie Mountains**, to the east by the **Richardson Mountains**. It is composed primarily of a gentle, rolling, unglaciated plateau with elevation ranging between 300 and 600 metres above sea level.

Vegetation is typical subarctic forest, consisting of open, often stunted stands of black spruce and tamarack. **Permafrost** is continuous, with high ice content. Almost half the region is covered by wetlands consisting of peat bogs, palsa bogs (round mounds composed of peat overlying mineral soil that can be 10 metres high), and fens. Wildlife here includes **caribou**, moose, grizzly and black bear, wolf, red fox, snowshoe hare, spruce grouse, beaver, **raven**, osprey, and many species of waterfowl. The **Dempster Highway** cuts through the southern portion of the plain, providing road access for the region's only permanent settlement—Eagle Plains, which has a full-service hotel with a store, a service station, and a landing strip.

Economy

Before the arrival of European explorers and fur traders, the Yukon **First Nations peoples** had an economy based on subsistence hunting and gathering. There was some trade in goods between Yukon First Nations and those of Alaska, British Columbia, and the Northwest Territory.

When European traders first entered the territory in the 1840s the economic base of the region began shifting toward resource extraction—principally furs and whale products. These two economic pursuits would dominate the territory's economy from the mid-1880s to the latter part of the century, with the whaling industry concentrated on the whaling port at Herschel Island. The **fur trade** led to the development of a network of trading posts scattered along the **Yukon River** and its tributaries. White traders operated the posts, while local First Nations hunters did the majority of the actual trapping.

The Yukon economy, as well as its society, underwent a major transformation in 1896 with the **gold** discovery that sparked the **Klondike Gold Rush**. Hereafter mining became the major economic force within the territory—an industry that retains the number one spot even today. Through the early and mid-1900s, however, a lack of all-season transportation routes into the territory hindered economic development. Transportation was centred on the sternwheeler riverboat operators using the Yukon River and limited services offered by the **White Pass & Yukon Railway**. The first could only operate in the short summer season when the river was ice free; the latter had only limited access to the territory. Not until the construction of the **Alaska Highway** was completed in 1942 was the Yukon linked by a land route to the rest of Canada.

Following the end of World War II, mining and petroleum exploration greatly expanded, leading to the opening of several large resource-extraction operations, of which the mine at **Faro**, opened in 1969, was the most significant. **Whitehorse** grew steadily as the centralized base for government, retail, trade, and educational services to the rest of the territory, ultimately dominating the rest of the Yukon politically and economically. Only in the mid-1980s did **tourism** begin to play a significant role in the territory's economy, emerging as the second-largest industry.

Today the Yukon economy continues to be driven primarily by the **mining industry**, tourism, and **government**. Yukon's gross domestic product (GDP) averages about $1.04 billion per annum. About $400 million is from mineral production. The retail trade sector, which encompasses most tourism-related economic activity, is valued at $280.4 million annually.

One significant factor in the Yukon's economy is its dependence on federal transfer payments from the Canadian government to the territorial government to fund **education**, medical services, highway maintenance, and many other governmental responsibilities. These transfers account for as much as 70 percent of territorial government revenue. Without this federal government support to the territory, the economic stability of the Yukon would be severely jeopardized.

The Yukon's long-range economic challenge remains the same as it was at the beginning of the 20th century—to develop an economy that is diversified and less dependent on resource extraction. To date, the only economic sector not based on resource extraction is the growing tourist industry. The territory's isolation and harsh northern **climate** mean that non-resource–based manufacturing industries are virtually impossible to attract in numbers that might lead to a reduction of dependence on resource extraction industries.

Even resource diversification is a problem. **Agriculture**, although practised, is hindered by limitations on arable land, difficult climatic conditions, and the lack of close markets outside the Yukon. The **forest industry** is hampered in development by the same distance-to-market problems and relatively poor timber values. While fur trapping remains an important Yukon economic factor, its total value averages between $270,000 and $290,000 per annum and is unlikely to grow significantly.

Ecosystems

There are 23 ecosystems in the Yukon, sometimes referred to as ecoregions. Ecosystems are categorized in terms of unique physiographic, geological, climatic, wildlife, and **vegetation** characteristics. Some ecosystems can be quite small, others very large. In the Yukon, for example, the **Mount Logan** and Yukon Coastal Plain ecosystems are relatively small and localized, while the North **Ogilvie Mountains** and Klondike Plateau ecosystems encompass thousands of square kilometres.

The Yukon's common environmental features are a combination of relatively cold, rugged and mountainous terrain, covered by sparse or stunted vegetation. This vegetation includes Arctic and alpine **tundra**, and subalpine and open subarctic forests. In the southern part of the territory, rich river valleys and boreal forest combine to create a more extensive diversity of forest types and vegetation. These, in turn, promote greater diversity in wildlife, particularly **invertebrates** such as insects (*see also* **Biodiversity**).

With so many ecosystems in the Yukon, many researchers consider it more useful to group the ecosystems into more broadly defined ecozones. There are five ecozones in the Yukon: Southern Arctic, Taiga Plain, Taiga Cordillera, Boreal Cordillera, and Pacific Maritime.

The Southern Arctic ecozone coincides with the Yukon Coastal Plain ecosystem fronting the **Beaufort Sea**. Glaciated during the Wisconsinan Ice Age, this zone features permanent **permafrost**. Its Arctic tundra vegetation is dominated by sedge and cottongrass tussocks. Small and moderate-sized lakes and large pockets of **muskeg** are common.

The Taiga Plain ecozone only enters the territory along its eastern border with the Northwest Territory. This zone comprises a flat plateau dominated by tundra, and subalpine and boreal forest. It encompasses the Peel River Plateau and Fort McPherson Plain ecosystems, with a small incursion in the extreme southeast corner of the territory.

Lying in the discontinuous permafrost zone north of the **Tintina Trench**, the Taiga Cordillera ecozone is underlain by sedimentary rock in the north and metamorphic rock in the south. Rugged mountain areas feature predominantly alpine tundra vegetation and were mostly glaciated in the last ice age. Its plateau regions are vegetated by taiga or subarctic forest. This area includes the British and Richardson mountains, Old Crow Basin, **Old Crow Flats**, **Eagle Plain**, North Ogilvie Mountains, **Mackenzie Mountains**, and **Selwyn Mountains** ecosystems.

The Boreal Cordillera ecozone lies south of Tintina Trench, falls within scattered permafrost zones, and is underlain by complex mixtures of sedimentary, intrusive, volcanic, and metamorphic bedrock. Most of this ecozone falls in the **Yukon River**'s drainage area. Boreal white and black spruce forest, subalpine spruce, willow, and birch forest, and alpine tundra are found here. This is the largest ecozone in the Yukon and includes the following ecosystems: Yukon Plateau—North, Yukon Plateau—Central, Klondike Plateau, Ruby Ranges, **St. Elias Mountains**, Yukon Southern Lakes, Yukon-Stikine Highlands, Pelly Mountains, Liard Basin, and the Hyland Highland.

In the Yukon's southwestern corner, the Mount Logan ecosystem falls within the Pacific Maritime ecosystem—the wet ecozone that dominates the Pacific northwestern coastal region. In the Yukon, this ecozone is primarily composed of the high-elevation icefields, alpine glaciers, and massifs of the Icefield Ranges of the St. Elias Mountains.

Education

The Yukon **government** spends about 21 percent of its total annual budget on education, averaging about $91 to $93 million, with about $13 million of this amount going to capital expenditures on new schools and improvements to existing facilities.

There are 29 public schools in the territory attended by about 6,200 children in kindergarten to grade 12. Their education is facilitated by teachers numbering the equivalent of 455 full-time instructors.

The territory has only one post-secondary institution—Yukon College. Its enrollment of full-time students stands around 800 and there are some 3,900 part-time students registered annually. The college's main campus is in **Whitehorse** and it also operates 12 community campuses: **Beaver Creek**, **Carcross**, **Carmacks**, **Dawson**, **Faro**, **Haines Junction**, **Mayo**, **Old Crow**, **Pelly Crossing**, **Ross River**, **Teslin**, and **Watson Lake**. Yukon College offers the first two years of university-level education and some specialized diploma and trade programs. Students who go outside the territory for further post-secondary education are provided with government financial support.

The Whitehorse campus's name, Ayamdigut, is Tlingit for "she got up and went."

A four-year First Nations education program is offered through the Yukon Native Language Centre, mandated to preserve **First Nations languages**. Aboriginal language training is also offered in the public schools system.

Endangered Species

Some biologists estimate that as many as 100 species of plants and animals around the world become extinct each day. Many other species are at risk, including some in the Yukon. Species considered at risk in the Yukon are identified through three bodies: the Committee on the Status of Endangered Wildlife in Canada (COSEWIC), the Convention on International Trade in Endangered Species (CITES), and the Yukon Wildlife Act.

COSEWIC is a national committee that evaluates the status of Canadian wildlife and plant species and identifies those most at risk within three categories: endangered, threatened, and vulnerable. Endangered species are those considered to have such low numbers they could disappear forever unless immediate action is taken. Threatened refers to species that will likely become endangered if no action is taken to bolster their populations. Vulnerable are species not actually threatened but existing in small numbers or possibly unable to withstand any pressures on habitat.

Yukon wildlife species considered at risk in the Yukon and all of Canada by COSEWIC are:

- Endangered—**bowhead whale**, anatum race of **peregrine falcon**;
- Threatened—**wood bison**;
- Vulnerable—grizzly bear, polar bear, wolverine, great gray owl, short-eared owl, trumpeter swan; tundra race of peregrine falcon, and Squanga whitefish.

CITES governs the cross-border movement of animal parts of species identified as being of international concern. Yukon populations of these species are not currently at risk but are carefully monitored to avoid being affected by the same problems that have extirpated or endangered them elsewhere. The grizzly bear is the only CITES named species considered to also be at risk in the Yukon. Other identified at-risk species, which occur in the Yukon but are not at risk there, are: wolf, black bear, lynx, river otter, gyrfalcon, and all birds of prey.

The Yukon Wildlife Act identifies several specially protected species. These include wood bison. With the exception of wood bison, none are at risk outside the Yukon. The species currently protected are: the tundra race of peregrine falcon, gyrfalcon, elk, muskox, mule deer, and cougar.

Little is known about the status of amphibian species in the Yukon but worldwide concern over declining amphibian numbers and species has raised awareness in the north. Currently, however, most monitoring of Yukon's four amphibian species is done by volunteers and no governmental action is being taken to protect their numbers. As is true elsewhere in Canada and the world, plant species also currently receive little attention with regard to endangered status and protection.

Ethnicity

As of the 1996 Census of Canada, the inclusion of Canadian as a source of ethnic origin was included for the first time in the census questions regarding ethnicity and status as a visible minority. Of the 30,650 Yukoners responding to the 1996 Census, 4,595 (15 percent) reported Canadian as their only ethnic origin. An additional 4,405 (14 percent) reported having Canadian and other origins. The Canadian average for these two categories was 19 percent and 12 percent respectively.

First Nations status was claimed by 3,615 Yukoners (11.8 percent) as their only ethnic origin, while another 2,575 reported partial First Nations heritage. The overall Canadian average for First Nations–only status was just 1.7 percent. This difference in percentages between Canada and the Yukon alone reflects the important role that **First Nations peoples** continue to play in the territory. First Nations ethnicity was the second-highest category of ethnic origin reported after Canadian.

The Yukon mirrors the Canadian average for those with origins in the British Isles, precisely 17 percent. More Yukoners claimed to have an exclusively English heritage than any other non-Canadian or non–First Nations origin— 1,865. Single-origin heritage was also reported by 690 Scots and 490 Irish residents. German was reported as the sole source of ethnic origin by 995 Yukoners. French-only ancestry was reported by only 700 residents or 2 percent of the population. This compares to a 9 percent French-only reporting average for the rest of Canada.

Only 1,000 Yukoners, 3.3 percent, identified themselves as members of a visible minority. This compares to a national average of 11.2 percent. Nationally, 28.6 percent of those claiming visible minority status were born in Canada. In the Yukon, 41 percent of people reporting visible minority status were born in Canada. Most visible minority Yukoners are of Asian origin, numbering 745. The Yukon black community numbers 125, while there are 50 people of Arab or West Asian ethnicity and 55 from Latin America.

Faro

A quintessential one-industry town, Faro's history since its construction in 1969 has consisted of cyclical booms followed by inevitable busts. The community consequently has emerged as a symbol for the perils accompanying the dependence of northern economies, and the Yukon **economy** in particular, on mining. Situated at the 414-kilometre mark on the Campbell Highway and 356 kilometres northeast of **Whitehorse**, Faro owes its existence to the nearby lead and zinc mine. When operational, the Faro mine, as it is informally known, is the Yukon's largest mine and, at varying times, has been the biggest producer of lead in Canada.

Faro's story begins in the early 1960s when two notably different men working in the **mining industry** came together to form Dynasty Explorations. Al Kulan was a rugged, veteran northern prospector, Dr. Aaro Aho a well-educated and well-connected mining industry executive. Both, however, were confident that the central Yukon contained major mineral deposits that remained undiscovered. Kulan was convinced those deposits lay underground somewhere near **Ross River**. By the mid-1960s Dynasty Explorations had begun test drilling near present-day Faro and the results were justifying the two men's belief. The company started **claim-staking** the area, a process that sparked a modern-day mineral rush as prospectors across the Yukon rushed in to stake out more than 17,000 claims in 1966 around the Faro site.

This mineral rush bore little resemblance to those of the 1890s, such as the **Klondike Gold Rush**. Dynasty had a crew of more than 100 in the field, supported by an air strip, helicopters, and river barges bringing supplies up the Pelly River. Development work was costing the company $50,000 a month.

Once it was certain that Dynasty had struck a motherlode lead and zinc find, the Yukon was ready to develop its first true world-class mining operation. All that was missing was the capital to bankroll the mine's establishment. Initial funding came from Cyprus Mines of Los Angeles. An eight-year agreement with two Japanese companies to purchase all the mine's concentrates further paved the way for its opening. The federal government kicked in about $28 million in subsidies and direct funding and granted a three-year tax holiday on corporate profits. The Cyprus-Anvil mine, as it was officially named, was scheduled to begin production in December 1969.

From the outset a tremendous operational obstacle facing Faro was its isolation. To provide the mining crews somewhere to live, an entire town had to be constructed from scratch. The miners themselves had to be recruited and induced to move from other parts of the country and the world to an unproven operation in the middle of nowhere. In addition, Yukon Territory had a relatively small power grid at the time and the mine's need for electricity threatened to exceed the territory's power capacity. Finally, the lead and zinc produced had to be shipped to market, requiring the construction of a road into Faro, with links into an expanded **White Pass & Yukon Railway** rail system. The improvements required of the railway alone cost $22 million, but breathed new, albeit temporary, life into the rail company. A new docking facility at Skagway, Alaska was built to ship the mine's production to world markets.

When the rapidly constructed town of Faro was almost completed a forest fire swept into the community and razed most of the buildings. Construction crews started over and by the end of 1969 Faro's first families were moving into their homes overlooking the Pelly River, with picturesque views of the Anvil Mountain Range in the background.

By 1978, Faro was the territory's second-largest community with a **population** exceeding 2,000. The mine also provided 40 percent of the revenues of the territorial **government**. Despite its prominence in the territory's fortunes, Faro itself remained an isolated enclave largely untouched by territorial issues or linked to the rest of the population. The miners were usually hired from outside the Yukon. They came for only a few years, vacationed in southern climes, seldom ventured outside their community to Whitehorse or elsewhere in the territory, and when they had accumulated sufficient savings left the area. The employment of local people was minimal, despite an early promise to hire significant numbers of Yukon First Nations.

Because of its isolation, which made mineral exportation costly, the Faro mine was a shaky proposition from the very beginning. There was, however, little incentive on the part of miners, the mine company, or the territorial or federal government to recognize this fact. Instead, everything possible was done to ensure the mine's ability to keep operating and to realize a profit. In 1975, the Northern Canada Power Commission constructed a hydroelectric dam on the Aishihik River at Otter Falls primarily to ensure power for the mine. The project cost about $42 million and backed up the Aishihik River to create a 3,045-square-kilometre reservoir. The capital investment required for the dam was paid by adding its cost to Yukon consumers' power bills.

In 1981, Cyprus-Anvil became a hapless victim of a corporate merger when its current owner, Hudson's Bay Oil and Gas Company Limited, was acquired by Dome Energy Limited, the wholly owned subsidiary of Dome Petroleum Limited. Dome viewed the Faro mine as a costly side show of little importance to its overall corporate plans, which revolved largely around the growth strategy of corporate acquisition and mineral and petroleum development rather than actual project operation. By 1982 a downturn in world lead and zinc prices, combined with Dome's teetering on the edge of bankruptcy, prompted the corporation to unexpectedly close the mine. A half-hearted attempt by Dome to refinance the operation by forcing workers to assume massive pay and benefit cuts prompted a strike. Dome was then able to shut the mine and avoid paying severance to the workers.

The closure devastated the Yukon economy. The White Pass & Yukon Railway closed in the wake of the loss of its major customer. By 1985, Faro's population had collapsed to about 320 residents. From 1982 to 1985, the territory fell into the deepest depression experienced since World War I. In 1986, however, the mine rose again when the federal and territorial governments struck a deal with Curragh Resources to enable the mine's reopening. This time, however, the mine was non-union and there were few worker subsidizations available. Employee turnover was high but the Yukon economy slowly edged back on track as the mine provided the backbone to finance more territorial development.

Since the mid-1980s Faro's fortunes have been less than sterling. At times the mine has boomed, then shut down entirely. Various mining corporations have tossed money into the venture in an attempt to keep it on track and realize some profit from the lead and zinc deposits. In 1996, for example, the Faro mine accounted for between 12 and 15 percent of the territory's gross domestic product and 75 percent of the $400 million total value of mineral production. It was the primary factor behind the Yukon economy's growth of 7.6 percent overall. In 1997, however, the mine was closed again and then partially restarted by an investment from Cominco Ltd.

Faro, it appears, is well named—its fortunes depend as much on the vagaries of chance as anything else. The name derives from a game of chance that was popular in saloons during the Klondike Gold Rush. Played with a regular deck of cards, often bearing the stylized face of an Egyptian pharaoh, Faro is one of the oldest card gambling games and has often been illegal. Winning or losing depends on the turn of a single card in a manner that cannot be predicted.

First Nations Art

Contemporary Yukon **First Nations peoples** arts traditions derive from historical patterns and methods of decorating clothing and other personal, ceremonial, and kinship-related objects. Clothing was decorated with fur trim and beads made from berry seeds, seashells acquired through trade with coastal peoples, porcupine quills, feathers, down, moose hair, beaver claws, and paint. When European traders established a presence in the Yukon, the clothing was further decorated with glass beads and occasionally small jewels and pearls. In southern Yukon, shirts and blankets often bore the emblems of the different clans (*see* **Raven**).

Unlike the Pacific northwest peoples, there was no tradition in the Yukon of carving poles. One possible reason for this was that Yukon First Nations were more migratory than their coastal counterparts and did not live in permanent villages. There was, however, a culture of carving wooden crests and images of animals linked to a person's matrilineal family. These images and crests were also painted on the walls and posts of houses, grave boards, boats, drums, and some items of clothing for ceremonial purposes. The images could be embroidered into the fabric of clothes. Wooden dance masks were created by the southern Yukon peoples, as well.

Today the mask-carving and animal spirit–carving tradition is being re-established as an art form in southern Yukon, as are many other forms of First Nations arts and crafts. Many Yukon First Nations artists and artisans are combining traditional practices and materials with modern methods to breathe new life into ancient art forms. Carvings are also created from mastodon horns and bones, **woolly mammoth** tusks, **caribou** antlers, and other animal bones and antlers. Every year **placer mining** and other mining operations unearth many

In 1851, British illustrator Alexander Hunter Murray drew this image of Yukon First Nations entitled "Dance of the Kutcha-Kutchi." (NAC C2263)

mammoth and mastodon bones and bone shards and some of these are purchased by First Nations artists. Beaded moccasins, baby belts, mukluks, jackets, and blankets are also common articles created by First Nations artisans. Some forms of First Nations art in the Yukon are unique to the north and sometimes to the Yukon alone.

Qiviuq, for example, is a craft form that involves spinning wool from the underhair of the muskox. This very soft and light wool has four times the insulating power of lamb's wool. The art of caribou tufting, usually referred to as moosehair tufting but more often using caribou hair, involves shaping the hair into intricate designs by sewing it in bunches onto an underlain fabric and then trimming to length.

The Society for Yukon Artists of Native Ancestry provides an important organizational structure to support the efforts of many of these artists, and holds regular exhibits throughout the Yukon.

Much of traditional Yukon art involved aspects of visual arts—music, dance, song, poetry, and drama. These forms of artistic expression are all alive and well today in the Yukon, with elders handing down the traditional forms and content to younger people. The Yukon International Storytelling Festival in **Whitehorse** and other festivals and art shows held throughout the year across the Yukon help to preserve these art forms.

First Nations Hunting and Gathering

Historically, Yukon **First Nations peoples** had a primary diet of meat and **fish**. Much attention was therefore given to developing effective means of killing various species of wildlife for food. The hides, sinews, and bones of animals were also important in the creation of tools, clothing, and shelter.

Most of the land-based animals hunted by Yukon First Nations were **mammals**. These included **caribou**, moose, mountain sheep and goats, beaver, muskrat, marmots, gophers, rabbits, and **bears**. Grouse and ptarmigan were also commonly hunted, as well as migratory waterfowl. In the regions of the territory drained by the Yukon and Alsek rivers, salmon were an important species; while in the regions draining into the Mackenzie River, where salmon are not present, hunters caught freshwater fish such as inconnu.

Yukon First Nations hunted caribou using group tactics. By constructing **caribou fences**, a family or clan could trap as many as 150 caribou at one time in a mass killing.

Because other animal species did not travel in large herds, as did the barren-ground and woodland caribou, hunters worked in smaller teams or even individually. Even here, however, fences were still a vital component in hunting some larger animals, such as moose. A fence designed to capture a moose was smaller but utilized the same basic principle as the caribou fence: the animal was driven through an opening toward a snare that would capture the moose by the neck and strangle it or hold it in place so the hunters could kill it with spears or arrows. Hunters also set snares along moose trails and sometimes stalked moose and killed them with bow and arrow. Hunting dogs were often used to run moose down in winter when the dogs could run on top of the crusted snow like **wolves**, while the heavier moose would break through and wallow clumsily, unable to escape the dogs.

Mountain sheep and goats were hunted mostly in late autumn when they were fattest from a season of grazing. Snares and bow and arrows were used to kill these animals, which were greatly prized for both their meat and thick fur coats. Because of their mountain habitats, however, both were considered difficult and dangerous to hunt.

Although larger animals were favoured by First Nations hunters, smaller animals provided a food mainstay for many people. Beaver were particularly popular for both meat and fur, with the fatty tail considered a special delicacy. In winter, beaver were often speared under the ice or captured in nets. As winter gave way to spring, beaver hunting increased because the thinning ice could be more easily cut. But the thin ice could also break and many hunters drowned when they fell through the ice into deadly cold water.

Muskrat, marmots, gophers, rabbits, and **birds** were all captured primarily with snares. Both men and women participated in hunting these animals. Until the European **fur trade** influenced First Nations' hunting practices, other fur-bearing animals that had less flavourful meat were seldom hunted only for fur. Not until the fur trade began did Yukon First Nations start regularly hunting marten, fox, wolverine, otter, mink, or wolf. Some of these animals, such as otters and mink, were believed to have strong spirit powers that would bring bad luck upon the hunters.

The most dangerous animal hunted by Yukon First Nations were bears, both because of their physical strength and because they were believed to possess great spiritual powers. Only the bravest hunters participated in bear hunts. Sometimes the hunters would discover a bear's wintering den and rouse the animal. When it emerged they could usually spear it to death before it could react. Strong snares were also utilized to catch both grizzly and black bears.

When the salmon were running on the **Yukon River**, Alsek River, and their tributaries, First Nations peoples in the region concentrated much of their hunting activity on capturing this vital food source. Fish traps were commonly used rather than spears or hooks. A typical trap was a cylindrical basket that was open at both ends and set in an eddy surrounded by a corral of posts and brush. The trap was canted on the downstream end so the fish would be swept up through its opening, where they could be easily speared.

Another trap was also basket-shaped and constructed of willow poles lashed together with roots and sinew so the opening formed a wide circle. Behind the opening the trap was fashioned into an ever narrowing funnel. When the fish reached the end of the trap it was unable to turn around and could easily be scooped out and killed. In some regions, dip nets and gill nets fitted with hooks were used to capture fish as well.

In winter, Yukon First Nations normally camped near lakes that were well stocked with fish. Usually two hunters worked together, first opening a hole in the ice. One hunter would then jig a line fitted with bait into the water and when the fish came to it the other hunter would dispatch it with a spear. The most common spearhead was made of caribou horn and had a central stiff prong with two springier, sharp prongs on either side. Gill nets were also used in winter fishing.

Some of the hunting techniques used historically by Yukon First Nations are still practised today, as are methods of gathering plants for food. A migratory people, Yukon First Nations never practised any form of cultivation; rather the women collected food from wild **vegetation**. In late summer, berries were an important food source with many kinds to choose from, including blueberries, soapberries, cranberries, raspberries, mossberries, and stoneberries. To avoid unwanted confrontations with berry-loving bears, the women worked in groups, singing and talking loudly to warn the bears of their approach.

Roots were also dug for food. "Indian sweet potatoes," known as *hedysarum*, were dug in the autumn after the first frosts or in early spring. Mushrooms, wild celery, and wild onion were also popular. The resinous gum or juice of spruce, pine, and fir trees was used as a sweetener and form of candy.

First Nations Land Claims

Before Europeans came, the Yukon was the dwelling place of 14 First Nations who spoke eight different **languages**. Although their traditional way of life was disrupted with the first arrival of Europeans in the 1840s, it was not until the 1950s that Yukon First Nations faced serious social change resulting from non-native incursions on their traditional lands. Until the 1950s, Yukon First Nations were generally able to employ their traditional uses of the land without Canadian or territorial **government** intervention. Most non–First Nations Yukoners had little interest in the land, confining themselves to small mining plots and a few townsites.

In the 1950s, however, industrial and economic expansion in the Yukon picked up steam. This coincided with a growing interest in the Canadian north by the federal government, which had until then largely ignored the territories. The Canadian government abruptly rejected aboriginal hunting and trapping as viable economic activities and began efforts to integrate Yukon **First Nations peoples** into the broader Canadian society. For the first time, issues of land ownership and tenure in the territory were raised by the government. Licensing of big-game hunting territories and registration of traplines were introduced in 1950. Such regulations meant that First Nations people could now be separated from lands which they and their ancestors had controlled for generations.

Land ownership policies were introduced rapidly throughout the territory. Huge oil and gas leases were granted in the northern Yukon to non–First Nations interests and hundreds of new mineral claims staked throughout the territory. Individual plots of land near towns and along lakeshores were deeded, particularly in southern Yukon. By the late 1960s, First Nations people were being told they must respect non-native claims to their lands and refrain from hunting on or otherwise using property legally assigned for individual use.

Decisions on First Nations issues were suddenly made primarily by non–First Nations people. In December 1958, for example, a meeting on Yukon First Nations welfare issues was convened in **Whitehorse** without a single First Nations person being invited. First Nations petitions to the government regarding territorial grievances were largely ignored. As the Department of Indian Affairs stated in an internal memo, its policy was: "The Yukon Indians have no stipulated land entitlement, land being provided as required to meet their needs." The government further held that most First Nations were merely "squatters on the land" who could remain there as long as the land was required for no other purpose by non–First Nations.

By 1962, only 1,943 hectares of the Yukon had been officially identified for First Nations use. Although some large blocks of land were granted to the First Nations over the next few years, the amount of the territory allotted for First Nations use remained slight.

Complicating matters was the fact that no land treaties had ever been struck by either the federal or territorial governments with the Yukon First Nations. The Canadian government claimed absolute dominion to the land, selling property deeds and granting mineral and petroleum licences without consulting any First Nations councils or paying any compensation for traditional territorial land lost.

Increasingly frustrated by attempts to negotiate some form of accord with the federal and territorial governments and facing increasing economic and social pressure on their people that was destroying traditional customs, values, and culture, the Yukon First Nations began to organize. In 1970, the Yukon Native Brotherhood was formed to represent status natives. In 1972, the Yukon Association for Non-Status Indians was formed. These two organizations forced the problems into the spotlight and slowly the federal government began to recognize that a land claim process had to be negotiated. As Elijah Smith, first chief of the Yukon Native Brotherhood, said, "We need a treaty to tell us what our rights are—where our land is—we want to plan for the future of our People."

In 1973, the Council for Yukon Indians (CYI), a coalition representing both status and non-status First Nations, tabled Canada's first comprehensive land claim. The document, entitled *Together Today for Our Children Tomorrow*, was accepted by the federal government for negotiation.

The negotiation process dragged on until 1980 when an agreement-in-principle was reached by the CYI, federal, and territorial negotiators. In 1984, the agreement was ratified by the federal and territorial governments but rejected by the CYI general assembly because there was insufficient land reserved for First Nations people, a condition that extinguished aboriginal title to many lands, and no provision included for First Nations self-government.

The following year the federal government's Federal Task Force to Review Comprehensive Claims Policy recommended changes to federal land claim negotiating policies that included concurrent negotiation of self-government agreements. In 1986, the task force's recommendations were largely accepted by the federal government, including the provision for negotiation of self-government agreements. Negotiations resumed in 1987 with a new agreement-in-principle being struck in early 1989 and ratified by the federal and territorial governments, as well as the CYI. Provisions of this agreement, known as the Umbrella Final Agreement (UFA), included: $242.6 million in compensation to be paid out over 15 years; 41,439 square kilometres of settlement land retained under aboriginal title and including all surface and subsurface title; participation of First Nations representatives assured on various wildlife and land boards and commissions; and a guarantee that Yukon First Nations would receive full rental revenue from surface leases and royalties from the development of nonrenewable resources on land to which First Nations held aboriginal title.

Although the CYI had accepted the agreement, it still needed to be individually negotiated and agreed to by the 14 Yukon First Nations. The UFA was ratified by the Yukon First Nations in 1991 at their general assembly. In 1992, agreement was formally initialled by negotiators for all sides. In 1993, the Yukon territorial legislative assembly passed enabling legislation, ratifying the UFA and self-government agreements. On May 29, 1993, at an outdoor ceremony in **Whitehorse**, the political representatives of Canada, Yukon Territory, and four Yukon First Nations met to officially sign what was now called the First Nation Final (Land Claim) and Self-Government Agreements.

As of 1997, 6 of the 14 Yukon First Nations had formalized agreements between themselves and the federal and territorial governments—all based on the UFA. Those nations are: the Vuntut Gwitchin First Nation, Nacho Ny'a'k Dun First Nation, Champagne and Aishihik First Nations, Teslin Tlingit Council, Little Salmon/Carmacks First Nation, and Selkirk First Nation.

The Yukon First Nations have all inextricably linked self-government to the successful conclusion of land claims negotiations.

First Nations Languages

Among the 14 Yukon First Nations there are eight different traditional **languages** spoken. Seven of these are Athapaskan languages, while the eighth is Tlingit. All are part of a superfamily known as Na-Dene. The Tlingit word *na* and the Athapaskan word *déné* both mean people. Also included in this linguistic superfamily was the language Eyak, which is now considered to have become extinct.

The Athapaskan language groups in the Yukon are divided into geographic regions. The north First Nations, extending south to about 64° north latitude and including **Old Crow**, speak Gwich'in (also spelled Gwitchin); near **Dawson**, and extending north through most of the **Ogilvie Mountains**, the language is Han; most of central Yukon speaks Northern Tutchone; from **Ross River** south to **Watson Lake** and east to the Northwest Territory border the language is Kaska; from **Whitehorse** to the western border with Alaska the language is Southern Tutchone, except for a small sliver of people near **Beaver Creek** who speak Upper Tanana. The people living near **Teslin** have Tagish as their native tongue. A small pocket centred on **Carcross** speaks Tlingit.

The Gwitchin people used to be divided by anthropologists and historians into two groups—the Loucheux and Hare. Another group referred to as Mountain is now considered to be part of the Kaska-speaking people. The extreme northern region of the territory bordering the **Beaufort Sea** was historically visited by Inuvialuit (western Arctic Inuit) peoples, but by 1920 disease and other calamities brought to these people by white whalers and fur traders drove the remaining Inuvialuit population east from the Yukon into the Northwest Territory. There is no Inuvialuit community in the Yukon today. (*See* **Herschel Island Territorial Park.**)

At one time Athapaskan-speaking peoples are believed to have dwelled close together and shared one common language. This ancestral homeland is thought to have been the western Yukon, which remained free of glacial ice during the Wisconsinan Age. Part of **Beringia**, it provided an ice-free corridor into the rest of North America from the Bering Sea land bridge. It is possible that during the volcanic-ash period, about 700 A.D. (*see* **Archaeology**), the Athapaskan people migrated in a number of directions to populate parts of Alaska, most of the Yukon, the Mackenzie River valley, and even the southwestern United States where they became known as Navaho, Apache, and Hupa peoples. Throughout all these regions today Athapaskan languages are spoken.

As generation succeeded generation, the Athapaskan language that had been commonly shared became fragmented, evolving into a series of languages that are not easily recognizable or even understandable to each other. Linguists further believe that the Athapaskan language itself was related to other languages from which it had split some thousands of years earlier. The greater language group, Na-Dene, can be compared to the Indo-European linguistic superfamily that incorporates English, French, German, and many other European languages.

All Na-Dene languages differ greatly from Canada's two official languages of English and French in grammatical structure. Plurals, pronouns, and assignment of gender are expressed within verb forms in Athapaskan or Tlingit. Verb forms provide far more complete information in these languages than in French or English, including even the subject to which a verb refers. If a Na-Dene speaker says he touched something, the verb form used will also tell the listener precisely what it was that he touched. If he touched another human the verb form will also identify gender and possibly whether that person was young or old. The role that verbs play in Na-Dene languages requires the speaker to have a highly developed vocabulary because there literally is one right verb for every occasion rather than a number of synonyms as is common in English or French.

Utilizing the expressive variety of the human voice to increase the number of words that could be formed, Na-Dene languages include sound variations and tones. Some sounds spoken normally could mean one thing, while the same sound combined with a popping noise generated by the glottis at the back of the throat might mean something else entirely. The use of tonality in language is a characteristic that Na-Dene speakers share with Classical Greek and many African and Asian languages.

Prior to European contact, Yukon First Nations had no written language. In recent times, however, steps have been taken to create a written form of the

Athapaskan and Tlingit languages. The Yukon Native Language Centre in Whitehorse publishes dictionaries, grammars, and reading books written so that they can be understood by most of the eight language groups in the Yukon.

The centre is also instrumental in an effort to ensure that Yukon traditional languages are not only preserved but become more commonly spoken by young First Nations people. As part of this initiative the Yukon Native Language Centre, housed at Yukon College, has developed a Native Language and Cultural Curriculum for school children. Such initiatives, however, face a difficult struggle because for most of the past 100 years or more First Nation languages were systematically weakened by a deliberate strategy on the part of Christian missionaries and the federal government. In missionary and government residential schools the speaking of Athapaskan or Tlingit was severely punished, as children were forced to learn English. Consequently, many people ceased to know their traditional language. Today, of 6,175 First Nations Yukoners, only 770 consider a First Nation language to be their mother tongue. Of these, 630 speak an Athapaskan language.

First Nations Peoples

Many Yukon First Nations tell legends and myths that claim their ancestors have dwelt within the territory since its creation. They often recount how a world of water was transformed into one of land by **raven** and this land, which encompassed the Yukon, was then populated by their ancestors. Some archaeologists believe these stories have their genesis in the great melting that began about 13,500 years ago when the Wisconsinan Age ended. During this period the land bridge connecting Alaska to Asia is believed to have been drowned under a resurgent Pacific Ocean and Bering Sea, severing the connection between the two continents.

Archaeologists generally believe the ancestors of today's First Nations peoples in the Yukon crossed the Bering Sea land bridge into what is called **Beringia** between 20,000 and 15,000 years ago. This was during the latter phase of the Wisconsinan Ice Age. As Beringia was never covered by glacial ice and stretched like a long finger for several thousand kilometres north and south of the present-day Bering Sea, it provided an ice-free corridor into the heart of North America for the early peoples migrating from Asia.

The Yukon was at the time girdled to the south by a vast ice sheet extending from the **St. Elias Mountains** in the west, encompassing the Pelly Mountains, and curving around to join up with another ice sheet in the eastern part of the territory that covered the entire Canadian Shield and was known as the Laurentide ice sheet. A large part of the Yukon was, however, ice free and consisted of a treeless **tundra** that provided excellent browse for ice age animals such as **woolly mammoths**, bison, horses, camels, **caribou**, and muskox. The people likely followed the migrational patterns of these animals and hunted them as their primary food source.

Whether First Nations peoples have always lived in the Yukon or migrated to it during the Wisconsinan Age, by 10,000 years ago the people of the Yukon were using distinctive tools known as microblades—tiny, specially shaped stone flakes with a keenly sharpened edge on the long side that rival a modern-day razor. Archaeologists believe these microblades were the product of a people who were among the last to cross the ice bridge before it was swallowed by the ocean. Microblade artifacts have been found in the Yukon that date from 10,000 to about 4,500 years ago. This would have been a period of great adaptation, as the people coped with the disappearance of the large **mammals** and the tundra receded before the advance of great spruce forests.

Between 5,000 and 4,500 years ago the making of microblades slowed, disappearing entirely about 4,500 years ago. Instead a new stone point with a notch on both sides near the bottom emerged. Such tools could easily be tied to wooden shafts to make spears or given handles for use as knives. Stone chopping tools were being used and nets for fishing and trapping game were produced. The archaeological record of this time shows many links to the historical culture of the Athapaskan people of the Yukon at the time of first European contact. For this reason, many archaeologists believe these people—whose culture is known by the term Northern Archaic Tradition—are the direct ancestors of the Athapaskan people.

For the next 1,500 years these people survived in a landscape that was often plagued by increasing cold and advances of glaciers out of the St. Elias Mountains, as well as the spread of ash over the land from volcanic eruptions in this young mountain range. Slowly, however, the climatic and geological period of disruption in the Yukon ended. With stability came new advances in technology, so that about 1,300 years ago a new culture had emerged out of the Northern Archaic Tradition that included the use of the bow and arrow and other more advanced tools. These peoples were also using copper to fashion tools and some ornaments. This period has been called the Aishihik Culture by archaeologists. The Aishihik Culture survived until about 1800 A.D., when it was supplanted by the Bennett Lake Culture.

The Bennett Lake Culture was directly linked to the traditions and practices of modern-day Athapaskan and Tlingit peoples of the Yukon. By this time the Athapaskan people in the territory were divided linguistically and socially into seven distinct peoples: the Gwitchin in the north, Han in the Dawson City area, Northern Tutchone in the Yukon's centre, Southern Tutchone in the southwest, Kaska in the southeast, Tagish in the **Teslin** region, and Upper Tanana in the **Beaver Creek** area. The Tlingit were centred near present-day Carcross. (*See* **First Nations Languages.**)

Within a few decades of this culture's emergence, contact with European cultures occurred—first Russian fur traders working from coastal ports and then Hudson's Bay Company traders journeying from the headwaters of rivers in the **Mackenzie Mountains** into the heart of the Yukon to the **Yukon River**. As the 1800s advanced, the number of white traders working in the Yukon increased and the influence of trade goods exchanged for furs taken by First Nations hunters affected their traditional way of life. Most influential was the gun, which enabled individual hunters to kill animals that had previously been hunted by groups using traps and snares, such as **caribou fences**.

Until the arrival of Christian missionaries, little effort was made by any of the whites entering the Yukon to change the ways of the First Nations peoples. Indeed, many of the traders, explorers, and soldiers admired the First Nations way of life and tended to emulate it as the most effective and practical way of surviving in a harsh land isolated from the rest of North America.

Although no Russian Orthodox missionaries are believed to have ever journeyed into the Yukon, they established missionary villages on the Alaskan coast that had some influence on the Yukon peoples through trade-related contact. The first Anglican missionary to gain direct access to the Yukon First Nations was William West Kirby, who arrived at Fort Yukon, located at the confluence of the Yukon and Porcupine rivers, in 1861. Kirby was soon replaced by Robert McDonald, who moved his missionary to Rampart House on the Canadian side of the border when the United States took over Fort Yukon in 1869.

Four years earlier, however, McDonald recorded the beginnings of the impact of white settlement among the Yukon First Nations. In 1865, he saw many First Nations people coming to Fort Yukon who were ill with scarlet fever introduced by the fur traders. Previous records show that such diseases as smallpox, measles, whooping cough, tuberculosis, and polio were all introduced to the region between 1838 and 1865 with devastating effect on the First Nations populations.

By the time of the **Klondike Gold Rush** in 1896–98, a number of Anglican missionaries were operating throughout the territory, many established by Bishop William C. Bompas. The missionaries, intent on converting the First Nations people to Christianity, paid scant attention to **First Nations spirituality**, making virtually no attempt to relate their religion to traditional beliefs. Instead they imposed their beliefs on the First Nations peoples and tried to convince them to abandon their spiritual relationship to the world, which emphasized living in harmonious balance. The schools established by the missionaries inculcated the Christian worldview into the minds of First Nations children, turning them away from their traditional beliefs.

With the arrival of more than 40,000 **gold** stampeders in the Klondike region, the traditional way of life practised by Yukon First Nations was essentially doomed. First Nations peoples could not help but be swept up in the fever of the gold rush. Three of the four people involved in the first discovery on Bonanza Creek in 1896 were Tagish First Nations.

By the turn of the century, much of the Yukon had been transformed by white development. **Sternwheelers** plied the Yukon River, **Whitehorse** was a major transportation hub and service centre to the growing mining operations throughout the southern territory, and whites were being granted ownership of large tracts of land without any compensation offered to the original people who had lived on the land for millennia. The lack of any formalized treaty with First Nations provided the grounds upon which most **First Nations land claims** in the Yukon are based.

Unlike their First Nations cousins in southern Canada and even in other parts of northern Canada, Yukon First Nations retained some strong links to their traditional lifestyles and spiritual beliefs. Myths and legends were preserved by elders and passed on to younger people. **Languages** were retained by sufficient numbers to keep them alive during the time when religious and government residential schools strove to eliminate the peoples' First Nations identity. Throughout the 1900s there were always some Yukon First Nations who still lived the traditional life of the **First Nations hunting and gathering** culture.

Partly this was possible due to the isolation of the territory during the worst

Caribou hides have always provided many essentials for Yukon First Nations peoples. Here, two Gwitchin women near Old Crow are pictured wearing caribou-skin coats. (Yukon Archives, Claude B. Tidd Collection, #7324)

decades of attempts to assimilate First Nations peoples into the European culture across Canada. Until World War II and the construction of the **Alaska Highway**, much of the Yukon was inaccessible by road and not easily reached by river transportation systems. Even today, the village of **Old Crow** has no road access and is a primarily First Nations' community, as are **Ross River**, **Pelly Crossing**, and other small Yukon communities that lie distant from any large white-dominated centres.

Yukon First Nations also have the advantage of being more numerous in relation to non–First Nations residents than is true for First Nations in southern Canada. Some 20 percent of Yukoners are First Nations, compared to a Canadian average ratio of only 2.8 percent. As well, Yukon First Nations have high numbers of young people in their **population**. Of 6,175 First Nations people in the Yukon, 2,395 are under the age of 19 and a further 1,715 are younger than 35, totalling 67 percent under 35 years old.

With a youthful population and a political movement toward strong self-government, Yukon First Nations are well poised to exert a profound influence on the political and social future of the entire territory.

First Nations Spirituality

The traditional spiritual or religious beliefs of Yukon **First Nations peoples** are intrinsically linked with their relationship to the land, the forces of nature, and the animals and plants with which they share the world. In this animistic view, spirits are believed to dwell throughout the natural world, in the land, the water, plants, animals, and the sky overhead. All these spirits and the forces of nature in which they are found must be maintained in a balanced state. Inherent in the animistic spiritual view is a deep respect for the natural world and a belief that humans are not quintessentially of more importance or value than any other part.

Although with the arrival of European missionaries many Yukon First Nations people were converted to Christianity, the traditional spirituality of their ancestors was often retained and blended with the Christian view in a manner that seldom was supported by the missionaries. Today, many young First Nations people are embracing their traditional spiritual practices and beliefs.

Traditionally, the Yukon First Nations peoples believed they had existed in the land since its creation by **raven**. The oral tradition of Yukon First Nations is rich in creation stories and others that explain how animals and humans came to differ from each other.

According to their beliefs, spirit powers existed virtually everywhere, with some more powerful than others. Some peoples believed that the spirits dwelt largely in their own distinct world, making occasional forays into the world populated by humans. Others believed the spirits always lived in the human world, though sometimes dwelling in some distant part unknown to humans. A spirit could grant good luck or added powers to humans to help them through life. Gaining the assistance of a spirit, however, depended on behaving in such a way as to please that spirit. Failure to do the right thing could bring bad luck upon a person.

Little or nothing existed that did not possess some form of spirit. Even inanimate objects created by humans, such as a bow or a knife, contained a spirit power that could be unleashed to a person's favour or sorrow depending on how it was approached and respected. Those who recognized and used spirit power positively could control their own destiny and influence that of others more easily than those incapable of invoking spirits on their own. Bad luck in hunting or contraction of serious disease was often attributed to an inability to invoke and benefit from the power of spirits. This belief meant that Yukon First Nations strove to live in harmony with the spirits of the world. They listened to the sounds of animals and watched their behaviour to try to learn the messages being imparted by the spirits within.

Because the world was so laden with meaning, and the potential for slighting a spirit so high, it was important to have a special relationship with one spirit who could serve as a personal guide. Known as spirit helpers, these guides were often linked to a specific animal. A young hunter, for example, might find his spirit helper during a dream in which a wolf brought him a special message. From that time on, he would believe himself to have access to the power and wisdom of **wolves**. It was possible to have more than one spirit helper. Indeed, the more spirit helpers a person could draw upon the more powerful, safe, and influential in the clan he or she would become.

Young men most often found their first spirit helpers at puberty. Some peoples, such as the Kaska, usually sent young men into the wilderness alone on a spirit helper quest. During this quest, the youth would fast and meet his fears of the wilderness directly and without cowardice. Before sleeping at night, he would pray for a visitation from an animal spirit to become his helper. With the visitation during a dream, his relationship with the spirit would be established. He often returned from the quest with a special song or words granted him by the spirit helper. The song or words would serve as a powerful talisman or incantation to work on his behalf.

A young woman found her spirit helper most often when she reached childbearing age. Menstruation was believed to be evidence of great internal power. Women generally did not rely so much on spirit helpers to enable them to cope in the world. They were expected to survive by their wits and the support of their clan.

Most clans had spirit doctors or shamans who provided medical and spiritual treatment and services. Sometimes the shaman was also the headman of a clan or family, but not always. Some were believed to be particularly powerful and capable of changing the weather, healing any illness, or guiding a lost soul back to its body.

Each living animal was believed to have its own spirit power dwelling inside. When an animal was killed, its spirit was believed to leave the body after a short period of usually four days. The spirit would then go to where other spirits of that animal lived and where the master spirit of the species also dwelt. Eventually this spirit power would return to earth and enter the body of a new animal.

Animal spirit powers were also capable of leaving the bodies they inhabited, especially during the hours of darkness. The powers could watch humans and, whether inside the animal body or not, know what a human was thinking or doing at all times. It was impossible to kill an animal whose spirit power opposed its death at the hunter's hands. It was therefore essential for a hunter to show proper respect to his quarry, both in thought and in treatment of the carcass. If a good relationship with the animals was not maintained, the hunter would have bad luck and would never have enough to eat.

If an animal's spirit could either prevent or aid in its own death at the hand of a hunter, the weather could also greatly influence the success or failure of a hunt. In a land with a **climate** as harsh and unpredictable as the Yukon's it was essential to understand the signs that indicated what weather patterns were developing at any given time. A ring around the sun, for example, meant rain or snow was imminent. The way clouds drifted off the peaks of specific mountains foretold of snow or rain and the direction from which the storm would come. It was also thought that specific actions could influence the weather. The Tlingit believed that a freeze-up could be encouraged by beating a wolverine skin because, according to legend, it was wolverine who had once stolen the north wind and controlled its release to, or withdrawal from, the human world. Improper behaviour could also influence weather. If a girl broke a taboo, a storm was sure to follow.

The world contained other creatures which were imbued with special powers and often posed dangers to humans. Among these were the bushmen, who had once been extremely numerous upon the land but were now rare and liked to steal young girls and women who wandered alone in the woods. What bushmen looked like varied greatly in the telling. Sometimes they were described as being humanlike, or as being very small and nimble, and yet again as taller than the highest tree. In some lakes water monsters were believed to dwell. Large worms were thought to live in glaciers that would emerge to cause glaciers to advance or floodwaters to run if they were annoyed by human actions.

Yukon First Nations all seemed to believe in reincarnation through the transfer of personal spirit powers. Those who had been reborn often remembered events from past lives and recognized places they had never been during their current existence. They also believed that a soul could be frightened away from the body of a living person or a soul could be stolen by a strong, hostile spirit power or an evil shaman. Failure to retrieve the soul quickly would result in the person dying. These unretrieved souls were thought to wander lost through the world and could pose a threat to the living. When the **northern lights** were unusually vivid some people believed they were the spirits of dead warriors or other humans who had suffered violent deaths.

To improve the odds of having a happy and full life untroubled by bad relations with the spirits inhabiting the world, it was important to behave properly. Generally this behaviour centred on the practice of moderation in all things to ensure balance. To overeat was to ensure starvation in the future, vanity would result in some injury to the face or body that would make the person ugly, and a spirit doctor who was allowed to gather too much spirit power would turn from doing good for people to harming them.

Fish

There are about 40 fish species found in the Yukon's rivers, lakes, and the **Beaufort Sea**. Twenty-eight of these species are fish that dwell in freshwater, including some, like salmon and Arctic char, that spend part of their lives in a saltwater environment.

Yukon waters provide four migration corridors for spawning salmon populations. Three of these encompass the **Yukon River** and its significant tributaries, the other the Alsek River. Some of the salmon spawning in the Yukon River complete a 3,200-kilometre trek to spawning grounds near the river's headwaters at Teslin Lake. Four species of Pacific salmon spawn in Yukon waters: chum, chinook, sockeye, and coho. Chinook, sockeye, and coho all spawn in the Alsek River, while chum and chinook spawn in the Yukon River. Chum and coho also spawn in the Porcupine River north of the **Arctic Circle**, a major tributary of the Yukon.

Chinook salmon are also known as tyee, king, or spring salmon. This species regularly exceeds 13 kilograms in weight and chinook weighing up to 30 kilograms have been caught in Yukon waters by commercial, sport, and First Nations fishing operations. Young chinook spend their first year in freshwater lakes or quiet backwaters of the Yukon River before migrating downstream as molts. After four to seven years in the Pacific Ocean they return to their birth waters to spawn.

Coho travel to the ocean before their first year is complete and generally return to spawn after less than two years in saltwater. They spawn in the Alsek-

Tatshenshini River system, especially at the Klukshu River, as well as in the Porcupine River. Most mature coho average a weight of 3.5 to 4.5 kilograms.

Often known as dog salmon because of the spawning males' doglike teeth and their popularity as a food for sled dogs, chum salmon spawn in the major Yukon tributaries of the Yukon River—the White, Stewart, Pelly, and Teslin rivers. The Porcupine River, including its Fishing Branch River tributary, also has a considerable spawning population. The chum migration appears at **Dawson** in mid-August and continues running after ice covers the river. Adult chum average about 2.2 kilograms. Immediately upon emerging from the spawning gravel in the spring, newborn fry migrate toward the sea and return to spawn in their third or fourth year of life.

Sockeye salmon live for two years in freshwater lakes before migrating to the ocean, where they live a further three years before returning to their spawning grounds. Because of its rich red, firm flesh, sockeye are the most sought-after salmon species despite their relatively small size. The average adult sockeye is only about 0.75 metres long and weighs about 2.2 kilograms.

In the Yukon, chinook salmon constitute the largest percentage of the commercial catch—about 59 percent in an average year. This species also represents about 75 percent of the First Nations fishery. The Yukon commercial fishery is based primarily at Dawson, with some smaller commercial fisheries operating at various freshwater lakes elsewhere in the territory.

Another freshwater spawning fish that spends some of its life in the ocean is Arctic char. One subspecies of this fish migrates into the sea in summer to feed and returns to freshwater in the winter; the other, known as non-anadromous Arctic char, lives its life entirely in freshwater. Both subspecies of Arctic char have elongated bodies that turn to a deep vermillion during the spawning phase.

Of the freshwater species in the Yukon those most favoured by sports anglers are Arctic grayling, lake trout, northern pike, whitefish, rainbow trout, and burbot or ling cod. During the **Klondike Gold Rush**, the demand for Arctic grayling became so great that the species was overfished on the Yukon River and many nearby lakes. Whitefish were also heavily harvested. At Tatlmain Lake, for example, more than 10,000 fish were harvested on an annual basis at the turn of the century. Some stocks never recovered from this intense fishery.

Most Yukon freshwater fish spend their lives in frigid, relatively unproductive lakes, so they are slow to grow and reproduce. A 20-year-old lake trout in Bennett Lake, for example, will average a weight of less than a kilogram. During the same lifespan, a lake trout living in an Ontario lake will exceed 1.5 kilo-grams. Because of their slow growth and reproduction rates, Yukon fish are more vulnerable to overharvesting than fish populations in more southerly North American lakes.

Yukon fish populations have been adversely affected by dams constructed on various lakes and streams. Dams on the North Klondike River, Mayo Lake, and Mayo River destroyed the upstream salmon migration populations. A dam at Aishihik Lake to provide power to the **Faro** mine eliminated East Aishihik River rainbow trout habitat and reduced whitefish populations. At Lewes River a dam constructed in 1899 disrupted migration patterns for generations. A fishway has since been installed, which has partly alleviated the impact of this dam. Despite the construction of the **Whitehorse Fishway** at Whitehorse Dam, fish mortal-ity remains high at this dam and a fish hatchery is required to replace the fish numbers lost.

Placer mining also has a major impact on fish populations. Rivers and creeks that have been intensively mined for many years cease to provide salmon-spawning habitat and become unsuitable for many other fish species. New stan-dards controlling placer-mining operations on fish-bearing streams have been enacted but in many cases the damage already done cannot be rectified. In some locations, the standards have already been relaxed to enable mining to proceed. Hardrock mining also has an impact on fish stocks because of the discharge of various contaminant metals and chemicals into streams. Road construction, log-ging, and residential growth are also reducing the number of viable fish habitats in the Yukon.

Five Finger Rapids

Situated at the 380.5-kilometre point of the Klondike Highway, Five Finger Rapids is a picturesque narrow gorge on the **Yukon River** divided into five sep-arate waterways by four columns of basalt rock. A trail and viewing platforms provide easy access to the rapids today. For river paddlers and other boaters trav-elling the river, the rapids are considered a moderate taste of adventure during what is generally a placid, easy run down one of Canada's major rivers.

During the **Klondike Gold Rush**, however, the rapids were viewed as one of the more dangerous sections of the trip down the Yukon River from Bennett Lake to **Dawson**. When **sternwheelers** began travelling from Dawson to

Whitehorse, the downward currents in the rapids were so strong that the boats could not pass through under their own power. They had to be dragged up the rapids by winches. Only the most easterly of the five fingers was passable to the larger riverboats.

Between 1899 and 1900, to make the passage for sternwheelers safer and more easily accomplished, the Canadian Department of Public Works blasted some of the eastern column away to widen the easterly finger. Two years later, department crews also dynamited most of the rocky obstacles at Rink Rapids, some eight kilometres downriver, to eliminate the danger these rocks posed to river traffic.

Prior to the gold rush, Five Finger Rapids was sometimes known as Rink Rapids. The name Five Finger was given to the rapids in 1882 by W. B. Moore, an early prospector who came to the region from Tombstone, Arizona. U.S. Army explorer Lieutenant F. Schwatka changed the name to Rink Rapids the following year. This name honoured Dr. Henry Rink, a Dane who was a world-renowned authority on Greenland and director of Copenhagen-based Royal Greenland Trade. Local miners resented Schwatka's displacing the Five Finger name with a Danish one they considered irrelevant to the Yukon so the name never took. In 1887, Canadian Geographical Survey Director George Mercer Dawson transferred the Rink Rapids name to the lesser obstacle downriver and resolved the dispute.

Forest Industry

The forest industry in the Yukon is relatively small, despite the fact that 281,030 square kilometres of the territory is forested land. Hampering efforts to expand the industry are a number of factors. First, Yukon forest is boreal forest comprised of black spruce and other species considered less valuable for lumber and other uses than timber in more southerly Canadian forests. Second, the Yukon's isolation and distance from major markets means harvesting and shipping costs combine in most cases to exceed market price. Third, trees in the territory grow slowly because of the **climate** and are extremely susceptible to destruction by wildfires before attaining maturity. Fires, mostly the result of lightning strikes, destroy millions of hectares of Yukon forests each year.

Despite these significant drawbacks the territorial **government** has, in recent years, embarked on various initiatives to attract more logging and milling operations. The main initiative has been to ensure that all lumber and other industrial wood products used in the territory are the product of Yukon forest company operations. The Yukon Forest Commission is working to develop effective partnerships between First Nations and federal and territorial governments to foster a larger, more diversified forest industry.

Currently most sawmill operations are based near **Watson Lake**, with a few smaller outfits near **Whitehorse**. The lumber from these mills is largely used in the territory or exported for use in Alaska. The Kaska Dene First Nations has, however, entered into a venture whereby raw logs are exported to Japan for processing.

Export initiatives, like the Kaska Dene's, are controversial among Yukoners, who fear such operations might be encouraged by a territorial government trying to increase employment opportunities without sufficient regard for preserving the territory's unique and largely untouched wilderness. These fears are augmented as territorial residents look south to northern Alberta and northern British Columbia, where boreal forest is being harvested at an increasing rate to feed the processing needs of southern-based pulp mills.

Fort Selkirk

In 1848, Robert Campbell of the Hudson's Bay Company (HBC) arrived at the junction of the Pelly and Yukon rivers via the Pelly River. Although uncertain that the **Yukon River** was the mightier waterway, he was sure their confluence would provide an ideal site for a fur-trading post that could dominate the northwest interior. Consequently, he ordered construction of Fort Selkirk, named after Thomas Douglas, Fifth Earl of Selkirk. In 1810, Douglas had gained control of the HBC and the following year founded the Red River Valley colony near present-day Winnipeg. The original Fort Selkirk was abandoned in April 1852 because of flooding and a new one was erected across the Yukon River.

Fort Selkirk's early history was stormy. The post broke the carefully managed monopoly the Chilkat people of the Alaskan coast had over the interior fur trade by providing an alternate market to which Yukon **First Nations peoples** could sell their furs. Angered, the Chilkats pillaged the post on August 19, 1852 but harmed none of the white traders. The abandoned post was later burned by local First Nations, reportedly so they could extract the iron fittings from the wood and use them for tools.

The HBC withdrew almost entirely from the Yukon for the next 50 years after this debacle. Not until September 1, 1889 would a new post be erected on the site, an independent operation founded by Arthur Harper. Still active when the **Klondike Gold Rush** began, the post became an important stop for those travelling downriver to **Dawson** by the Yukon River. The **Yukon Field Force** also established its headquarters here in 1898 and for a time it was rumoured that Fort Selkirk, rather than Dawson, would become the first territorial capital. Its fortunes faded, however, with the end of the Klondike rush and a subsequent depopulation as many of the residents rushed off to Alaska to chase **gold** during the Nome Gold Rush, which started in 1899. Meanwhile, the Yukon Field Force left to chase glory in the Boer War and the post was kept alive only by the presence of a few traders and missionaries.

In 1938, the HBC returned and operated a post until 1950. Steamboat traffic was also languishing about this time, as the **Alaska Highway** provided more economical means for moving people and goods. Within a few years Fort Selkirk was abandoned.

Today, however, many of the old buildings dating from the 1890s to the 1940s have been restored. First Nations in the area have also made a point of re-establishing their presence here to underscore the fact that before Campbell and the other Europeans arrived this had been a traditional meeting place for hundreds of years. Fort Selkirk is a unique historic site, as it is only accessible by air or water. Several outfitters offer a two-hour river cruise to the fort from Minto, about 40 kilometres south on the Klondike Highway.

Frances Lake

In 1840, Hudson's Bay Company (HBC) trader and explorer Robert Campbell travelled by boat up the Liard River and its tributary, traversed the continental divide and descended what he named the Pelly River in hopes of reaching the Pacific Ocean. Campbell's journey failed to take him to the ocean and he withdrew, returning to a long lake lying adjacent to today's Campbell Highway north of **Watson Lake**. Campbell named the waters Frances Lake after Lady Frances Simpson, then wife of the governor of HBC's trading territories in British North America, Sir George Simpson.

When Campbell reported on his journey to Simpson, the governor decided that the Pelly River either led to Cook Inlet or was the **Yukon River**. Either possibility promised the HBC a backdoor means to invade the Russian fur-trade empire that encompassed Alaska and was jealously guarded by both coastal First Nations and the Russians. If the HBC established a trading post inland from the coastal fur trails and seaside trading posts it could hope to divert some of the furs captured by non-coastal peoples without causing an international diplomatic crisis.

Consequently, in 1842 Campbell opened the Yukon's first fur-trading post on the southern shores of Frances Lake. But the route from the Liard River to Fort Frances was extremely arduous and dangerous. The Frances River, linking the Liard to Frances Lake, was chockful of submerged sandbars, steep canyons, racing currents, and wild rapids. At least 14 traders died trying to travel between the Liard and Frances Lake. In 1851, when a new route to the Yukon River, via what became known as the Rat River portage, was discovered by Campbell, Fort Frances was abandoned.

Today, Frances Lake is a popular fishing and boating lake. It also serves as a launching point for whitewater adventurers who travel the 200 kilometres from the lakehead to the village of Upper Liard about 12 kilometres west of Watson Lake.

Francophone Yukoners

The first French-speaking people came into the Yukon as fur traders working either for the Hudson's Bay Company or the Alaska Commercial Company. Among the latter were two brothers, François and Moise Mercier. François Mercier served as the general agent for Alaska Commercial for 17 years, beginning in 1869 when the U.S. government asserted control over Alaska and took possession of Fort Yukon. From St. Michael on the Alaska coast, Mercier exerted control over a trading region and series of posts that extended far up the **Yukon River** into the present-day Yukon. Other *coureurs de bois*, as the French-Canadian fur traders were called, constituted a significant portion of the first white settlers who established themselves near the fur-trading posts. Although there was an early francophone presence in the Yukon, the emergence of a strong Métis population that was significantly distinct from the First Nations did not take place. Rather, the First Nations tended to absorb the francophones who married native women, or the women moved south with their husbands when the traders transferred out of the territory or left the HBC.

With the beginning of the **Klondike Gold Rush**, more francophones were attracted to the Yukon and soon the territory was peppered with French place names, such as **Lake Laberge** and La Biche River. For most of the early- and mid-20th century, however, francophone Canadians living in the Yukon had little formal community presence. That changed in 1979 when the *Association franco-yukonnaise* (AFY) was formed. Beginning initially as a social club, AFY soon expanded its mandate into the field of political and social advocacy for francophone rights. In 1982 it adopted a constitution and was incorporated.

One of its first priorities was to identify means to breathe new life into the francophone cultural heritage, which was in jeopardy of being subsumed by the more dominant anglophone culture. A major initiative on this front was the launching of the French-language newspaper, *l'Aurore boréale*. In 1984, a French school, *École Émilie-Tremblay* in **Whitehorse**, opened and by 1991 was offering French-language instruction up to the grade 10 level. Today, it offers French-language education through grade 12.

In 1988, the territorial **government** enacted the Languages Act, which recognized the legitimate existence of a French-speaking community in the Yukon. Amendments to the Education Act followed, allowing for creation of a francophone school board. In 1993, the territorial government implemented French-language services within the public service.

Today, a total of 1,172 or 3.8 percent of the Yukon's **population** report French as their mother tongue. This is an increase of 0.5 percent from 1991 and indicates a gradual, but strong, growth in the number of francophones living in the Yukon as French-speaking people.

Fur Trade

The oldest industry in the Yukon is the fur trade, tracing its roots back to 1840 when the first Hudson's Bay Company traders entered the territory via the Liard River and soon established trading posts on the **Yukon River** and its tributaries. Prior to that there had been some trade by Yukon **First Nations peoples**, through intermediary First Nations tribes on the British Columbia and Alaskan coasts, with Russia. When the Russian Empire ceded Alaska to the United States on March 30, 1867 for $7.2 million, American traders replaced the Russians and pushed into the interior up to the current border that Alaska shares with the Yukon. Because the American traders could quickly reach the Yukon River from its mouth on the Bering Sea, they were more effectively able to exploit the fur trade throughout Alaska and most of the Yukon than the Hudson's Bay Company traders, who had to move furs and trade goods across thousands of kilometres of river and overland routes to the east coast of North America.

By the turn of the century, **gold** had replaced fur as the most important commodity in the Yukon. The **Klondike Gold Rush** brought thousands of non–First Nations into the territory and changed its face forever. But the fur trade remained a significant part of the **economy** and continues to be important today.

There are about 800 people—mostly First Nations—employed in the Yukon as fur trappers or processors and the industry is valued at about $275,000 annually. Fur prices vary dramatically from one year to the next. In recent years, marten has been the most valuable fur trapped in the Yukon in terms of overall industry value. In 1996, for example, $193,596 of the $274,540 total fur value harvested in the territory came from marten. Beaver pelts were the next most valuable fur, but totalled only $18,176.

The average price of a marten fur in 1996 was $52.00, while a beaver pelt fetched $32.00. Wolverine skins were the most valuable individual pelt in that year—valued at $218.00.

Glaciation

During the Wisconsinan glaciation from 40,000 years to about 13,000 years ago, much of the Yukon was covered by three vast ice masses known as the St. Elias, the Cordilleran, and the Canadian Shield or Laurentide ice sheets. The ice covered southern and eastern Yukon and lobes of ice extended westward into the area of the **Tintina Trench**, Bonnet Plume basin, and Arctic coastal plains. At the same time, alpine valley glaciers originated in the Ogilvie, Wernecke, British, and, scientists believe, possibly the Richardson mountains.

Acting like a massive bulldozer that pushed all loose earth and rocks before it, the Laurentide ice sheet transported massive rocks from the Canadian Shield and deposited them over the northern glaciated areas. The ice of all three sheets worked to smooth the topography of plateaus; rounded lower mountains; scoured valleys; trapped large, temporary lakes; redirected some rivers; and spread vast deposits of moraine over large tracts of the Yukon landscape.

But, unlike the majority of Canada, not all of the Yukon was glaciated. Due to a lack of sufficient precipitation, a large area in the northwestern portion of the territory remained ice free. It consisted of the Klondike, Porcupine, and Arctic plateaus and portions of the Ogilvie, Wernecke, and British mountains, and the western slopes of the **Richardson Mountains**. Unaffected by the extreme scouring action of glaciation, this region of the Yukon has been subjected to only the erosion resulting from normal weathering, such as rain, freezing, and wind.

This ice-free area of the Yukon is known as **Beringia** and was part of the corridor linking North America to Asia that is believed to have been used as a land bridge by prehistoric humans coming into North America.

Gold

A bright yellow metal valued for its lustrous beauty and relative scarcity, gold has profoundly influenced the history of the Yukon. Undoubtedly the territory's development would have proceeded in an entirely different manner had it not been for the discovery of gold that sparked the **Klondike Gold Rush**. This led to a gold-based development in the last decade of the 19th century that was as fevered as it was transitory.

Gold is an element, meaning it occurs naturally and cannot be broken down into component substances by ordinary chemical means. It is considered a noble metal, meaning it is inert and unaffected by most chemicals and acids. Extremely durable, it is immune to corrosion and will not rust. Gold is also ductile, which renders it an excellent conductor of electricity even when stretched into filament-thin threads for use in microchip circuitry or as the skin of a satellite. It is possible to hammer 16 cubic centimetres of gold into a sheet capable of covering 103,225 square centimetres.

In nature, gold is seldom as pure as it is when transformed into a piece of jewellery or a bar of bullion. Usually it is alloyed, or fused, with metals such as copper or silver. Such fusion transforms the colour of gold. If alloyed to silver the gold is usually quite pale; when alloyed to copper it takes on a reddish hue. It can also be coated by iron oxide and so appear dark and rusty or, if coated with manganese, black.

Gold also comes in many shapes and sizes in its natural state. It can be as finely grained as flour, shaped like a flake, or formed into a nugget as large as a human fist. Often it is embedded in rock as part of what is known as a vein or lode. Other times it is found loosely mixed in deposits of sand or gravel. To add to the gold-identification problem there are other minerals that mimic its appearance—the all too common fool's gold that has humbled many naïve gold-seekers over the course of human history. The most exact test of whether a mineral find contains gold or fool's gold, such as pyrite or marcasite, is to measure its specific gravity. Gold's specific gravity is high—19.3—compared to a specific gravity for pyrite of only about 5. Although gold's specific gravity is high, it is softer than the lookalike minerals, enabling it to be easily shaped to make fine jewellery. Combined with its lustre, this characteristic has most contributed to gold becoming a precious metal known around the world as a symbol of wealth.

In the Yukon most commercial gold is refined, meaning the impurities or alloys mixed with it are removed. The more pure the gold the more valuable it is. Some Yukon gold mined from creeks has been as pure as 98 percent. Most, however, is of a lower purity, which can drop to 65 percent. Gold broken down by the washing action of water over many centuries into flour gold, commonly called dust, is often virtually pure and consequently extremely valuable.

Much of the gold in the Yukon is found in placers, which are deposits of sand, gravel, or other materials that contain recoverable amounts of gold and other minerals. The heavy minerals found in placers are loosely held in other materials and so more easily separated than minerals contained in veins or lodes that must be mined by hardrock or quartz technologies. **Placer mining** is the only form of mining that can reasonably be carried out by an individual using simple methods.

If the Klondike River and its tributaries had not contained large deposits of gold in the placers along their shores there would have been no gold rush. Although there are many 19th-century tales of individual goldseekers striking it rich by finding and tapping into a gold "motherlode," few prospectors ever searched for such strikes. They looked instead for heavy concentrations of placer gold in creeks and streams. It was to these gold strikes that thousands of prospectors—veterans and novices alike—would rush whenever word of a placer find leaked out.

Gold Dredges

Not all **placer mining** during the **Klondike Gold Rush** entailed individual prospectors working with relatively primitive sluice boxes and rockers to extract the gold from the creekbeds. As the peak period of the rush ended, new forms of mining technology were introduced that enabled a claim to be worked more quickly and efficiently than by traditional placer mining techniques. One of these methods involved the use of a dredge.

A gold dredge functioned somewhat like a giant sluice box. Floated on a barge, its giant cast-iron buckets dug up gravel from the bottom of the stream, which was then processed through a long trough, like a sluice box.

The first dredge was put into operation at Otago, New Zealand in 1867. It was powered by current wheels. In 1881, a steam-driven dredge was constructed on the Molyneux River in New Zealand and this served as the model for most of the dredges built in North America.

In 1899, the Yukon's first dredge was built at Cassiar Bar on the **Yukon River**, then moved to Bonanza Creek where the first strikes of the Klondike Gold Rush had been made in 1896. This dredge operated on the creek for several years, often reworking ground that had been mined less thoroughly by sluice box and rocker techniques.

Twenty dredges were built in the Yukon before technology and the costs of operation rendered the devices outmoded. The records vary, but there may have been as many as 35 gold dredges deployed on Klondike creeks until the last one closed down in the late 1950s. The Yukon dredges, measured by the cubic-metre capacity of each bucket, ranged in size from .07 to .45 cubic metres.

One of these dredges remains relatively intact and is a tourist attraction on Bonanza Creek, outside **Dawson**. Known as No. 4 dredge, it now rests on Claim 17, below Discovery Claim. It is the biggest wooden-hull, bucket-line dredge in North America and was designed by the Marion Steam Shovel Company. Owned by the Canadian Klondike Mining Company, it was first deployed at Claim 12 below Discovery Claim on Bonanza Creek in May 1913. The dredge dug a path that remains marked by the tailing piles bordering the creek from Claim 12 to the Boyle Concession, where it sank in 1924. Three years later the dredge was

The massive structure of Gold Dredge No. 3 at the time of its deployment on Bonanza Creek.
(NAC C3089)

refloated and continued operating up the Klondike Valley to Hunker Creek. At the mouth of Hunker Creek the dredge produced more than 800 ounces of gold in a single day. Operation at Hunker Creek continued until 1940.

The following year its new owners, the Yukon Consolidated Gold Corporation, moved the dredge back to Bonanza Creek where it worked until 1959. It was the last dredge to cease operating in the Yukon. At the time the dredge was working on Claim 17 and was abandoned there, becoming mired in about 5 metres of silt. In 1991, as part of the Klondike National Historic Sites initiative of Parks Canada at Dawson, restoration of the dredge was undertaken. The following year the dredge was released from its bed of muck and ice and floated to a crib, where it now rests.

No. 4 dredge has a 43-metre-long hull that is 20 metres wide and ranges from 3.5 to 5 metres deep. Its total height from hull bottom to the highest point on the roof is 23 metres. Its displacement weight is 2,722 tonnes.

Gold Panning

To test the **gold** content of placers, prospectors have traditionally used a technique known as gold panning. This is not a mining technique, as it is virtually impossible to pan enough gold to make it worthwhile. Panning for gold is, however, an essential method of discovering gold and assessing the potential of a strike.

Traditionally, gold pans were made of heavy-gauge steel which required careful maintenance to avoid rust. Many prospectors today favour pans made of high-impact plastic, some with built-in ridges known as riffles that trap gold more easily than a smooth-surfaced pan.

A prospector usually works in an upstream direction when panning, hoping to follow a gold trail to its source. The prospector moves along the stream edge, panning wherever there appear to be good placer deposits. Scooping up some of the gravel from the stream bottom and keeping the pan immersed in the water, the prospector rotates the pan in a circular motion combined with up and down movement. Gold has a high specific gravity and will sink to the bottom of the pan, while the gravel is suspended in the pan's water.

After about five minutes of panning a sample, the prospector removes the pan from the water and skims off the top layer of gravel using the edge of one hand. This process is repeated several times. When only the heaviest materials are left in the bottom of the pan, little should remain in the pan but some black sand and whatever gold was in the sample.

If only two or three flecks of gold are found, the prospects for that section of streambed are poor; six to eight flecks indicate a good prospect; and 30 to 60 flecks mean the prospector has hit paydirt and should immediately start **claim-staking**.

There are many sites in the Yukon where people can practise gold panning. These include the Klondike Visitor Association's site on Bonanza Creek where the **Klondike Gold Rush**'s discovery strike occurred.

(*See also* **Placer Mining**.)

Government

Yukon's government derives its modern-day structure from British parliamentary tradition, but unlike the provinces of Canada that democratic structure was only recently attained. Until 1870 the Yukon was part of the large Hudson's Bay Company territory known as Rupert's Land, and the North-Western Territory, of which the Yukon was a part. In 1870 these lands were acquired by Canada through a transfer negotiated with Great Britain.

The Northwest Territories, as this vast land was identified by the federal government, was governed by a territorial council appointed by the federally appointed lieutenant-governor. There was no allowance for true self-representation within the structure of the territorial government. The capital was based in present-day Saskatchewan at Regina.

Considered a territory within the Northwest Territories, the Yukon received little governmental attention until the **Klondike Gold Rush** suddenly brought a great influx of prospectors. Although most of the prospectors were Americans, there were enough Canadians of European descent to raise the issue of governmental self-representation in the territory. **First Nations peoples** were at the time denied the rights of Canadian citizenship and so could not vote. Soon the complaints by whites against the distant Northwest Territorial council in Regina grew loud enough to reach Ottawa's ears. There was another pressing reason that encouraged Ottawa to consider making the Yukon a distinct political territory independent of the Northwest Territories. The costs of policing the **gold** rush were putting a mild strain on the national treasury. By creating a distinct territory, Ottawa could ensure that the revenue being generated at **Dawson** by the government liquor tax was retained to cover those costs rather than lost to territorial coffers.

Consequently, on June 13, 1898 the Yukon Territory Act was proclaimed, establishing the territorial boundaries then in existence as constituting the boundaries of a new territory. The Commissioner of the Yukon was appointed by Ottawa, the first person holding this position being Major James Morrow Walsh. The Mountie was renowned for his role in assuring the peace when Sioux chief Sitting Bull and his army sought refuge in Canada after their victory over the U.S. army at the Battle of the Little Bighorn. Walsh arrived in the new capital of Dawson to assume his position and proceeded to become embroiled in arguments with the **North-West Mounted Police** superintendent Sam Steele and other leading figures. Resigning in a huff within months of his arrival, Walsh left the territory and was replaced by William Ogilvie. The new commissioner was popular, having worked as the mining commissioner who oversaw the early development of the Klondike gold fields.

Although the territorial council was appointed and included such government administrators as Sam Steele, it differed from that of the Northwest Territories in that all its members were Yukon residents. Still, meetings of the council were at first closed to the public.

One year later, however, in response to local pressure, the Yukon Territory Act was amended to allow for the addition of two elected members. This brought the council up to eight members. Its responsibility was to oversee public health,

education, local administration, and the building and maintenance of roads and other services.

In 1902, three more elected members were added to the council. This coincided with the federal government granting the territory the right to elect its own member of parliament. James H. Ross became the Yukon's first federal MP, stepping down from his post as the current Yukon commissioner to assume the seat in the House of Commons.

Pressure for a fully democratic territorial council continued and in 1908 a fully elected council numbering 10 members was established. Elections were to be held every three years. But the Yukon was facing a crisis in the form of a dwindling **population** as miners left the gold fields at the end of the major gold rush. New technology being used to extract gold required fewer miners than the individual **placer mining** operations that had existed on the Klondike creeks. World War I further depopulated the territory as many of the non–First Nations residents headed off to war.

In 1916 the office of the commissioner was disbanded and its duties assumed by the territorial gold commissioner, who was little responsible to the elected territorial council. Two years later the federal government sought to disband the council altogether but recanted the following year, even though, because of the drastically diminished population, it was reduced to only three members.

From 1918 to the end of World War II the political fortunes of the Yukon seesawed dramatically back and forth according to the rise and fall of its population and economic prospects. World War II brought the construction of the **Alaska Highway** and in the wake of this and other economic developments, the territory regained a territorial commissioner in 1948. In 1951, the territorial council was increased to five elected members.

Two years later the council decided to shift the capital from Dawson to the newly emerging economic centre of **Whitehorse**. Bitter opposition to this plan from Dawsonites went largely unheeded and the move spelled the community's worst period of economic decline.

Not until 1970 did the Yukon receive what is termed responsible government. At this time an executive committee of the Yukon territorial government was formed. It included members of the elected assembly—which replaced the former territorial council. For the first time in the territory's history, elected representatives controlled day-to-day governmental affairs. Assembly members were responsible for advising the commissioner on territorial issues. Even then, the commissioner—still an appointed official—could ignore their advice.

In 1979 the federally appointed commissioner's office finally became responsible to a wholly elected executive committee, now referred to as the cabinet or executive council. The move was not entirely popular among all Yukoners. The commissioner of the day, Ione Christensen, declared that she was now no more than a figurehead and resigned. But there was no turning back the clock and the commissioner survives in a position akin to that of provincial lieutenant governors elsewhere in Canada.

The cabinet today is responsible for the governing of the Yukon. As is true of provincial cabinets, it can only continue to govern if it has the confidence of the legislative assembly. There are currently six members of Cabinet drawn from the elected political party that captures the most seats in the legislature. Party politics came to the Yukon in 1978, one year before the government was made entirely responsible to the electorate.

The legislative assembly is composed of 17 members, who hold terms not to exceed four years. Parties that are commonly present in the legislature are the New Democratic Party, the Yukon Party (formerly the Yukon Conservative Party), and the Liberal Party.

The Yukon government consists of 12 departments, as well as a Women's Directorate and four Crown corporations. Each takes direction from a cabinet minister and is responsible to the cabinet. Government departments and agencies are responsible for a similar range of activities as in Canadian provinces, including education, economic development, municipal affairs, social services, housing, **tourism**, **justice**, renewable resources, and finance.

Administration of some programs, mostly in the field of natural resources, remains federally controlled. Some of these, however, are gradually being transferred to territorial jurisdiction. In recent years transfers have been completed for the Northern Canada Power Commission, freshwater fisheries, mine safety, inter-territorial roads, the Alaska Highway, oil and gas management, and airports.

The Yukon has one member of parliament in the federal House of Commons and one member in the federal Senate.

Grizzly Bears. *See* **Bears.**

Haines Junction

With a **population** of about 850, Haines Junction stands at the crossroads of the Haines and Alaska **highways**. It is also the headquarters for **Kluane National Park Reserve** and provides an access point to Tatshenshini-Alsek Wilderness Provincial Park in British Columbia. Overlooking the community are the towering peaks of the **St. Elias Mountains**. The village has well-developed services for travellers and numerous backcountry guiding operations that offer hiking, whitewater rafting, kayaking, canoeing, and other trips into Kluane, the Tatshenshini-Alsek, and other wilderness regions.

Haines Junction was born during the **Alaska Highway** project, serving as a U.S. army base to house engineers working on the road's construction. It was named after the community of Haines, situated on the Alaska coast. The 257-kilometre Haines Highway connects Haines and Haines Junction via the 1,065-metre-high Chilkat Pass. This highway was originally constructed to provide a direct route for transporting supplies shipped into Haines to the Alaska Highway project.

Parts of this road follow the path of the historic Dalton Trail, slashed out of the wilderness by **Klondike Gold Rush** entrepreneur Jack Dalton as a toll route to the Klondike. This was the only trail over which livestock could successfully be herded to **Dawson**. Dalton charged $250 per person to travel the road.

The Dalton Trail is probably most famous as the route used by a U.S. government–inspired rescue mission to provide food to Dawson in the winter of 1897–98 to relieve the near-starvation conditions reported there. The government purchased 539 reindeer in Norway, shipped the herd to New York City, moved it by train to Seattle, then by boat to Haines, and in May 1898—long after the starvation winter had passed in Dawson without a single casualty—proceeded to drive it over the Dalton Trail on a 1,200-kilometre trek through harsh wilderness. The reindeer were accompanied by Laplander herders brought

from Norway. Along the way the reindeer fell prey to **wolves** and other predators, succumbed to diseases, drowned in river crossings, and perished from
other calamities. Many starved for lack of appropriate food along the route, a fate
that also nearly claimed the lives of the Laplanders. The herders were reduced to
eating the reindeer and food given to them by stampeders who stumbled on this
bizarre party en route to Dawson.

On January 27, 1899, the reindeer herd finally reached Dawson. Only 114
animals were still alive, these so gaunt from hunger they were considered not
worth eating. The remnant herd of the Klondike Relief Expedition, as it was
known, was sent on to Alaska to provide food for miners there.

Herschel Island Territorial Park

In July 1987, the 100-square-kilometre expanse of Herschel Island became the
Yukon's first territorial park, created out of the settlement of Inuvialuit land
claims. The park is maintained by the Yukon government in cooperation with
First Nations peoples of the region.

The island lies just off the northern coast of the Yukon mainland within the
Beaufort Sea. Ninety kilometres north of Herschel Island begins the permanent
pack ice of the Arctic Ocean, which moves slowly in a clockwise direction due
to a prevailing current known as the Beaufort Gyre. At times, but most often during the winter, if prevailing winds are blowing out of the north the pack ice can
press in and surround the island.

Herschel Island was so named on July 17, 1826 when Arctic explorer John
Franklin sighted it from his ship and named it after British chemist and
astronomer Sir John Herschel. Inuvialuit peoples, however, who had camped on
this island for millennias knew it as *Qikiqtaruk,* meaning "it is island."

The waters around Herschel Island provide a rare Arctic haven for **fish** and
marine **mammals**. Although Arctic waters are usually less productive than more
southerly oceans, the nearby drainage of the Mackenzie River into the Beaufort
Sea provides a warmer, nutrient-rich flow that drifts westward to Herschel
Island's shores. **Invertebrates** and other small sea creatures feed on these nutrients and are, in turn, eaten by larger fish, seals, and whales. The Mackenzie River
also provides the northern coast's only source of driftwood, carried into the
Beaufort Sea from the mainland interior. This wood has long been considered a
vital resource for use as firewood and building materials.

The crew of Maid of Orleans *numbered among some of the whaling crews who wintered at Herschel Island in the early 1900s.* (Yukon Archives, Ernest Pasley Collection, #9211)

Archaeological evidence on Herschel Island and the neighbouring mainland coast here reveals that about 1,000 years ago a large population of people, known as the Thule, had developed a sophisticated culture that included villages of more than 2,000 people. Houses were dug into the beach gravel and had walls constructed out of driftwood covered with hides and sod. The Thule people are believed to have been drawn to the area from the east by the migration of the **bowhead whale** to this area during a period of climatic warming.

When Franklin visited the island, he found descendants of the Thule who knew themselves as the Qikiqtarukmiut or "island people" living in three villages. Some 60 years after Franklin's visit came American whalers who, in 1890, established a major whaling station on the southeast side of the island in the deepwater harbour of Pauline Cove. The only protective harbour between the Mackenzie River Delta and Point Barrow, Alaska, Pauline Cove was considered a vital port for western Arctic whaling operations.

At the time, bowhead had been hunted to near extinction in more southerly waters. Within a few years, the whaling station's population was about 1,500. Houses and warehouses were constructed. The use of driftwood for these structures and for firewood to heat the ships and buildings quickly depleted the island's wood resources, forcing the whalers to begin importing coal. Local Inuvialuit supplied the whalers with food and clothing in exchange for manufactured goods and such southern foods as tea and sugar.

The introduction of alcohol and diseases to the Inuvialuit population on Herschel Island had a devastating effect. Many died. In 1893, responding to reports of whalers abusing the local population, the Anglican missionary Isaac Stringer visited the island. In 1897, he returned with his wife and established a permanent mission. The **North-West Mounted Police** arrived in 1903 to exert Canadian sovereignty over the whalers. Lacking their own patrol boats, however, the Mounties were dependent on the whalers for all forms of marine transport. The only way they could maintain an independent line of communication with Canada was via an annual winter patrol, when a small group of Mounties travelled by dog sled between Herschel Island, Fort McPherson, and **Dawson** (*see* **Lost Patrol**).

By 1907, the whaling era came to an abrupt end when the market for bowhead whale oil suddenly collapsed and the whaling station was completely abandoned by 1914. The mission remained open sporadically, but the Mounties continued to maintain a permanent post here until 1964 to enforce Canadian sovereignty over the western Arctic. When the police left, no permanent **population** remained, as the last Inuvialuit had left many years previously.

Forty-one years earlier, Herschel Island had been the scene of a controversial trial that led to the execution in a transport shed on the island of two Inuvialuit men—Alikomiak and Tátimagana—convicted of murdering four other Inuvialuit in a dispute over women. The two men had also killed Royal Canadian Mounted Police officer W. A. Doak and Hudson's Bay Company employee Otto Binder during an escape attempt. Despite many appeals in the southern press for the release of the convicted men, the federal government decided that capital punishment was required to convince the Inuvialuit people that they had to obey Canadian law. The two men were the first Inuvialuit to be condemned and executed in Canada.

Herschel Island today is home to a rich mixture of marine and land wildlife. Polar **bears** live there and ringed seals are common. The island is an important denning site for Arctic foxes. **Caribou**, muskox, and grizzly bears also cross to the island on the ice in winter or occasionally swim across during summer. Bowhead and beluga whales are recovering their populations in this region and are often seen offshore. The island is also home to the largest western Arctic colony of black guillemots, which have expanded their nesting sites to include the rafters of the abandoned Anglican mission house. Arctic terns, golden plovers, sandpipers, and red-necked phalaropes all nest on the island in summer. One of the most productive breeding populations in North America of rough-legged hawks is found in the island's cliffs and gullies.

From late June to early August, the island's humid maritime **climate** supports a lush growth of **tundra** flowers. Almost 200 species of vascular plants occur on the island, including vetch, lousewort, arctic lupine, arnica, and forget-me-not.

Herschel Island is undergoing constant and extreme erosion along its shoreline. The effect of waves, pack ice, and sun all combine to break down the island's steep slopes, open **permafrost**, and massive convex walls of ice and wash them into the sea. The island itself is termed a polar desert because it receives little precipitation. In January temperatures average -27^0 to -30^0 Celsius, but in July the temperature averages about 13^0 Celsius.

From early July to late September, Herschel Island is accessible by boat or float plane charter from Inuvik or Dawson. Visitors are required to be equipped for self-sufficient Arctic wilderness camping. Park rangers maintain limited services at Pauline Cove.

Highways

Much of the Yukon is inaccessible by highway. Those that do exist are primarily confined to the southern part of the territory, with the exception of the Klondike Highway to **Dawson** and the **Dempster Highway**, which branches off the Klondike Highway to cut through the northern heart of the Yukon before entering the Northwest Territory en route to Inuvik.

The Yukon portion of the **Alaska Highway**, extending from south of **Watson Lake** to the Alaska border west of **Beaver Creek**, is the territory's primary road access. Until its construction in 1942, the Yukon had no road connection to the rest of Canada. This highway is paved throughout. The Klondike Highway branches off to the south and north of the Alaska Highway, providing a road link to **Carcross** in the south and access to the majority of the territory's communities north of **Whitehorse**, including **Carmacks**, **Pelly Crossing**, **Stewart Crossing**, and Dawson. The Klondike Highway is paved from start to finish.

The Campbell Highway runs from Watson Lake through **Ross River** and **Faro** to a junction with the Klondike Highway just north of Carmacks. This 582-kilometre route is mostly unpaved, except for the section between Faro and the Klondike Highway junction. At the 110-kilometre point north of Watson Lake, Nahanni Range Road #10 provides rugged, unpaved access to the Logan Mountains but is closed from 134 kilometres because of washouts and a lack of road maintenance beyond this point.

Extending from Johnson's Crossing on the Alaska Highway to Ross River and then beyond to the Northwest Territory border is the 472.4-kilometre-long **Canol Road**. This historic road is unpaved, with a ferry crossing at Ross River.

At **Stewart Crossing** on the Klondike Highway, Highway 11—known as the Silver Trail—provides a scenic, mostly paved loop from **Mayo** through the silver-lead mining communities of **Elsa** and **Keno**. Accessible by ferry from Dawson is the Top of the World Highway, which is open in the summer only and provides road access to Alaska and the option of driving a loop from Dawson through Alaska to the Alaska Highway at Tetlin Junction. The Top of the World highway is entirely unpaved.

Several other small highways provide access to Aishihik Lake and to Atlin in British Columbia, and link **Tagish** to the Klondike and Alaska highways.

Historical Overview

The first European to reach any part of what is today the Yukon Territory was probably Sir John Franklin. He followed the Yukon's **Beaufort Sea** shoreline, visiting First Nations settlements on Herschel Island in 1826. Previous to Franklin's explorations, **First Nations peoples** of the Yukon may have had passing contact with Russian fur traders who operated posts on the Alaskan coast. It is more likely, however, that their trade with the Russians was through intermediary Chilkat people of Alaska, who jealously guarded their fur-trading links with the Russian traders.

The first fur traders of the Hudson's Bay Company (HBC) arrived in the Yukon by travelling up the Liard River, then down the Pelly River to its junction with the **Yukon River**. In 1848, Robert Campbell of the HBC completed this trip and constructed a fur-trading post. He subsequently explored the upper waters of the Yukon River. Soon a network of fur-trading posts was strung along the Yukon River and its tributaries. The commercial **fur trade** in the Yukon was never highly profitable for the HBC because of the vast distances the furs had to be transported from the territory to Britain. Consequently, the posts were often abandoned after only a few years' operation.

Meanwhile, American whalers had established a whaling station on Herschel Island and American fur traders were moving into the territory from Alaska, following the purchase of Alaska from the Russians in 1867. With an all-water route to the Alaskan coast via the Yukon River, the Americans were better able to commercially exploit the Yukon fur trade than the HBC, leading to the company's slow withdrawal from the region.

In 1870, the HBC ceded Yukon, then part of the North-Western Territory and Rupert's Land, to Canada. It became a territory within the larger North-Western Territory. From 1870 to 1896, its inhabitants were mainly First Nations peoples. They lived as they had for millennia, with little contact between themselves and whites, other than traders seeking to buy their furs and missionaries intent on converting them to Christianity. The Canadian government was content to virtually ignore the Yukon and most of northern Canada.

The discovery of **gold** on a Klondike River tributary in August 1896 suddenly brought the Yukon to the attention of the world. The greatest of the 19th-century rushes—the **Klondike Gold Rush**—was soon underway. By 1898 the **population** of the Yukon exceeded 40,000 and **Dawson** was the largest city west of Winnipeg and north of San Francisco. The gold rush forever changed the face of the territory, bringing with it an influx of people, a highly developed river-based transportation system, the **White Pass & Yukon Railway** link to

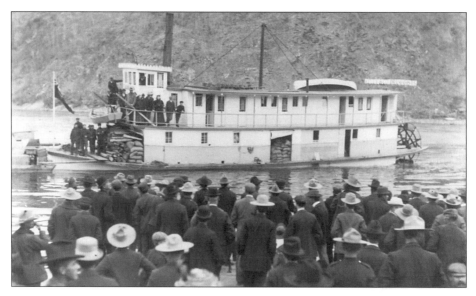

A sternwheeler steams into Dawson during the gold rush era. (NAC PA-16201)

the Pacific Ocean, and a place in Canada's dominion as a full-fledged territory of its own when the Yukon Territory Act was proclaimed on June 13, 1898.

Although the gold rush's end and the depopulating effect of World War I greatly reduced the Yukon's political stature, the territory survived as a political entity and began a slow process of economic diversification based on mineral exploration and development. Although gold mining would remain important to the territory, the **mining industry** would also be based on silver, lead, and zinc extraction.

With the outbreak of World War II and the bombing of Pearl Harbor by Japan on December 6, 1941 followed by Japan's capture of the Aleutian Islands, the United States government decided it needed an all-weather highway link to Alaska. Such a road had to pass through the Yukon. The Canadian government agreed to its construction and the **Alaska Highway** was completed on October 28, 1942. Its construction brought thousands of American and Canadian soldiers, construction workers, and support personnel into the territory. Communities such as **Watson Lake**, **Whitehorse**, and **Destruction Bay** served as major operational bases. At war's end, Whitehorse emerged as the territory's primary service and supply centre, ultimately eclipsing Dawson, which lay well to the north of the Alaska Highway where most commercial and resource development was focused. In 1953, Whitehorse's ascendancy would be formally recognized when the provincial capital moved there from Dawson.

Mining fuelled the territory's development in the postwar years, centred first on the **Keno** and **Mayo** silver mines and in 1969 on **Faro**, where lead and zinc were the main minerals extracted. The late 1960s also marked the beginning of the **tourism** industry, which is today the second-biggest single contributor to the territory's **economy**.

Not until 1979 did the Yukon attain true political independence from the federal government when an entirely elected Cabinet was made directly responsible to the territorial assembly, rather than to a federally appointed territorial commissioner. The devolution of federal authority to the territorial **government** has continued to be an ongoing process. Almost 10 years earlier, Yukon First Nations launched efforts to have their land claims recognized and settlements negotiated. Negotiations between First Nations and the federal and territorial governments have so far resulted in the involvement of Yukon First Nations in most governmental, economic, and environmental issues.

Today, about 70 percent of the Yukon's population lives in Whitehorse, leaving the rest of the territory largely unpopulated. While most Yukoners live a primarily urban day-to-day existence, they sustain and claim a close connection to a wilderness that has largely been lost to the majority of Canadians who live in a narrow, densely populated strip along the Canada–U.S. border.

Invertebrates

Between 90 and 95 percent of all animals living on earth are invertebrates, creatures lacking a backbone. Apart from this absence, invertebrates have little in common. They are generally soft-bodied animals without a rigid internal skeleton, but often have a hard outer skeleton (like most molluscs, crustaceans, and insects) that serves, as well, for body protection. Every year new invertebrates are discovered and classified by wildlife specialists.

The most numerous subgroup of invertebrates is the arthropods, comprising insects, crustaceans, and spiders and their relatives. Roughly 85 percent of all invertebrates are arthropods. North America is known to have about 100,000 arthropod species.

Yukon's number of arthropod species is unknown, as is the total number of invertebrate species. Less is known about insects in the Yukon than any other region of Canada. Yet the Yukon is particularly important to the understanding of invertebrate species in North America and the world because of **Beringia**, the ice-free corridor that connected North America to Asia during the Pleistocene glaciations. The Yukon was also the northernmost limit of fauna extending its reach from the south after the continental ice sheet dissipated. These animals came into contact with those that had sheltered inside Beringia, resulting in an increased number of wildlife species in the territory.

The diversity of the invertebrates is amazingly prolific when compared to other forms of animal life. There are only 61 mammal species in the Yukon and about 40 species of **fish**. This compares to a minimum of 22,000 insect species alone. In 1988, for example, two researchers identified 245 species of noctuid moths within the confines of the territory. Many of these were identified as "Beringian endemics," species that have not extended their range beyond the ice-free zones since deglaciation occurred over most of the North American continent some 10,000 years ago.

In the Yukon, 297 species of spiders are known to exist, 157 oribatid mites, 33 species of dragonflies, 71 species of stoneflies, 17 species of grasshoppers, 216 species of true bugs (Heteroptera), 145 species of leafhoppers, 53 species of aphids, 913 beetle species, 64 species of weevils, 76 black fly species, 20 robber fly species, 518 species of butterflies and moths, 145 caddisfly species, 153 species of wasps (estimated as only 80 percent of probable species present), and 19 recognized species of ants.

Ivvavik National Park

Established in 1986, this 10,000-square-kilometre park lies on the far northwestern edge of the Yukon, by the **Beaufort Sea**. Flowing through the park's rugged heart is the Firth River, one of the premier wilderness rafting waters in the world. Off the park's northern coast lies **Herschel Island Territorial Park**. Ivvavik Park encompasses a large portion of the British Mountains and is renowned for its isolated northern alpine terrain, which protects a great diversity of wildlife living in **tundra** and Arctic wilderness environments.

The shores of the Firth River provide prime grizzly bear habitat, and much of the park falls within the migrational range of the Porcupine barren-ground **caribou** herd.

Services in the park are minimal to nonexistent and visitors should be completely self-sufficient in terms of food and camping supplies. There are no accommodation facilities other than camping sites, no road access, and few marked trails. Two landing strips on the coastline provide the only outside access to the park. Charter flights to Ivvavik Park can be booked from **Dawson** or Inuvik.

Justice

The administration of justice in the Yukon is carried out through three permanent courthouses, located in **Whitehorse**, **Watson Lake**, and **Dawson**. Court circuits regularly visit most of the territory's other communities. The Yukon Justice Department spends slightly more than $30 million annually on its operations.

In 1960, a special Court of Appeal for the Yukon was established. It consists of the British Columbia chief justice, B.C. justices of appeal, and the judges from the Territorial Court of the Northwest Territories. This appeal court has all the powers of provincial courts of appeal in southern Canada.

Court services, the sheriff's office, the coroner's office, the law library, and probation services are all based in Whitehorse. So, too, is the territory's only penitentiary for adults, along with a smaller facility for juveniles. Anyone sentenced to more than two years' imprisonment is transferred to federal prisons in the south, just as offenders in the provinces sentenced to more than two years are confined in federal facilities. Territorial inmates participate in mobile work camps that complete community-related work projects.

First Nations communities are also involved in sentencing First Nations offenders. This form of justice draws on traditional First Nations' practice and the knowledge of elders. With self-government, it is expected that First Nations will take a greater role in administration of their own justice and sentencing systems. First Nations' sentences can include such punishments as banishment to a wilderness area for a specific period of time or studying traditional ways of life with elders.

Keno

On July 10, 1919, prospector Louis Beauvette staked out a claim identified as Roulette on Sheep Hill near Mayo Lake. He renamed the hill Keno, after a form of bingo game that was popular in North American mining camps. The hill contained rich deposits of silver and lead. Beauvette, as was true of many prospectors, lacked the finances to develop the claim, so he turned to Yukon Gold Company (YGC) engineer A. K. Schellinger, who convinced the company to invest in establishing a mining operation. When word of the YGC deal leaked out, a minor rush was sparked and more than 600 claims were filed in 1920 on and around Keno Hill.

From the outset the Keno mines were plagued by their isolation. **Yukon River** ships were unable to ascend the fast-running and shallow Stewart River and smaller draught vessels were unable to proceed past where the river became impassable to boats beyond **Mayo**, about 60 kilometres away from the mines. This made the cost of hauling the ore to Mayo almost prohibitively expensive. If the ore deposits had not been so rich, the shipping costs would have made the entire operation unfeasible without expensive concentration facilities at the mine site. YGC was unwilling to make such an investment and limited its development to extracting only the richest silver veins.

In 1924, the company leased the mine's operation to newcomer Treadwell Yukon Company. Treadwell assigned geologist Livingston Wernecke (for whom the nearby Wernecke Mountains are named) to manage the operation. Wernecke realized the operation required a long-term development strategy to make the mine cost-efficient. Deployment of a caterpillar tractor train to the mine in 1922 had solved the problem of how to haul the ore to Mayo efficiently and construction of a concentration mill in 1924 allowed the company to exploit milling-grade ores as well as high-grade silver. Treadwell also began buying up adjacent mining operations, such as United Keno Hill Company, so that by 1930 it controlled most of the Keno Hill mining operation.

In that year, Treadwell's Keno operations accounted for 14 percent of all Canadian silver production—some 3.7 million fine ounces. Two years later, however, a world collapse in silver prices and the depletion of the principal deposits led to the closure of the concentration mill and by 1934 Treadwell permanently shut down its operations.

The effect on the nearby community of Keno was severe. Having grown from the success of the YGC and Treadwell operations, Keno had evolved from a tent town to a community with log houses, a hotel, school, liquor store, and assay office. By 1934 school and liquor store had both closed and Keno seemed destined to become another ghost town.

But the town enjoyed a respite in 1935 when Treadwell discovered several rich new veins on nearby Galena Hill. The price of silver suddenly increased as the U.S. government enacted a silver-purchasing plan. In the midst of a world depression, Treadwell confidently announced it would expand its Keno operations. A concentration mill was constructed at Elsa, a small mining community established in 1929. The expansion ground to a quick halt, however, when world silver prices collapsed toward the end of the 1930s. In 1939, the Elsa mine and other Treadwell operations near Keno were all closed. In May 1942 the Treadwell Yukon Company was formally dissolved.

Keno today is a shadow of its former self, with just a handful of permanent residents and a hotel. The Keno City Mining Museum recounts the area's history. Nearby Elsa enjoyed a brief resurgence when its United Keno Hill mine was reopened in the 1980s but depressed silver prices led to its closure again in 1989. The townsite there is largely mothballed, with just a small security crew remaining.

Klondike Gold Rush

In the summer of 1896 prospector Robert Henderson was realizing good results from a gold-mining claim he had staked on Gold Bottom Creek, a tributary flowing into the Klondike River. In a few weeks he and some companions netted $750 worth of **gold** before running short on supplies. Henderson restocked at Joseph Ladue's trading post on Sixtymile River, advising the trader, who had backed many of Henderson's mining forays into the surrounding creek country, of his good fortune. He then started back toward Gold Bottom Creek with his

A group of prospectors working their claim on Bonanza Creek. (Anita John Collection, Klondike National Historic Site photo 610)

supplies, soon coming to the confluence of the Klondike and Yukon rivers. Here, a fateful meeting took place that would lead to the most famous gold rush in history.

Camped at the Klondike River's mouth was George Carmack and his three First Nations relatives, Dawson Charlie, Skookum Jim Mason, and Carmack's wife Kate, who was also Skookum Jim's sister. The group had set up camp on the site where Ladue—acting on Henderson's tip—would soon establish **Dawson** and were using nets to catch fish because in a dream Carmack had seen two fish covered with gold nuggets instead of scales and with twenty-dollar gold pieces for eyes. Upon seeing Carmack, Henderson told him about the good returns he was realizing at Gold Bottom Creek. He invited Carmack to try his hand there but added that none of Carmack's First Nations relatives were welcome. Henderson believed some First Nations people had robbed one of his food caches and had decided all were untrustworthy.

Carmack set out the next day with Jim and Charlie to check on Henderson's report. Instead of following the Klondike up to Gold Bottom, however, they took what they thought might be a shortcut up a small stream called Rabbit Creek. Along the way they did a bit of **gold panning**, struggled through dense bush, and were swarmed by **mosquitoes**. Not far from where they would soon establish the claim that sparked the Klondike Rush, Jim and Charlie panned about ten cents in gold from the stream. Encouraged, the men decided if nothing came of the Gold Bottom find they would return and work Rabbit Creek. Carmack advised Jim and Charlie not to disclose what they had found to Henderson's party because he wanted to make sure the find had some prospects to it first. On August 11, Carmack's group staked a couple of claims near Henderson's operation on Gold Bottom Creek that showed less promise than Rabbit Creek, so decided to return there for further panning.

Before leaving Henderson's camp, however, Jim and Charlie approached the other miner and asked if they could buy some tobacco from him. Henderson gruffly refused in a way that Carmack considered a direct insult of his relatives. Carmack would later write, "his childish unreasoning prejudice would not even allow him to stake on the same creek with the despised 'Siwashes' so his obstinacy lost him a fortune."

Returning to Rabbit Creek, the three men panned their way downstream but after three days ran out of supplies. Jim, however, managed to kill a moose. While Jim was waiting for his partners to join him by the creek, he paused for a drink and saw more gold lying on the bottom than he'd ever seen in one place. The three men set to panning and soon had a shotgun cartridge bulging with gold. Carmack proceeded to write in pencil on the flattened side of a spruce tree: "TO WHOM IT MAY CONCERN: I do, this day, locate and claim, by right of discovery, five hundred feet, running up stream from this notice. Located this day of August, 1896. G. W. Carmack." Carmack's claim was for the discovery portion of the creek and another directly above it. He registered another claim in Jim's name above his highest claim and one below the lowest claim for Charlie. The men then rushed out to file their claim with the **North-West Mounted Police** (NWMP) at Fortymile Creek. On the way they told passing prospectors of their luck and provided directions to Rabbit Creek. Carmack, however, made no effort to send word to Henderson, an act that has been explained either as an oversight or as deliberate revenge on Henderson for slighting Carmack's First Nations relatives.

Upon reaching Forty Mile, Carmack reported his luck first to fellow miners in a saloon and then to the NWMP across the street. By dawn the following day Forty Mile was a ghost town, the miners scrambling to get to Rabbit Creek before all the best claims were snapped up. Even some of the members of the NWMP convinced their superiors to grant them leave to join the rush to stake claims.

On August 22, 1896, some 25 prospectors met on a hillside downstream from Carmack's group's claims and formally renamed the creek Bonanza Creek. Using a length of rope that was improperly measured they proceeded to mark off claims along the creekside. Eventually this length of rope would become the centre of a controversy over the legitimacy of some claims and government surveyor William Ogilvie would spend many weeks legitimizing and restaking claims to adhere to government regulations.

Meanwhile, Carmack, Jim, and Charlie had returned to their claims along with Kate and set to work. They diverted water down a three-metre-long sluice box with pole riffles in the bottom. Jim and Charlie lugged gravel on their backs to feed into the sluice box. Carmack worked the box, removing the tailings produced. The system was primitive and more gold was lost than recovered by this method. Still, the recovery rate was five ounces a day and after three weeks they had yielded $1,400 in gold.

As winter set in, about 300 men were working Bonanza Creek. By November 20, 1896, the number of claims filed stood at 338. The rush continued through the winter, men struggling up the frozen rivers to Bonanza by dogsled and on snowshoes. By January 6, 1897, the number of claims had reached 500.

Henderson, meanwhile, only heard of the strike a couple of weeks after the discovery had been made. Desperately trying to cash in on it somehow and knowing that soon no section of any of the Klondike's tributaries would be free of a claim, Henderson identified three different sites that seemed to have promise and headed out to file his claims. According to the regulations, Henderson could file either discoverer's claims or secondary claims. Of the claims he planned to file, two were discoverer's claims, which could be double the size of a secondary claim, and one was a secondary claim located alongside another prospector's profitable-looking claim on Hunker Creek. At Forty Mile, however, Henderson learned that the law had been changed and he was only allowed to file one claim. He decided to forego filing on either of the discovery claims and take the smaller, but more proven, claim at Hunker Creek.

Embittered by the whole experience, Henderson never really bothered to work this obviously profitable claim but rather sought to find a strike that would rival Carmack's in the surrounding hills. Eventually he became ill and was forced to sell the Hunker Creek claim for $3,000. Ultimately, this claim was reported to net $450,000 for the buyer, who then sold it for another $200,000. Henderson would spend the majority of his remaining years campaigning for recognition as a co-discoverer of the gold that started the Klondike rush. The Canadian government, responding in part to a formal affidavit filed by prominent Yukon residents, officially acknowledged his claim and granted him a yearly pension as recognition. But the decision was made primarily on patriotic grounds. Carmack was an American, Henderson from Pictou, Nova Scotia. Jim and Charlie, of course, were First Nations and denied the rights of Canadian citizenship. Eventually, Henderson would be recognized officially in many histories as a co-discoverer of Klondike gold.

Carmack, for his part, never claimed to be the first to find gold in the Klondike. He always credited Andrew Madden, who had discovered gold on the Klondike River in 1889. During that same year, several other prospectors also found traces of gold on the Klondike creeks, convincing many that there were large strikes to be found. The trouble was finding it. There were many creeks, and prospecting by panning was a haphazard and imperfect technique for systematically surveying a creek's potential. The Carmack strike was the first to prove that the region had bonanza-grade gold deposits and, like most strikes that sparked gold rushes in the 1800s, it was made entirely by chance. Carmack always acknowledged this fact.

In early 1897 few people were much concerned about who should be credited with the discovery. Outside of the Yukon and Alaska word of the strike had yet to leak out. But already the majority of the good claims had been staked and the town of Dawson established by Joseph Ladue. Fortunes were being made and squandered in the saloons and through bad business deals in mere days and weeks. The extreme isolation of the Yukon ensured that the gold rush would remain little known until the first **sternwheelers** could come up the river after the spring melt to carry out the news and about 80 of the newly wealthy prospectors. Each of these prospectors had a fortune ranging from $25,000 to $500,000 in gold stuffed in boxes, suitcases, jam jars, medicine bottles, old cans, blankets, and sacks made from **caribou** hides.

At St. Michael on the Alaska coast they transferred to two coastal steamers, the *Excelsior* and *Portland*, bound for San Francisco and Seattle respectively. The *Excelsior* reached dock first on July 14, 1897. When news spread of the wealth that was offloaded from that ship, newspapers around the world rushed to cover the docking of the *Portland* in Seattle. Thousands turned out to watch the unloading of what the *Seattle Post-Intelligencer* claimed was "a ton of gold" from its holds and decks.

The resulting gold fever that swept across North America was unlike the response to any of the previous rushes of the 19th century. In part this was because the world was in the grip of a major depression and there were no wars underway to distract attention. The morning after *Portland* docked, the *New York Herald* proclaimed that "Seattle has gone stark, staring mad on gold." Within days the rest of the continent followed suit.

In Seattle, thousands swarmed the dockyards trying to book passage to St. Michael. The price of such a journey skyrocketed overnight, becoming too expensive for all but the most well-off stampeders. Other routes to the Klondike had to be found that were less expensive. Across the continent, people from all walks of life quit their jobs, abandoned families or dragged them along in tow, and started a mad dash toward the Klondike. In Canada, many looked at maps and saw that Edmonton was the farthest north of the western railheads. So they headed there. Others caught trains to Vancouver, which doubled its population during the rush. Edmonton's population also doubled to 2,000 people. About 1,600 men and women left the town in a usually vain effort to cross more than 2,400 kilometres of wilderness to reach Dawson.

In all, about 100,000 people joined the international stampede to the Klondike, but only about 40,000 successfully traversed the **Trails of '98** that led into the region. Many of the rest would get no closer than Seattle, Vancouver, or Edmonton. Thousands of others would run out of cash or determination, or become ill on the northern coast of Alaska and British Columbia and turn around. Others would fail to complete the harsh trips over the trails and retreat or die along the way.

Through the winter of 1897–98 and the following year stampeders poured into Dawson and set out into the countryside to try their luck. Already there were few profitable claims left to be staked and only a few of these late arrivals were destined to become rich from mining. Some turned to mining the miners instead by setting up businesses in Dawson. The majority, however, ultimately returned south with nothing to show for joining the rush except participation in one of the last great mass adventures.

Despite the vast numbers of people pouring into the Yukon, the Klondike Gold Rush was the most peaceful in North American history. This was directly attributable to the efforts of the North-West Mounted Police, who allowed none of the gun-slinging violence common in gold rushes south of the Canada–United States border. Although the majority of gold stampeders were Americans, they largely abided by the Canadian laws. Ogilvie's efforts to ensure that the claims staked were properly marked, filed, and recorded also reduced greatly the potential for violence arising out of **claim-staking** feuds.

By the summer of 1898 it became clear that the hurly-burly days of the early gold rush were over. Few new claims were being staked that showed any promise. The Spanish-American War broke out and another gold strike on the beaches at Nome, Alaska prompted a mass exodus of the miners from Dawson and the Klondike. By then about $50 million had been taken out of the creeks at a price of only $20 an ounce.

Although the rush was over, the creeks would still continue to offer up gold—another $50 million over five years. But after 1899 the gold was mostly mined through more technologically sophisticated and expensive mining techniques that required few miners to operate. Professionals arrived who knew how to work the new mines and most of the amateur prospectors departed for other parts of the north or returned to southern Canada and the United States.

Today, gold is still mined on the Klondike River and its tributaries. Gold mining operations are also found in other parts of the territory. About 700 people are employed by the gold mines which realize about $65 million annually. This, of course, is $65 million at a time when gold sells for an average of $375 to $400 U.S. an ounce, 20 times the amount paid during the Klondike Gold Rush.

Kluane National Park Reserve

Eighty-two percent of Kluane National Park Reserve's 22,015 square kilometres is dominated by mountains and ice. Canada's highest and most massive mountains, the **St. Elias Mountains**, are divided within the park into two ranges— the Kluane Range and the soaring giants of the Icefield Ranges. Lying between them is the Duke Depression.

The eastern boundary of Kluane Park is skirted by the Alaska and Haines **highways**, which front the lower Kluane Range. Beyond the Kluane Range, the massifs of the Icefield Ranges are sometimes visible from the highway. The valleys and slopes followed by the highways contain northern Canada's greatest diversity of **vegetation** and wildlife. The forest is montane, composed primarily of white spruce, trembling aspen, and balsam poplar. The treeline ends at 1,050 to 1,200 metres, changing from low-growing and stunted shrubs such as willow, dwarf birch, alder, and other smaller plants to alpine **tundra**. The tundra zone is home to more than 200 varieties of alpine flora, including many species of wildflowers.

Wildlife found in Kluane National Park Reserve includes the park's most abundant large mammal—Dall sheep. Mountain goats, North America's largest subspecies of moose, a small **caribou** herd, black **bears**, and grizzly bears also live within the park's boundaries, as well as smaller **mammals**, such as wolverine, muskrat, mink, marmot, red fox, lynx, otter, coyote, beaver, snowshoe hare, and Arctic ground squirrel. There is a transient population of **wolves**. About 150 species of **birds** have been identified within the park and 118 species use the park for nesting. Bird species include falcons, bald and golden eagles, thrushes, yellow-rumped warblers, and mountain bluebirds.

The majority of this wildlife dwells in the valleys bordering the Kluane Range, a chain of mountains that averages 2,500 metres in height. Rising to the west of the Duke Depression, and inaccessible to motor vehicle traffic, are the giants of the Icefield Ranges. This range is home to Canada's highest peaks, 5,959-metre **Mount Logan**, 5,489-metre **Mount St. Elias**, 5,226-metre Mount Lucania, and many others of similar height.

Draped across and around these peaks are the world's largest nonpolar icefields, a legacy of the Wisconsinan Ice Age. They are sustained today by massive quantities of snow that accumulate here virtually year-round as moist Pacific air traverses the St. Elias Mountains and flows inland. Radiating from these icefields are immense valley glaciers, such as 65-kilometre-long Lowell Glacier, known as *Naludi* by **First Nations peoples**. The advance of this glacier between 1725 and 1850 blocked the Alsek River near Goatherd Mountain with a vast ice dam, transforming much of the river's length into a long lake. It is believed that, when the dam inevitably broke, the lake drained in a two-day flood with a flow rate comparable to the present-day Amazon River. Huge gravel ripples and wave-cut lake benches 10 kilometres north of **Haines Junction** provide evidence of the devastation this flood caused.

Because of its size, rugged terrain, and proximity to the Pacific Ocean, Kluane National Park Reserve experiences sudden and dramatic climatic changes. Most of the park falls within the dry, cold continental **climate** typical of the Yukon. The southeastern portion, however, is subject to more coastal influences, including greater rates of precipitation. Temperatures range between 33° Celsius and –50° Celsius. The average June temperature is 11° Celsius, while the January average is –21° Celsius. In the Kluane and Icefield Ranges winter temperatures are usually colder and the weather more unpredictable. Throughout the park, frost can occur any time of year. Most lakes have ice coverings by the end of October. The Icefield Ranges can experience heavy snowfall throughout the year.

Access to Kluane National Park Reserve is via roads leading out of Haines Junction to the park boundary. There is a day-use and camping area on the Haines Highway at Kathleen Lake. Most of the park, however, is accessible only to hikers. There is also limited accessibility to some areas by mountain bike, horseback, boats, and whitewater rafts. One of the most popular activities in Kluane is commercial rafting trips down the Alsek River to the Tatshenshini River. Because of the park's many massifs, mountaineers from around the world are attracted to the park.

Kluane National Park Reserve forms a major part of a conglomerate of linked parks that together constitute the world's largest international protected area— a total of approximately 8.5 million hectares. The other parks in this area are Alaska's Wrangell–St. Elias and Glacier Bay national parks and British Columbia's Tatshenshini-Alsek Provincial Park.

Kluane (pronounced *kloo-wah-nee*) is a Lu'An Mün Southern Tutchone word for "lake with many fish" and refers to the Yukon's largest lake, Kluane Lake, which covers about 399 square kilometres.

Labour Force

Of the Yukon's total **population** of 33,580, about 15,200 are counted among the labour force by the territorial **government**. About 13,200 of these are employed at any given time and the remaining 13 percent are unemployed—giving the Yukon a relatively high unemployment rate in comparison to most other parts of Canada. In the latter part of the 1990s, the unemployment rate has risen and fallen in relation to economic changes. Generally, however, it has remained about three percentage points above the national rate of unemployment.

A high percentage of Yukoners are employed by the federal, territorial, or municipal governments—about 4,600. The majority—3,200—work for the territorial government. Most of the rest are federal employees, with only about 325 employed by municipalities.

Private-sector employment accounts for the rest of the Yukon's work force. Although the **mining industry** is the Yukon's largest single economic force, there are seldom more than 1,000 people working directly in mining and exploration. **Tourism** is actually the second-largest sector of employment, providing about 3,400 jobs. The nontourism-related service and construction sectors account for approximately another 2,500 workers.

The territory's work force is almost evenly divided by gender, with only about 500 more men in the labour force than women. This is perhaps not surprising as males in the Yukon outnumber women by only about 1,000.

Wages in the Yukon are relatively high compared to the rest of Canada. Average annual income is about $36,375. In weekly terms, the average is about $695 compared to a national weekly average of $585. Goods-producing salaries are much higher in the Yukon, averaging slightly more than $940, while trade sector wages hover in the area of $500 a week. Government sector employees average salaries of $800 a week.

Although wages are higher in the Yukon than in most other parts of Canada, prices in the territory more than offset this advantage. Prices in **Whitehorse**, for example, run about 10 percent higher than prices in Vancouver, British Columbia and about 23.5 percent higher than Edmonton. The rest of the territory has consistently higher prices than Whitehorse.

Lake Laberge

More than 50 kilometres long and averaging a width of 1.5 to 2.5 kilometres, Lake Laberge is situated about 40 kilometres north of **Whitehorse**, adjacent to the Klondike Highway. It was named after Michael Laberge, an explorer for the Western Union Telegraph Company, who hailed from Chateaugay, Quebec. It is unclear if Laberge actually reached the lake itself during his 1867 exploration up the **Yukon River** for a possible telegraph link to Alaska, or just had it described to him by **First Nations peoples**. Upon returning to Fort Yukon, he and companion Frank E. Ketchum learned the telegraph project was cancelled and Laberge never ventured again up the Yukon River. The lake was named after him by Western Union Telegraph Expedition Scientific Corps director William H. Dall in his report of 1870.

During the **Klondike Gold Rush**, many stampeders travelled the length of the narrow lake aboard hastily constructed log rafts. If the waters remained calm the trip was an easy drift. But Lake Laberge lies within a narrow, steeply walled valley running almost exactly north to south that serves as a perfect wind tunnel. Calm waters can change in a moment to waves running to heights exceeding two metres. A good number of stampeder rafts were swamped during such storms and some of the hopeful prospectors perished.

Lake Laberge is well known to many thousands who have never seen it and haven't even the vaguest idea where in the Yukon it is located because it serves, with more poetic spelling, as a setting in one of Robert Service's most famous poems, "The Cremation of Sam McGee." In the poem, Sam McGee, who longed for the warmth of his Tennessee homeland but froze to death in the Klondike, is cremated in the boiler of a sternwheeler wrecked on the "marge of Lake Lebarge."

Languages

Most Yukoners declare English as their first language. In the 1996 Census of Canada, of the total 30,215 single respondents to the language question, 26,405 or 86.8 percent cited English as their mother tongue. Despite the number of Yukoners speaking English as a first language, the percentage has dropped from the 1991 census, which recorded 88.8 percent.

A total of 1,172, or 3.8 percent of the **population**, reported Canada's other official language of French as their mother tongue, up 0.5 percent from 1991.

Although 6,190 Yukoners are of First Nations descent, only 770 reported a First Nations language as their mother tongue, reflecting the unfortunate "success" of residential schools in eliminating **First Nations languages**. Of those 770 people, 630 spoke an Athapaskan language.

The third-most-spoken language in the Yukon is, according to the census figures, German with 890 or 2.1 percent claiming it as a first language. Other languages trail far behind, reflecting the homogeneity of the territory's population. All Asian languages, for example, were spoken by only 560 people.

Even those Yukoners for whom English is not the first language generally use it as their language of choice at home. Fully 95.4 percent, or 29,238 respondents, most often spoke English at home. French was the home language of choice for 542 people, or 1.8 percent of the population.

With regard to Canada's official languages, those Yukoners speaking only English numbered 89.2 percent of respondents. Those who were bilingual in French and English numbered 10.5 percent. Only 0.2 percent of the population spoke French only, while just another 0.2 percent knew neither English nor French.

Bilingualism is, however, on the increase in the Yukon. In 1996, 3,210 Yukoners were bilingual compared to only 2,570 in 1991. Still, the Yukon's rate of 10.5 percent trails the Canadian bilingual average in 1996 of 17 percent.

Legal System. *See* **Justice.**

Lost Patrol

On December 21, 1910, four members of what was then the Royal North-West Mounted Police (RNWMP) set out with three dog teams from the Hudson's Bay trading post at Fort McPherson, Northwest Territories on the seventh patrol between the post and **Dawson**. Their trip was intended to take them over a route of 765 kilometres in the middle of a harsh winter. The temperature as they left the fort was, at −29° Celsius, considered relatively balmy. Leading the patrol was veteran inspector Francis J. "Frank" Fitzgerald, who was 41. He was accompanied by 41-year-old former-RNWMP constable Sam Carter, who was to serve as the guide, and constables George Francis Kinney, 27, and Richard O'Hara Taylor, 26. They had 15 dogs in the traces, five pulling each of the three sleds. This was the first patrol to start at Fort McPherson. As always, the purpose of the patrol was to carry dispatches and mail between the Arctic posts of Fort McPherson and Herschel Island and Dawson, where a telegraph and regular postal service provided the nearest links from the north to the rest of Canada. A minor additional purpose was to check on the condition of **First Nations peoples** and, more importantly, prospectors who might be wandering the wilderness of northern Yukon.

The route Fitzgerald planned to follow differed in its southern portion from the one he had taken when, as staff sergeant, he had been a member of the second patrol of the winter of 1905–6. This patrol had left Dawson and run southeast to **Mayo**, then almost straight north through the Wernecke Mountains and down the Wind River. Where the Wind River met the Little Wind, it picked up the route pioneered by the first patrol of 1904–5 to turn north to Fort McPherson along the Peel River. The trip was slowed by heavy snow and bitter cold, taking 56 days—the longest of any patrol the RNWMP undertook.

All other patrols had taken another route, which ran northeast from Dawson to cross the Blackstone River, veered due east to the Hart River and then across the Hart River divide to intersect the Wind River, and continued to Fort McPherson. Fitzgerald had never, of course, travelled this route but Carter had in 1906–7 and was confident he could retrace the route. For this reason, perhaps, Fitzgerald made the decision to undertake the journey without the services of a First Nations guide, which was normal practice. Past patrols had benefited significantly from the ability of their guides to hunt and trap food along the trail to supplement the supplies they carried.

The total weight of provisions was about 590 kilograms, split evenly among the sleds. This included 40 kilograms of food per man, enough for the estimated 30 days that Fitzgerald had allotted for the trip. The diet, however, was largely composed of meat—other foods being hard to come by at isolated Fort McPherson. Patrols departing Dawson usually had a better variety of food to help sustain the men's strength and endurance. The total weight of gear per sled was 272 kilograms. For some unexplained reason the party also carried only one rifle—a .30-30 calibre—despite the fact that usual practice was to carry at least an additional .22-calibre rifle or a shotgun.

Fitzgerald's patrol faced another difficulty no earlier patrol had experienced—it had to start breaking trail from the moment of departure. Patrols leaving Dawson were supported initially by a horse and sled which were used for the first 23 kilometres to break trail and carry much of the supplies while the men and dogs found their "trail legs." They also faced heavy snow conditions and extreme cold. Still, the journey appeared to be proceeding satisfactorily when they completed the first 240 kilometres in 12 days. Although if they continued to manage only their current rate of 20 kilometres a day, the trip would take 9 days longer than the 30 planned, Fitzgerald is believed to have been confident that the worst mushing was over and their pace would improve.

Unfortunately, the patrol was beset by a bone-chilling cold snap that saw average daily temperatures plunge to −46° Celsius and that persisted for seven days. They also encountered increasingly deep snow, stretches of open water, and piles of driftwood on the river ice that made passage extremely difficult. They mushed on, managing only 112 kilometres, or 16 kilometres a day.

When the patrol reached the junction of the Little Wind and Wind rivers the weather improved and Fitzgerald remained confident they could complete the trip with their remaining supplies. They now needed to link up with a creek named Forrest and follow it through the Hart Divide to Waugh Creek on the other side. Carter, however, failed to recognize which of a number of creeks off the Wind River was Forrest Creek and the party became lost. For the next nine days the patrol wandered for 158 kilometres back and forth on the Little Wind River seeking the right creek with no success.

With only 4.5 kilograms of flour, 3.6 kilograms of bacon, and some dried fish remaining, Fitzgerald realized on January 17 that their only hope of survival lay in returning to Fort McPherson. Even then, he confided in his diary, they would have to kill and eat some of the dogs and maybe fail if they could not find some First Nations people to give them food. Again plagued by terrible cold and dreadful trail conditions, the patrol struggled northward. By January 20 they had exhausted their flour and bacon supply. They began killing dogs to supplement the sparse supply of dried fish and tea that remained. Frostbite, starvation, and scurvy began taking their toll, weakening the men terribly. By February 5 they had only five dogs remaining and were still 112 kilometres from Fort McPherson. On that day Fitzgerald made his last diary entry, which concluded that they could "only go a few miles a day."

A rescue team led by corporal W. J. D. Dempster left Dawson on February 28. On March 21 the team discovered the bodies of Kinney and Taylor in a small camp about 56 kilometres from Fort McPherson. Kinney appeared to have succumbed to hypothermia. Taylor had committed suicide with the .30- 30. Sixteen kilometres farther along, Dempster's party found the bodies of Carter and Fitzgerald. Carter's body was neatly arranged with his hands crossed over his breast and a handkerchief covering his face. Fitzgerald lay next to the remains of a small fire. Nearby a piece of paper was found on which Fitzgerald had scrawled a will with a bit of charred wood. Three sentences long, the will ended, "God bless all. F. J. Fitzgerald, RNWMP."

The disastrous seventh patrol was not the last undertaken by the RNWMP. These continued until 1921 when the demise of the whaling industry at Herschel Island and the establishment of radio communication ended their need. One final patrol was, however, undertaken in 1945 from Dawson to Herschel Island and there was a commemorative patrol in 1970.

Measures were taken after the patrol's loss to ensure that a similar disaster did not occur. Food caches were established along the trail and trees were slashed to serve as trail markers. Why the trail had never previously been marked by the Mounties was never determined. Undoubtedly, had the Wind River–Forrest Creek junction been marked, the party would not have become lost.

In his official report on the tragedy, Dempster blamed the patrol's demise on the small stock of supplies Fitzgerald took, the lack of a First Nations guide, and the loss of time spent trying to find the trail rather than immediately retreating to Fort McPherson.

Mackenzie Mountains

The Mackenzie Mountains straddle the boundary of the Northwest Territory and the Yukon for 800 kilometres. This range is a northern continuation of the Rocky Mountains, which terminate in British Columbia about 45 kilometres south of the province's border with the Yukon.

Composed almost entirely of sedimentary rock, the main core of the Mackenzie Mountains is known as the Backbone Ranges. These ranges encompass a series of rough peaks and ridges that reach a maximum height of 2,759 metres at the summit of Mount Sir James MacBrien (the highest peak in the Northwest Territory).

The Mackenzie Mountains stand in the rainshadow cast by the more westerly **Selwyn Mountains**, so experience a relatively dry **climate**. The timberline is low, leaving many slopes bare and rocky. Black spruce is the most common tree, with lodgepole pine occurring in the more exposed, sunny areas. Several woodland **caribou** herds range onto the western slopes of the mountains, moose are numerous in the valleys, and both black and grizzly **bears** are present, as are **wolves**, most small **mammals** found in the Yukon, and a great diversity of **birds**.

The Mackenzie Mountains are named after Alexander Mackenzie, the second prime minister of Canada, who served for one term from November 7, 1873 to October 8, 1878.

Mammals

There are 46 land-dwelling mammal species in the Yukon and 15 species of marine mammals. Mammals are generally regarded as the most evolved or advanced of the vertebrate species (animals having a backbone). They share a number of characteristics, including being warm-blooded and possessing mammary glands that produce milk for nourishing their young. Mammal species in the Yukon are less numerous than in most other parts of Canada, but for some mammal species the territory is one of the last refuges where they are not endangered or threatened due to habitat loss. Grizzly **bears**, for example, are generally considered endangered or extirpated from most other regions of Canada but are considered to have a stable, although at risk, population in the Yukon of about 6,000 to 7,000. **Wood bison** are also present in the territory, but are considered endangered.

The majority of mammals in the Yukon, as elsewhere, are small species—shrews, voles, mice, and other rodents. One species of bat—the little brown bat—occurs in the territory. Larger mammals include all three species of Canadian bears, about 4,500 **wolves**, 55,000 moose, over 200,000 **caribou**, 2,000 mountain goats, 19,000 Dall sheep, and 3,000 stone sheep. Some species that are extremely numerous in southern Canada are relatively rare in the Yukon. There are, for example, only about 80 muskox, 500 mule deer and 100 elk. These three species are all protected under the Yukon Wildlife Act. The Arctic fox population of the Yukon is estimated at only 50 animals, concentrated mainly on the **Beaufort Sea** coastline and **Herschel Island Territorial Park**. Cougar occur occasionally in the southern portion of the territory. One recent newcomer to the Yukon is the coyote, which appeared in the late 1800s and is now widely distributed throughout the territory.

In the Beaufort Sea, **bowhead whales** are stabilizing their numbers after being nearly hunted into extinction in the early 1900s. There are approximately 21,500 beluga whales in the Beaufort Sea and some harvesting of this population by Inuvialuit peoples is permitted. Narwhals were once common in the Beaufort Sea but are seldom seen in these waters today. Several species of seals occur as well along the Beaufort coastline, including ringed seals. The ringed seal is the most common coastal mammal in the Yukon.

(*See also* **Endangered Species**.)

Mayo

Situated in the central Yukon, Mayo lies in the traditional heartland of the Nacho Ny'a'k Dun peoples' territory. The town is home to about 450 people. Mayo is situated at the 53-kilometre point of the Silver Trail highway, which extends through what was once one of the richest silver mining regions in Canada. The first mining undertaken here, however, was for **gold**, discovered at the mouth of the Mayo River in 1902. Silver was discovered at **Keno** in 1919 and then at Elsa in 1929.

Many years earlier, the first prospector to enter the region was New Brunswick native Alexander McDonald. In 1887, he came across a large lake and named it Mayo after his friend, Captain Alfred S. Mayo. The captain owned a small steamboat christened *New Racket,* probably reflecting his career change from circus acrobat to steamboat owner. Mayo would later become a founding member of the Yukon Order of Pioneers.

Although Mayo is today connected to the rest of the territory by a paved road that was first constructed in the 1950s, the only previous link to the rich silver mining operations was provided by steamboat. The ships arrived on the Stewart River laden with supplies and left more heavily laden with sacks of ore. About eight kilometres beyond Mayo the pavement ends and the rest of the road to Keno and Elsa is gravel.

Mayo is a popular recreation area that offers good swimming and boating in nearby lakes and hiking in the surrounding wilderness. It is the main service area for all travellers venturing up the Silver Trail. The Village of Mayo operates the Binet House Interpretive Centre, which houses a collection of historic photos, an extensive geology display that includes sections on **permafrost**, bedrock geology, rock deformation, glacial history, and hard rock and **placer mining**.

McArthur Wildlife Sanctuary

This 1,700-square-kilometre preserve was first designated in 1948 to ensure a hunting sanctuary for fannin sheep and other wildlife. Today, it is closed to all hunting. Situated at the southern base of the **Tintina Trench** and southeast of **Stewart Crossing**, the sanctuary is inaccessible by road or plane. Visitors usually enter the area in the company of a guide.

The sanctuary has been a major focal point of the **First Nations land claims** negotiations with the Nacho Ny'a'k Dun peoples. Under the final agreement between the Nacho Ny'a'k Dun, the federal government, and the territorial government, McArthur Wildlife Sanctuary will become a special management area with territorial and First Nations administrations working together to ensure its preservation and the protection of its wildlife species.

Medical Facilities

There are two 24-hour hospitals in the Yukon, one at **Whitehorse** and the other at **Watson Lake**. Twenty-four-hour medical service is also available at the clinic in **Dawson**. Most other communities have a nurse or doctor on call 24 hours a day, connected to the territory's eight health treatment centres, three public health centres, and four nursing stations.

The Yukon is home to about 110 licensed physicians and some 18 licensed dentists.

As of 1998, except for some health care services provided to First Nations people by the federal Department of Indian Affairs, all health care facilities and services in the territory were funded and operated by the territorial **government**. Total spending on health and social services in the Yukon is about $108 million annually.

Metric System

The Yukon uses the metric system of measurement, as does all of Canada.

The decision to replace the historic British imperial system of units (based on yards, pounds, and gallons) with a metric system was made by the Canadian government in 1971. The metric system chosen is known as the Système international d'unites (SI). Conversion to metric was prompted by rapidly advancing technology and expanding worldwide trade, both of which made it clear that a country as dependent upon import and export trade as Canada needed an international measurement system.

Converting to the metric system in Canada was a gradual process allowing for the re-education of a public used to the British imperial system. The first extension of metric unit measure into the realm of everyday Canadian life had the unfortunate timing of being introduced on April Fool's Day (April 1), 1975, when all temperature announcements were given only in degrees Celsius during weather forecasts. In September 1977, road signs showed distances in kilometres and speed limits in kilometres per hour. The national process of converting to metric was not completed until December 1983.

The adoption of the metric system has been controversial from the outset, both because of the mandatory nature of the government regulations and the fact that it was seen by many Canadians as an attack on the British-Canadian heritage. In the mid- to late 1980s some regulations were relaxed so that the two measures could be posted side by side and small businesses could continue to operate to a limited degree using the imperial system. But the metric system is clearly here to stay.

The following chart shows common conversions.

To change	To	Multiply by
centimetres	inches	.39
metres	feet	3.28
kilometres	miles	.62
square metres	square yards	1.20
square kilometres	square miles	.39
hectares	acres	2.47
kilograms	pounds	2.21
kilometres	nautical miles	.54
inches	centimetres	2.54
feet	metres	.30
miles	kilometres	1.61
square yards	square metres	.84
square miles	square kilometres	2.59
acres	hectares	.41
pounds	kilograms	.45
nautical miles	kilometres	1.85

Miles Canyon

Although much tamed today by the Whitehorse Dam's calming of the **Yukon River** running through it, Miles Canyon and the two sets of rapids immediately beyond constituted one of the most dangerous obstacles faced by stampeders rushing toward the **Klondike Gold Rush** in the late 1890s. As the river descends into the canyon it narrows to one-third of its width and, before the dam's construction in 1957, the water was shoved upward into a foamy crest as much as a metre high that was riddled with small erupting geysers. Log jams, jagged boulders, and sandbars all added to the dangers of making a passage through the canyon in a raft or small boat. Near the canyon centre was a whirlpool, and then for the last nine metres the walls narrowed in so much that the river literally squirted out to enter Squaw Rapids and the Whitehorse Rapids beyond. Squaw Rapids was notorious for rushing across a series of jutting rocks, while Whitehorse Rapids was so named because the surface foam resembled white steeds leaping and dancing in the sunlight.

Initially many of the stampeders plunged into the canyon with little or no reconnaissance of its hazards. Some 150 boats were either capsized, sunk, or smashed to pieces and a dozen miners drowned in the first weeks of 1897. Eventually order was brought to the entire process of circumnavigating the canyon by the **North-West Mounted Police**, which enforced safety standards on the boats passing through and forbade women and children from making the trip. These measures were rendered unnecessary when two tram lines went into operation at **Canyon City** in 1898, to pull the miners' vessels and supplies safely through for a fee.

Not all women abided by the police prohibition on their passage through the canyon by boat. Among these was Emma Kelly, a reporter for the Kansas City *Star*, who risked a possible $100 fine for running the rapids in defiance of the police edict. Kelly was so thrilled by her first trip through the canyon in a small boat that she hiked back up to the beginning and rode another boat through.

Although the basalt walls of Miles Canyon rise only about 30 metres, it was

Klondike river raft shoots the rapids at Miles Canyon. (Adams and Larkin photo, NAC C15022)

initially known by miners coming into the area as Grand Canyon. The name was changed in 1883 by U.S. army lieutenant F. Schwatka to honour his superior, Brigadier General Nelson A. Miles, Commander of the Department of the Columbia, which included the jurisdiction of Alaska. Schwatka called the canyon "a diminutive Fingal's Cave . . . resembling a deep black thoroughfare paved with the whitest of marble."

The canyon and its following rapids presented the only obstacle that barred navigation of the river by **sternwheelers** and other steamships from the Yukon's mouth to Bennett Lake in British Columbia. Miles Canyon thus played a fundamental role in the birth of **Whitehorse** because its presence necessitated the establishment of a major transportation staging centre below the canyon. If it were not for the canyon, **Carcross**, farther upriver than Whitehorse, would have been the logical terminus for the **White Pass & Yukon Railway** and its link with the sternwheeler fleet. Instead, Whitehorse filled this role and eventually blossomed into the major **population**, commercial, and administrative centre of the Yukon.

(*See also* **Five Finger Rapids**.)

Mining Industry

The Yukon mining industry contributes about $400 million annually to the territory's gross domestic product. Although in most years there are fewer than five operating hardrock mines in the Yukon, there are always about 50 other sites where mineral deposits are being examined or are known to occur in quantities that may warrant development when market conditions are right.

Gold **placer mining** and other **gold** mining operations continue to play an important role, reaching back to the mining industry's roots in the prospecting that led ultimately to the **Klondike Gold Rush** of the late 1890s. Gold mining in the territory is valued at about $65 million annually and employs about 700 Yukoners.

When the Anvil Range mine at **Faro** is in operation, zinc is usually the dominant mineral being extracted in the territory. In 1996, for example, when the Anvil Range mine was open for most of the year, zinc production totalled $202 million. The previous year, however, when the mine was closed, production of zinc was a little less than $60 million. Lead and silver, the other two minerals that most contribute to the territory's **economy**, tend to be hit with the same downturns and upswings that influence the operation of the Faro mine.

Despite the uncertainty that is endemic in mining operations throughout the world, the Yukon economy continues by necessity to depend on this industry for its economic fortune. There is little indication that economic development in other sectors will result in a significant decline in mining's importance any time soon.

Mosquitoes

There are at least 74 species of mosquitoes in Canada. About 25 of these are found in the Yukon. Worldwide, there are more than 3,000 mosquito species with most occurring in the tropics.

Dominant species in the Yukon are all from the genus *Aedes*. These include *A. punctor* and *A. communis,* which concentrate in the boreal forest regions, *A. hexodontus* in the sub-Arctic, and *A. impiger* and *A. nigripes* in the Arctic. *A. punctor* prefers acidic water lying over peat, while *A. communis* is more often found near pools underlain by alluvial clay and in stream valleys. *A. hexodontus* occurs mostly along the sub-Arctic treeline, while the two common Arctic species, *A. impiger* and *A. nigripes,* are more likely to be feeding during warm days. *A. nigripes* occurs only in the **tundra** regions.

Some mosquito species have ancient origins. *Aedes pullatus*, for example, is believed to have found refuge in **Beringia** during the last glacial period, which ended about 10,000 years ago, and to have spread outward from there throughout most of western Canada.

The first appearance of mosquitoes in the spring varies throughout the Yukon and is dependent on temperature and the speed of the snow melt. Usually mosquitoes appear first in the Yukon valleys and the extreme southern boundary of the territory—sometime between June 1 and June 10. The southern mountain regions begin to see mosquitoes about 10 days later. The **Eagle Plain** and other regions around the **Arctic Circle** undergo mosquito outbreaks most years between June 20 and June 30, while the shores bordering the **Beaufort Sea** are host to active mosquitoes in the first days of July.

Male mosquitoes feed only on nectar, while most female mosquitoes require blood to add to carbohydrate foods for egg development. The blood is ingested directly into the midgut. Here, it is enclosed in a transparent sheath of thin cuticle called the peritrophic membrane. The swelling of the gut caused by the blood helps initiate the production of hormones necessary to stimulate egg development, which occurs when the blood is digested and assimilated. Egg development can take between 24 hours and 15 days depending on average temperatures—the higher the temperature, the faster the development process. When one batch of eggs is laid, the female may again seek blood to repeat the process. The average life span of an adult mosquito is about three weeks. However, some Yukon species can survive freeze-up by overwintering as larvae within the ice for up to nine months, emerging as mature mosquitoes in the late spring or early summer.

Mosquitoes will feed upon just about any blood-carrying animal. **Birds**, **mammals**, and **amphibians** are all subject to attack. There does seem to be a slight preference among most mosquito species for mammal blood. That makes humans favoured prey and is the primary cause for the struggle between humans and mosquitoes.

In the Yukon, mosquitoes seldom carry or transmit diseases that are harmful to humans. There are, for example, no malarial-infected mosquitoes in Canada. The danger mosquitoes pose in the Yukon results more from blood loss and extreme irritation resulting from swarming. Humans, **caribou**, **bears**— almost every mammalian species in the Yukon—can be driven to hysteria by thick clouds of female mosquitoes swarming them in search of blood.

Female mosquitoes have been known to fly as much as 300 to 500 kilometres in search of a good blood meal. The female is attracted to other animals by their discharge of carbon dioxide. As the mosquito gets closer to its prey, it senses heat if the victim is warm-blooded before it is able to see its target. After landing, the mosquito will probe the skin a few times, searching for a capillary. It drives the tips of its needle-sharp mandible into the tissue. Engorgement takes only a few seconds as many mosquitoes absorb an amount of blood equalling their own weight. In some species the weight of blood taken may be triple their body weight.

The mosquito season in the Yukon is mercifully quite short, which helps to offset its intensity. Often by late August most regions of the territory are experiencing a rapid decline in mosquito numbers and by September the Yukon is relatively mosquito free.

In addition to utilizing commercial mosquito repellents, some Yukoners claim that effective deterrents include liberal covering of the skin with a mixture of black spruce pitch and bear fat.

Mount Logan

At 5,959 metres above sea level, Mount Logan is the highest point in the Yukon and Canada. It is the second-highest mountain in North America, after Mount McKinley (6,194 metres) in Alaska. Lying within **Kluane National Park Reserve** in the Yukon's southwestern corner, Mount Logan is part of the **St. Elias Mountains**.

The mountain is the world's single most massive mountain block, composed of granite and featuring multiple summits which rise above a snow and ice plateau found at altitudes ranging from 4,500 to 5,400 metres. This plateau sprawls over 19 kilometres. Three of the summits are higher than 5,890 metres.

Until 1992, Mount Logan's height had been estimated at 6,050 metres. In 1992, however, as part of the 150th anniversary celebrations of the Geological Survey of Canada, the nation's 125th birthday, and the 50th anniversary of construction of the **Alaska Highway**, a team of mountaineers and scientists ascended the mountain. They then measured the mountain's height using highly accurate Global Positioning System satellite technology. On July 1, 1992, Mount Logan was officially declared to be 5,959 metres high.

Eternally wreathed in cloud, snow and ice, Mount Logan is the world's most massive mountain block. (Marten Berkman photo)

The mountain was named after Sir William Edmond Logan by Professor I. C. Russell, who saw the edifice in 1890 while attempting to climb nearby **Mount St. Elias**. A geologist, Logan was the first director of the Geological Survey of Canada, Canada's first public scientific endeavour, serving from 1841 to his retirement in 1869.

The mountain was first successfully climbed by a joint Canadian-American team in 1925. Led by American Alpine Club of Canada member Albert H. MacCarthy, the expedition took 65 days to complete the ascent, including a punishing two-way trek through Alaska and the Yukon. Two climbers, MacCarthy and his partner W. W. Foster, then Alpine Club of Canada president, reached the summit on June 23, 1925.

Since then, the mountain has been climbed by 13 different routes. Because of its remote location, it is still considered one of the most difficult and forbidding climbs in North America. Many expeditions have failed due to supply logistics problems or to the onset of fierce storms that can strike even in the middle of summer and leave the region deep in heavy snows.

From 1970 to 1980, Mount Logan was the site of a high-altitude physiology research program conducted by a joint Canadian–U.S. medical team operating from a camp established at the 5,503-metre level. This project was funded by the Arctic Institute of North America and the Canadian Armed Forces.

Mount St. Elias

At 5,489 metres, Mount St. Elias is Canada's second-highest mountain. It straddles the border between Alaska and the Yukon, 43 kilometres south of **Mount Logan** in the heart of the **St. Elias Mountains**, in the territory's southwest corner.

Mount St. Elias is reported to have been the first feature in the Yukon ever named by Europeans. It was so named by Vitus Jonassen Bering, a Dane who served in the Russian navy. In 1728, Bering had sailed through the Bering Strait, proving that Asia and North America were not joined by a land bridge. On a subsequent expedition in 1741, Bering sailed his ship *St. Peter* from Siberia eastward into the Gulf of Alaska, becoming the first European navigator to sight both Alaska and Mount St. Elias. It is believed the mountain sighting took place on July 16, 1741, which was St. Elias Day.

St. Elias was a prophet in 800 B.C. who, according to Russian and

A solitary mountaineer treks across the glacial expanses near Mount St. Elias. (Marten Berkman photo)

Greek Orthodox faith, subjected the Israelite King Ahab and his wife Jezebel's kingdom to a three-and-a-half-year drought for building a temple to the pagan idol Baal. He later parted the Jordan River after taking counsel from God on Mount Sinai. Both these acts have led to his often being compared to Moses. He later prophesied that Ahab's blood would be licked up by dogs and Jezebel eaten by dogs. According to the Bible, both fates consequently befell the royal couple. The Bible further testifies that St. Elias never died, but ascended to Heaven in a fiery chariot.

On St. Elias Day, Bering sent a party ashore and they succeeded in slaughtering several sea otters. The discovery of the sea otters and their rich pelts ultimately led Russia to establish fur-trading stations on the Alaskan coastline, beginning the first European settlement in the northern Pacific region. The first of these stations opened in 1784 at Three Saints Bay, near present-day Kodiak.

Bering never returned from this expedition. Not far from Kamchatka, from which the expedition had set out in June 1741, the *St. Peter* was caught in a storm and wrecked on the shores of the island Bering had named after himself. Bering and many of the survivors contracted scurvy. The expedition's captain succumbed to the illness on December 19, 1741. A few survivors managed to reach Siberia, bringing with them the news of the sea otters they had killed on the shores of Alaska and of the massive mountain they had seen far inland.

In May 1778, Captain James Cook spotted the mountain as he sailed along the western coast of North America. The intrepid explorer and cartographer, working from the deck of his ship, calculated the mountain's height at 5,517 metres—an error of just 28 metres.

The first mountaineering expedition to tackle Mount St. Elias was undertaken by U.S. Army lieutenant F. Schwatka in 1886. The badly planned attempt was forced to quit after only a few days. The peak was finally climbed in 1897 by Prince Luigi Amadeo of Savoy, the nephew of Italian King Humbert I. Known as the Duke of Abruzzi, the prince was a famous mountain climber. He made the ascent with the help of many climbing partners and a small brigade of native packers required to carry all the equipment and supplies necessary for the expedition.

Museums. *See* **Burwash Landing; Dawson; Keno; Mayo; Northern Lights Centre; Teslin; Watson Lake; Whitehorse; Yukon Archives; Yukon Beringia Interpretive Centre.**

Muskeg

The term muskeg applies generally to areas of natural and undisturbed peat mosses, tussocky sedges, and sparse scrubby trees. It is an Algonquin First Nations word meaning grassy bog. Muskeg is usually viewed in northern Canada as an area of deep mud that promotes fly infestations, often sucks up industrial equipment, and in many other ways impedes human progress. One industrial analyst described muskeg as "smeared across Canada like leprosy. The machine hasn't been invented that can get through it consistently. It slurps up roads and railways, gobbles buildings and airfields, swallows the least trace of humanity. In summer, it's a rotting mushland of blackflies and **mosquitoes**, and the odor akin to backed-up septic tanks. In winter it's an eerie half-world, a frozen lifeless wasteland defying civilization."

Before the end of the Wisconsinan Ice Age there was no muskeg in Canada, except within a few areas that were not glaciated. This included the region of the

Yukon known as **Beringia**. As the ice melted, however, the muskeg range expanded to 1.295 million square kilometres—the largest expanse of muskeg found in any nation. This area includes more than half of the Yukon—and small pockets of muskeg are present in the other portions of the territory. The primary muskeg range is generally linked to black spruce boreal forest areas.

Curiously, muskeg does not occur in areas that are very dry or very wet. Nor is it related to any specific type of surface mineral or soil. Instead, muskeg is created by a complex process that scientists are still trying to understand. A variety of factors must interlink in such a way that peat moss accumulates faster than it decomposes. Precipitation plays an important role in promoting peat moss accumulation, in combination with temperature variations, sufficient water inflow from streams, and the creation of nutrients by wildfires, biological, and geological processes. Muskeg development is slowed by the rate of evaporation due to hot weather and winds, the runoff of water, and the natural process of peat decomposition. Depending on how these and other factors combine, muskeg can occur on relatively dry slopes in one place but be entirely absent in a marshy valley floor elsewhere.

The majority of Yukon muskegs are found in rock basins. Muskeg is closely associated with **permafrost**, especially in the Yukon, where it is unlikely to occur without permafrost also being present.

Despite its commonness, Yukon muskeg is not as extensively developed or as profusely distributed as in most other parts of northern Canada. This is believed to be due to the **glaciation** period having been too dry and cold in the territory to allow for optimal peat development. Most of the region of the Yukon that has extensive muskeg fields was unglaciated, so the muskeg here is also very ancient.

Where oil and gas are found in the north, muskeg is almost certain to be the surface overlying it. This is one reason that oil, gas, and mine developers tend to love and hate muskeg simultaneously. Fortunes have been and will continue to be made in its muck, rendering it, as one wag said, "both prize and plague, a crazy mixed-up quagmire with a split personality—not all bad. The sooner we realize it the sooner we'll reap its riches."

In recent years, concern for the effects that construction of roads, railways, and pipelines on this highly sensitive environmental habitat for **birds** and many other animal species has become an issue. The impact of even seasonally accessed roads on muskeg regions is permanent and significant. Mineral mining and oil and gas development also can have serious environmental impacts, as does peat moss and other sphagnum moss extraction for commercial use in **agriculture** and landscaping.

Northern Lights

The scientific term for northern lights is aurora borealis. They appear as a stunning and haunting display of multicoloured luminescence in the day or night sky in high latitudes of the northern hemisphere. Auroras are commonly visible throughout the Yukon, but can on rare occasions be seen as far south as Miami, Florida.

Northern lights are arrayed along a band known as the aurora oval centred on the northern geomagnetic pole. This band is usually about 500 to 1,000 kilometres wide, giving it a southern extent of approximately the sky over **Carmacks** and **Faro** in the Yukon. During periods of intense activity, however, the band expands and the whole territory may be overlapped by its presence.

The northern lights originate in interplanetary space, the product of solar wind, which is sometimes called interplanetary gas. Solar wind is composed of thin, invisible streams of charged subatomic particles, mostly protons and electrons. The particles vary in density, depending on their position in the solar system. Near the sun, for example, solar wind travels about a thousand times faster than near Earth. During solar flares, particles are projected outward from the sun at speeds of 300 to 1,000 kilometres per hour. When these particles penetrate the Earth's upper atmosphere near the magnetic poles they react with and excite oxygen and nitrogen contained in the atmosphere, creating the colourful, shimmering lights. In the southern hemisphere the same phenomenon occurs and is known there as aurora australis, or the southern lights.

The colour of the lights is influenced by the atmospheric gases with which the particles interact. For example, green or red light derives from excited atomic oxygen, while purple light emanates from excited molecular nitrogen.

For centuries humans seeing the northern lights have been haunted by their flickering or pulsating glow. **First Nations peoples** often viewed the lights as ancestral spirits dancing before the Great Spirit, and the Inuit said they were sky people playing a form of ball game.

Northern Lights Centre

Situated in **Watson Lake**, this planetarium houses the only theatre of its kind in North America. The 110-seat ElectricSky theatre offers the latest in domed video projection to present a multimedia experience of the **northern lights**, exploring the science, myth, and folklore surrounding this natural phenomenon. The theatre also features a star projection system capable of projecting 2,354 stars onto the 15-metre dome, including the 88 recognized constellations and all 57 navigational stars located in both the northern and southern hemispheres.

Many other state-of-the-art laser and sound technologies make this theatre the first in the world to have such an integrated panoramic video system. Opened in 1997, the Northern Lights Centre includes interactive exhibits describing the folklore and science of the aurora, displays on the history of Canadian rocket technology and its role in early Northern Lights research, Canada's space research activities, and ongoing studies of the northern lights.

North-West Mounted Police

In September 1886, two American miners found **gold** at the mouth of Fortymile River. The following year, Alaska Commercial Company trader Jack McQuersten established a fur-trading post near the discovery site and in a short time Forty Mile became the largest settlement on the Yukon River. Although it lay inside Canada, it was mostly American in **population** and even had an American post office. The only Canadian official at Forty Mile was surveyor William Ogilvie, who increasingly believed that the federal government must exert Canada's sovereignty over the post or risk the gold-rich region being annexed by the United States. In April 1894, the government reacted to Ogilvie's entreaties and ordered the North-West Mounted Police (NWMP) to conduct a fact-finding mission. Within a month, NWMP Inspector Charles Constantine and Staff Sergeant

The presence of the NWMP in Dawson during the gold rush years of 1897-1899 ensured that both Canada's sovereignty and an un-American peacefulness prevailed over the Klondike gold rush fields. (Yukon Archives, Macbride Museum Collection, #3782)

Charles Brown left Ottawa for Forty Mile. Constantine's orders were to investigate the liquor trade operating there, establish a customs collection post, and check the condition of First Nations in the region.

Crossing the Chilkoot Pass, Constantine arrived at Forty Mile on August 7, 1894. He stayed a month before catching the last steamer to St. Michael, Alaska prior to freeze-up. Constantine recommended that the federal government send 40 Mounties to enforce the peace. Ogilvie disagreed and recommended that only 10 men be sent. Ottawa compromised, authorizing the dispatch of a 20-man force.

The Yukon's first NWMP detachment, with Constantine in command, left Regina on June 1, 1895 and arrived by steamer at Forty Mile on July 24. Just downriver from Forty Mile the force built a post, christened Fort Constantine. In his annual report of January 1896, Constantine stated that the fort was "the most northerly military or semi-military post in the British Empire."

Construction of Fort Constantine was no sooner completed than the **Klondike Gold Rush** started. Within days of the discovery on Rabbit Creek (soon renamed Bonanza Creek), Forty Mile was reduced to a near ghost town. Realizing this rush would bring thousands more prospectors into the region, Constantine sent a plea to Ottawa for reinforcements, so he could establish a post closer to the new gold fields and ensure Canadian sovereignty over what would surely be a flood of American prospectors. To quell a possible uprising against his small force, Constantine requested a Maxim machine gun be immediately sent from Regina. His request for the gun was denied, but the newly promoted superintendent received 80 reinforcements. In the spring of 1897, the NWMP constructed Fort Herchmer at the new community of **Dawson**. Fort Herchmer became the headquarters for the NWMP in the Yukon. From 1897 to his relief on June 23, 1898, Constantine built the NWMP presence up to 264 men and established 31 posts in the territory and in northern British Columbia. As he sailed from Dawson to southern Canada aboard the sternwheeler *C.H. Hamilton*, Constantine wrote, "Thank God for the release."

Constantine was replaced by Superintendent Samuel Benfield Steele, whose name remains inextricably linked to the maintenance of peace and good order during the Klondike Gold Rush. Although he played a critical role in its resolution, by the time Steele assumed command the sovereignty issue had been resolved. In 1897, Alaskan officials claimed that Bennett, at the head of Bennett Lake, was part of the United States and that a Canadian customs collection post situated there was operating illegally. Acting on orders sent by Canada's Minister of the Interior, Clifford Sifton, Constantine ordered two NWMP detachments— now armed with Maxim machine guns—to establish customs collection posts at the summits of the Chilkoot and White passes. The U.S. army responded by posting 200 soldiers at Skagway and demanded the NWMP withdraw from the summits. The Mounties refused. Steele, who commanded the summit detachments, met his counterpart, a U.S. army colonel, in March and negotiated an agreement whereby the summits were recognized as a temporary boundary. By May, the majority of the U.S. troops had been withdrawn and Steele sent the machine guns back to Fort Herchmer.

The Mounties at the summit posts faced difficult circumstances. Snow piled up so quickly and deeply at the Chilkoot post that the command tent was often buried under about three metres of snow and the entrance required shovelling out at 15-minute intervals. Between February and June 1898, Chilkoot-summit commander Inspector Robert Belcher collected customs' tolls totalling $174,470.32. In late June, the NWMP turned its toll operations over to civilian authorities.

Meanwhile, Steele was enforcing Canadian law on the **Trails of '98** and in Dawson. In some cases this meant inventing laws on the spot, such as his edicts requiring that every boat passing through **Miles Canyon** pass a police-administered seaworthiness inspection, and that each prospector coming over the Chilkoot Trail be provisioned with a year's supplies. In Dawson and other communities, he enforced laws against the open carrying of firearms, regulated the prostitution trade, and prosecuted bootleggers.

By 1900, the gold rush was nearly over and most of the stampeders had left Dawson. Steele followed them a year later. Thousands of Dawsonites lined the shoreline to bid the "lion of the north" farewell and the town's dignitaries presented him with a purse of gold nuggets in appreciation of his service.

Four years later, the Yukon's population numbered only about 10,000, down from over 40,000 at the peak of the gold rush. Federal spending on the territory decreased and many NWMP posts were closed. The only new Yukon post opened during this time was at Herschel Island, where American whalers had established a whaling station and presented a new threat to Canadian sovereignty. With the outbreak of World War I, many Yukon Mounties defied orders to remain at their posts and volunteered for service overseas. By this time, the NWMP's golden era in the Yukon had drawn to a close.

Today the NWMP's descendent, the Royal Canadian Mounted Police, is the territory's only policing authority.

(*See also* **Lost Patrol**.)

Ogilvie Mountains

The Ogilvie Mountains form the most westerly and northerly portion of a broad mountainous band that runs across north-central Yukon in an arc reaching down the eastern flank of the territory almost to its southern border with British Columbia. The other components of this band are the Wernecke portion of the **Mackenzie Mountains** and the **Selwyn Mountains**. These mountains together present a major barrier to the prevalent winds out of the Arctic, resulting in increased cold and precipitation on their north slopes and more moderate temperatures to their southwest. They contribute significantly to the warmer **climate** that more southerly territory communities, such as **Dawson** and **Whitehorse**, enjoy in comparison to northern communities such as **Old Crow**. The mountains also pose a barrier to transportation, with only the **Dempster Highway** crossing them to link the northern portion of the Yukon to the south. The majority of the territory's **population** lives to the south of this band of mountains.

The southern portion of the Ogilvie Mountains is extremely rugged, with ridges linking precipitous peaks that flank deep valleys. Seldom does elevation drop below 1,500 metres, while mountain peaks exceeding 2,100 metres are rare. The highest peak in the Ogilvies is 2,362 metres. The northerly portion of the Ogilvie Mountains features fewer true mountains. Rather, the terrain consists mostly of flat-topped hills that are eroded remnants of a former plateau. Elevations here range between 900 and 1,350 metres, with the highest peak reaching only 1,803 metres.

All of the Ogilvies lie within the **tundra** region and the entire system experiences discontinuous **permafrost**, with continuous permafrost in the northern ranges. Below the continuous permafrost zone, black and white spruce grow in protected valleys, with aspen and poplar found in well-drained warmer valleys.

There is no permanent and scarcely any semi-permanent human habitation in the Ogilvie Mountains.

The mountains were named in 1966 after William Ogilvie, who surveyed many parts of the Canadian west between 1875 and 1898. In 1896, he was working out of Fortymile Creek when the initial discovery was made that set off the **Klondike Gold Rush**. The only Canadian government representative in the territory other than **North-West Mounted Police** Inspector Charles Constantine, Ogilvie played a vital role in ensuring that the claims staked by prospectors during the rush were lawfully registered, thus defusing many disputes that could otherwise have been settled with violence. Ogilvie became the second Commissioner of the Yukon Territory in September 1898 and held the post until his resignation in 1901. He left the Yukon that same year and died on November 13, 1912 in Winnipeg.

Old Crow

Old Crow, located at the junction of the Porcupine and Old Crow rivers, is the only community in the Yukon without road access. It does have a landing strip and is serviced by regular flights out of **Dawson** and Inuvik. Old Crow lies north of the **Arctic Circle**, and is about 1,000 kilometres north of **Whitehorse**.

The eroding banks of the Old Crow and Porcupine rivers are considered a treasure trove by anthropologists, archaeologists, and palaeontologists. Large quantities of Pleistocene vertebrate fossils have been unearthed here over the past 20 years. Archaeologists have also uncovered evidence of human life at Old Crow dating back to about 20,000 years—the oldest known signs of human habitation in North America (*see* **Archaeology**).

Old Crow has a **population** today of about 285, mostly **First Nations peoples** of the Gwitchin nation. Their livelihood comes chiefly from fur trapping, hunting, fishing, and a small amount of **tourism** and employment with the Gwitchin council and federal and territorial governments.

Old Crow's modern settlement history begins in 1911, but the roots of this population date back to 1847 and the beginnings of the **fur trade** in the Yukon. In that year, Fort Yukon was established as a Hudson's Bay Company (HBC) post at the confluence of the Yukon and Porcupine rivers in present-day Alaska. In 1869, when the HBC was ousted from all American territory, the Gwitchin residents remaining loyal to the British Crown moved up the Porcupine River to a trading post called Old Rampart House. This post, however, proved to be still inside the American boundary, so the people moved once again to New Rampart House, near the site of Old Crow. But in 1911 a smallpox epidemic devastated the community. The survivors burned the post and moved to the Porcupine–Old Crow rivers' confluence.

They named the community after a Gwitchin chief in the 1870s, Te-Tshim-Gevtik (Walking Crow), who was known for the high standards and moral principles he expected the people to live by. It should be noted that crows do not occur this far north and the term crow is used interchangeably to denote ravens, which are extremely common.

Despite its small size and remote location, Old Crow is familiar to many Canadians—the result of the columns by Order of Canada recipient Edith Josie, a Gwitchin resident, which appeared in the *Whitehorse Star* for 30 years, beginning in 1962. Known as the "Old Crow News," the columns usually began with the statement, "Here are the news" and ended with "This is end the news." Her vivid, laconic, and ungrammatical style dramatically expressed the essence of Old Crow life and history.

Old Crow is officially a "dry" village, meaning that no alcohol can be sold or consumed within its boundaries. The principal diet of Old Crow residents remains **caribou** meat. Most residents report eating caribou in at least one meal more than 200 days a year.

Old Crow Flats

Situated to the north of **Old Crow**, the Old Crow Flats encompasses an amazing network of wetlands, ponds, and lakes clustered in a 600,000-hectare region. "The Flats," as the area is known locally, contains more than 2,000 lakes. Its altitude averages only about 300 metres above sea level, but experiences some of the lowest average temperatures found anywhere in North America. Average annual temperature is –10° Celsius with averages in summer of 7.5° Celsius and winter of –27° Celsius. The ecoclimate here is considered high subarctic.

The wetlands covering most of the area are made up of peat bogs with basin fens and shore fens. In better drained areas, black spruce, tamarack, and some white spruce are found. **Permafrost** is continuous with a high ice content in the form of ice wedges and chunks.

Old Crow Flats is home to a great diversity of wildlife, including grizzly and black **bears**, moose, beavers, muskrats, foxes, **wolves**, hares, ravens, rock and willow ptarmigan, and bald and golden eagles. This rich diversity of wildlife makes the flats important to **First Nations peoples** as a hunting, trapping, and fishing area.

The Old Crow Flats are a major breeding ground for ducks and other **birds**. In 1991, for example, about 575,000 ducks were counted in the area. On average, annual duck counts identify 350,000 to 400,000 ducks using the area as a summer feeding and breeding ground. It is one of four Yukon wetlands that is protected through legislation. Much of the region is included within the boundaries of **Vuntut National Park**, while an area south of the Old Crow River is protected as a special management zone under the authority of the Vuntut Gwitchin Final Agreement (*see* **First Nations Land Claims**).

Parks. *See* **Coal River Springs Territorial Park; Herschel Island Territorial Park; Ivvavik National Park; Kluane National Park Reserve; Vuntut National Park.**

Pelly Crossing

With a population of 300, Pelly Crossing is the home of the Selkirk First Nations band. It is situated at the 465-kilometre point of the Klondike Highway between **Whitehorse** and **Dawson**. Consequently, the community is an important service centre for travellers and a popular launching spot for canoeists and other boaters planning to journey down the Pelly River to its junction with the **Yukon River** and from there down the Yukon to Dawson.

The community derives its name from the river, which was named after Sir John Henry Pelly, governor of the Hudson's Bay Company (HBC) large Northern Department, in 1840 by Robert Campbell, an HBC explorer who passed through the region. Campbell also named two lakes at the headwaters of the Pelly River and the high bluffs that overlook the stream opposite the mouth of Big Campbell Creek after his employer.

Peregrine Falcon

Two subspecies of peregrine falcon are listed as being at risk in the Yukon. The tundra peregrine falcon is identified by the Committee on the Status of Endangered Wildlife in Canada as vulnerable and the anatum peregrine falcon is one of only two animal species in the territory listed as endangered (the other is the **bowhead whale**).

Peregrine falcons are among the fastest creatures on Earth, capable of flying up to 200 kilometres per hour. This speed enables peregrines to effectively hunt their preferred prey of other **birds**. Peregrines are crow-sized falcons with pointed wings, long tails, dark heads and backs, and contrasting wings and underparts. In the Yukon, peregrines nest on cliffs overlooking major rivers. The anatum subspecies summers in the interior regions, while the tundra subspecies spends summer north of the tree line.

The plight of the peregrines has come to symbolize the unforeseen implications of environmental degradation by humans. In the 1960s, peregrine falcon populations throughout North America suddenly plummeted for no apparent reason. Researchers soon discovered the problem. Peregrines were unable to produce offspring because thin egg shells were breaking prematurely so that the embryos perished before hatching. All the unusually thin egg shells were found to contain high concentrations of pesticides, especially dichlorodiphenyl-trichloroethane (DDT).

Peregrine populations in the Yukon were devastated. From 1971 to 1974 no anatum peregrines at all were counted in the territory. By the mid-1970s all peregrine races had been extirpated from most of North America. In the Yukon, both tundra and anatum subspecies survived in remnants of their original population, with only about 18 anatum pairs counted in 1975. Of these, slightly less than half were pairs producing young. With respect to tundra peregrines, by the early 1980s no breeding pairs were counted in the territory.

By this time the commercial use of DDT had been banned throughout North America and, in a desperate move to save the species, some of the last young peregrines found in the wild were captured and used to establish a captive breeding program. In 1978, a recovery team comprising biologists and other specialists from across Canada drafted the Canadian Peregrine Recovery Plan. The same year, the first peregrines raised in captivity were re-introduced to their former range in the Yukon.

By the early 1980s, peregrines were exhibiting the first documented population recovery in North American history. The number of anatum peregrines in the territory rose steadily until by 1990 an estimated 110 breeding pairs summered along Yukon rivers. This subspecies remains endangered or extirpated in much of its former range. Placing the species even more at risk is the fact that it winters in Central and South America, where dangerous pesticides, including DDT, are still used. Residues of DDT are also still present in the Yukon environment.

Meanwhile, the tundra peregrine has been slowly recovering, as well. Currently in the Yukon, its population numbers about 20 percent of historic counts, but only three breeding pairs have been identified within the territory. In the eastern Arctic, however, the tundra peregrine is recovering more quickly, which has led to its downgrading from threatened to vulnerable in Canada.

(*See also* **Biodiversity; Endangered Species.**)

Permafrost

All of Yukon Territory lies within the Canadian permafrost zone. Simply put, permafrost is ground that has remained at or below 0° Celsius for at least two years. It may be comprised of cold, dry earth; cold, wet earth; ice-cemented rock; or frozen subsurface and surface water. If the ground is dry, ice will not form no matter how low the temperature drops. In permafrost regions, an upper surface layer may undergo some thawing in the summer and then refreeze in the winter. This layer is known as the active layer. Below this is the permafrost layer. Where permafrost underlies more than 80 percent of the ground, it is known as continuous permafrost. If the permafrost underlies 30 to 80 percent of the ground it is referred to as discontinuous permafrost.

The continuous permafrost region in the Yukon covers all the ground north of a rough line cutting across the territory through the Peel River Valley from the east into the heart of the **Ogilvie Mountains** in the west. Below this line, the ground is affected by discontinuous permafrost.

The depth of permafrost in the continuous zone can be astonishing. In most areas it runs to depths of more than 100 metres, and even in the southernmost continuous permafrost zones the depth tends to be 60 to 90 metres. Even in areas of continuous permafrost, however, the active layer will experience seasonal thawing and freezing. The depth of the active layer varies with latitude. The farther south the area, generally the deeper the active layer. At high latitudes it is common for the active layer to only reach a depth of 15 to 30 centimetres, while farther south it might be as much as 1.5 metres deep. It is this thawing within the active layer that allows **tundra**, boreal forest, and other **vegetation** types to grow in permafrost zones. Because the active layer is resting on frozen ground, the surface tends to be marshy, with water pooling common. This promotes the breeding and distribution of **mosquitoes** during summer months when thawing peaks.

Permafrost presents many challenges to human activities. No materials, other than gravel and clean sand, are immune to the heaving action caused by the seasonal freezing and thawing. For this reason houses often list to one side or sag in the middle, as the shifting of the ground is seldom even over any significant area. Many pioneer homes were built on platforms, which could be propped up each summer to compensate for the inevitable shifting.

Agriculture is also hindered. The inability of roots to grow deeply because of the permafrost underlay causes stunted growth. Greenhouses need to have insulated floors to protect the plants from the cold emanating upward out of the permafrost layer.

Road, highway, and pipeline building creates special challenges. Where vegetation is scraped away, the active layer will deepen as the ground gets warmer in the absence of plant cover. This causes increased rates of soil sinkage and pooling of water, resulting in **muskeg** and deep mud, which in turn causes construction vehicles to become mired and sections of roadbeds, runways, and pipe lines to sink, crumble, or crack. The **Alaska Highway** construction during World War II was particularly plagued by problems resulting from permafrost disturbance. Permafrost also creates unique problems for mining, ore drilling, and hydroelectric development.

On the positive side, however, **First Nations peoples** and some non-First Nations have long enjoyed natural refrigerators by digging holes into the permafrost layer and storing food there.

(*See also* **Pingos; Polygons.**)

Pickled Toes. *See* **Sour-Toe Cocktail.**

Pingos

In the **permafrost** zones of northern Canada are many ice-cored hills that take on a conical shape similar to that of a volcanic cone. They are not, however, formed by lava eruptions. Rather, pingos result from water collecting under the surface of the earth and then freezing in winter so that the earth pushes upward—the same process that creates frost heaves in asphalt-surfaced roads. Pingos, however, can reach up to 50 metres high and 200 metres or more around.

The world's greatest concentration of pingos is found in the Mackenzie Delta's Tuktoyaktuk area, where there are some 1,450 of the hills. Some of the largest pingos here are more than 1,000 years old. In the Yukon, pingos are concentrated in the **Eagle Plain** region, north of **Old Crow** in **Vuntut National Park**, and at various locations along the Alaska-Yukon border.

Pingos are of two types. The larger pingos rise up in flat ground where there was once a lake that has either dried up or drained away. This situation produces the largest pingos, like those common in the Mackenzie Delta, and takes hundreds of years to complete the building process.

Other pingos are formed in wet, poorly drained areas underlain by permafrost. Most of the pingos in the Yukon are of this type. The largest of these pingos often nurture the growth of birch and aspen, which thrive on the well-drained soil that covers the slopes and summit of the pingo. On the surrounding terrain, the **vegetation** growing in the boggier soil is usually willow, alder, and black spruce.

Most smaller pingos eventually weather away as erosion by rain and wind, and melting of the ice core itself, slowly reduces the soil cover to expose the ice core to melting during the short but hot summer months.

Pingo is an Inuit word meaning "small hill." It was applied to the ice-cored hills in 1938 by botanist A. E. Porsild.

Placer Mining

A great deal of the **gold** found in the Yukon was placer gold, meaning it was contained within a loose mix of materials, most commonly gravel. Gold contained in placers can be mined by amateur prospectors using relatively crude techniques. It was discoveries of rich concentrations of placer gold that sparked most of the major gold rushes of the 19th century, such as the **Klondike Gold Rush**.

Placer mining entailed first making the strike by **gold panning** to assess the potential of a stream bed. Once a creek site was proven by panning, the prospector would proceed with **claim-staking** and start mining.

Because gold has a high specific gravity it sinks in a moving mixture of gravel and water to the bottom, providing a fairly simple means of separating the gold from other materials. To take advantage of this gold characteristic, placer miners of the 1800s developed two types of mining tools—the sluice box and the rocker.

A sluice box creates an artificial miniature stream. It is basically a long, narrow, open-ended box that is slightly inclined to allow water to flow through.

Placer gravel is shovelled into the upper end and mixed with water that is flushed through the box. As the mixture of water and gravel flows down the box, the gold falls to the bottom and is captured by a series of riffles or ridges built into the bottom. The mixture captured by the riffles is usually composed of heavy, black sand and gold flakes. To separate the gold from the sand, the prospector usually finishes the process by panning the material to wash the sand away from the gold without any gold loss.

A rocker is a wooden boxlike device that is rocked back and forth like a child's cradle to create a flow of water. While rocking with one hand, the miner pours water on the gravel, which rests on a screened surface. The finer materials are washed through the screen into a lower, riffled chamber. When the lower chamber is nearly full, the top half of the rocker is removed and the black sand below is panned to separate it from the gold.

In the Klondike Gold Rush and other rushes of the 19th century, most miners threw away the black sand in which the gold was concentrated after panning

Prospectors work a sluice box at Claim 67 below Discovery on Bonanza Creek in 1901. (H.J. Woodside photo, NAC PA-16277)

it. But this sand often contained large amounts of gold flour (or dust) that was more valuable than the gold removed during panning. Today, most miners take the time to separate the gold from this concentrate, which is usually composed of magnetite, hematite, cassiterite, and ilmenite, as well as occasional concentrations of platinum. The concentrate is run through successively finer screens, each separating some gold from the sand. When no more gold can be seen by the naked eye, the miner thoroughly dries the concentrate in a pan set over a fire. This is always done outdoors because the concentrate may contain mercury, which evaporates when heated and has highly toxic vapours. Once the concentrate is dried, the magnetite is separated off with a magnet and the rest of the nongold materials are removed by blowing them gently to one side.

Placer gold can be sold by miners directly to some banks in the Yukon, to several commercial gold buyers, to jewellers, or as concentrate to refining companies. Before gold can be shipped out of the territory, a royalty must be paid to the **government**. This means that all gold recovered must be weighed at a District Mining Recorder's Office, the royalty paid, and an export licence received before it is exported.

Polygons

Occurring commonly in areas of **permafrost**, polygons are produced in the saturated wet ground that lies on top of most permafrost terrain. Polygon construction can take hundreds of years and is generated by the combined actions of large-scale thermal contraction in the ground and seasonal freezing, which causes ice movement and expansion.

The result is deep water- or ice-filled fissures in the ground bordered by surface ridges that are arranged in polygonal outlines—hence the name. Each polygon may measure from 15 to 30 metres across. Usually polygons occur in large clusters that are easily recognized from the air, appearing as a network of hundreds of small lakes forming intricate and regular geometric shapes.

Population

There are no reliable estimates of how many **First Nations peoples** traditionally made their home in what is today the Yukon Territory. Most archaeologists and ethnologists estimate the 19th-century population of Athapaskan and

Tlingit peoples here in the low thousands, possibly as low as their modern-day numbers of about 6,000. Other researchers argue that there might have been as many as 40,000 in the territory. This seems unlikely given the need for clans to range quite far to find sufficient food and other resources. In addition to the Athapaskan and Tlingit peoples dwelling in the Yukon, there was until recent times also a small migratory population of Inuvialuit—or western Arctic Inuit—living on the **Beaufort Sea** coast. Whalers at Herschel Island estimated their population at about 400 to 500 in 1890. But by the early 1920s, disease and other disruptions caused by the whalers had resulted in the deaths of many of the Inuvialuit and the survivors fled eastward out of the territory. There are no Inuvialuit settlements remaining in the Yukon, although some members of this people do come into the extreme northern part of the territory on hunting expeditions.

Until the beginning of the **Klondike Gold Rush**, the non–First Nations population of the Yukon consisted of a scattering of fur traders, missionaries, and prospectors. Within two years of the strike it jumped to more than 40,000. With the end of the gold rush, the population collapsed to 27,219 by 1901. The downward spiral continued through 1911 when only 8,512 people lived in the territory to an ultimate low in 1931 of 4,230. From then on the population slowly grew, reaching 14,268 in 1961 and then rising steadily to the current population of about 33,600.

Of this population, 24,000 live in **Whitehorse** and the rest are concentrated in small clusters within the territory's 3 towns, 4 villages, 2 hamlets, 13 unincorporated communities, and 9 rural communities. **Dawson**, with 2,150 residents, and **Watson Lake**, with a population of 1,790, are the second and third most populous communities.

The Yukon has a young population, with an average median age of 33. Some 7,600 Yukoners are under the age of 15; about 10,400 are between 15 and 34; 14,000 range from 35 to 64; and only about 1,500 are older than 65. There are about 1,000 more males than females in the territory.

Post-Secondary Education. *See* **Education.**

Potlatch

Yukon **First Nations peoples** in the southern part of the territory hosted potlatches as a memorial ceremony held an average of a year or two after a death in a clan. The southern peoples of the Yukon divided their society into two halves, a practice that some anthropologists call a moiety system after the French word *moitié*, which means half. Each clan would belong to either the Wolf or Crow moiety. In the Tlingit language, for example, the halves were *Yéil* (**raven**, or crow) or *Gooch* (wolf).

Moiety membership was traced matrilineally, as was clan membership. If one was from the Wolf moiety, that person's opposite moiety was Crow and its members were part of the person's patrilineal lineage. Traditionally, a Wolf was required to marry a Crow or vice versa. Intermarriage within a moiety was strictly forbidden. It was important to be able to identify each First Nations person by moiety to recognize who was a member of the individual's mother's side and who was from the father's side. Southern Yukon First Nations believed that to get through life people required the assistance of members of their father's moiety as well as their mother's.

If a Wolf died it was the responsibility of the Crow relatives of that person to prepare the body for burial or cremation. The Wolf moiety would then host a potlatch as a memorial ceremony for the deceased, and as a means to give the Crows, who had carried out their last duties, payment for their services.

Potlatches in the Yukon, then, differed significantly from those held by First Nations of the northwest coast, which were primarily a means of establishing and confirming rank, status, lines of privilege, and power. There was no element of competition on the part of the holders to outdo previous potlatch holders by being more generous with gift-giving and more lavish in the celebrations.

The process of preparing for a potlatch in the Yukon was a long one—seldom would one be held until at least a year after a person's death. During the time between the death and the potlatch, members of the matrilineal family and direct relatives would trap for furs, prepare skins, sew fine fur robes, make moccasins and other clothes, and trade for other goods that would all be given away as presents to the members of the opposite moiety. Large quantities of food also had to be accumulated and prepared for the celebration. Because food was most plentiful and available in late summer, potlatches were usually held in this season.

Guests attending a potlatch always wore their finest clothes and sang as they arrived. After a formal greeting by the headman of the host moiety, the guests and their hosts would make speeches, dance and sing for each other, and display articles of clothing and headdresses bearing the clan crests. There would be much feasting, with all the guests eating and drinking symbolically for their dead ancestors. When the feasting was complete, the dead person's closest matrilineal relatives would pay those from the opposite moiety who had helped with the funeral ceremony. Each guest would receive a gift. All presents that had been collected for the potlatch had to be given away for fear that bad luck would be invoked if everything was not distributed.

When European missionaries arrived in the Yukon they joined those on the northwest coast in lobbying the federal government to enforce a ban on potlatch ceremonies, which they believed were shameless, wicked, pagan celebrations interfering with the ability of the missionaries to convert First Nations peoples to Christianity. In 1884, the federal government amended the Indian Act accordingly and until 1951 the holding of potlatches was illegal and the hosts subject to imprisonment.

Today potlatches are again held in the Yukon, reinforcing the underlying principle of social organization among First Nations that people from differing clans, moieties, or nearby bands should help each other.

Princess Sophia Sinking

In 1918, 268 Yukoners boarded the SS *Princess Sophia*, bound from Skagway to Vancouver. Some were leaving the territory for good, but most were leaving for the winter with plans to return the following spring or in a year or two. The majority were residents of **Dawson**, which had undergone a dramatic **population** decline in the wake of the end of the **Klondike Gold Rush**.

Among those aboard were a former dance hall queen, a mine owner, and some families that had been present in Dawson since 1897. The *Princess Sophia* was not long out of Skagway when it became mired in a blinding snowstorm on October 23 and ran aground on Vanderbilt Reef. For a full day and a half the ship hung on the reef while the crews of other ships that had raced to its aid tried to decide whether to risk a rescue attempt by taking the passengers off the reef in the face of heavy swells or to hope the stranded ship could be floated free when the storm abated.

On the night of October 25, however, the decision was taken from the rescuers' hands as the wind suddenly changed direction and blew the ship off the reef in one violent slide that ripped open the *Princess Sophia*'s bottom plates. She sank quickly, leaving no survivors. The passengers and 75 crew members drowned, were suffocated by spilled bunker oil, or succumbed to exposure before they could be pulled from the frigid water. In all, just under 10 percent of the non–First Nations population of the Yukon died in less than 30 minutes.

At a time when the Yukon was already suffering from a serious economic depression and the loss of many people to the battlefields of World War I, the impact of the sinking of the *Princess Sophia* was devastating. A once-thriving territory, buoyed by **gold** rush fortunes and its elevation to a near self-governing territory, was too demoralized to offer significant resistance as the federal government continued a program of stripping the territorial **government** of much of its powers, reduced the territorial budget by 50 percent, and closed many federal offices. For many Yukoners, the sinking of the *Princess Sophia* became synonymous with the end of the territory's period of good fortune.

Qikiqtaruk. *See* **Herschel Island Territorial Park.**

Raven

In the Yukon the common raven is also often referred to as a crow because its smaller southern cousin has no presence in the territory. For this reason the legends, myths, and stories of **First Nations peoples** in the territory often refer to crow when the subject is actually raven. The raven is Yukon Territory's official bird and is ubiquitous throughout most of the territory.

Ravens and crows are remarkably similar and both of the same genus, *Corvus*. Both are all black with a purplish or violet lustre. The raven is significantly larger, though, and has a much heavier bill. Its tail is wedge-shaped, clearly noticeable when it is in flight. To become airborne, a raven usually needs to take two or three sharp hops before take-off. During flight, it is graceful and agile, often performing barrel rolls, sharp dives, and tumbles between long periods of gliding and soaring.

One of the most distinctive characteristics of a raven is its voice—a hoarse, far-carrying, wooden-sounding croak that is quite different from the sharper caw of the crow.

Ravens nest in pairs on cliff ledges and in tree cavities, especially those of conifers. Their nest is a large mass of sticks lined with soft grass and moss. The female will lay three to five eggs, which hatch after an incubation period of about 20 days.

Scavengers, ravens do well in the urban areas of the Yukon, feeding on garbage and carrion. They are fierce and clever birds, which are extremely protective of their young and will feed on other birds' young and eggs. Like crows, they seem to have a highly developed sense of play that even includes body-surfing on their backs down snow-laden slopes.

The cunning nature of ravens undoubtedly contributed to their being considered tricksters in most First Nations myths. The black colouring, many myths claim, was a punishment visited on Raven by the gods for his mischievous behaviour.

Yukon First Nations, like most northwest coast First Nations, attribute Raven with having created the world in which humans came to dwell. The creation story takes many varying forms but the essence of most stories is the same. There was a time when the world was flooded and there was no game to be found or place for Raven to land and rest. Eventually Raven spots a bright light in the dark night sky. Flying to it, he finds a woman sitting by a fire on top of a small summit above the flood, which is often said to have been in the heart of the **St. Elias Mountains**. The summit is barely larger than the woman and the fire burning next to her. Beside the woman is a baby.

Seeing the child, Raven swoops down and grabs it. The woman and Raven argue, Raven offering to surrender the baby only if the woman, known as Sea Woman, gives him some land like her own. Finally, after refusing four times, the woman agrees to make the long journey entailed in finding the land in return for Raven's promise to stay with the child and not harm it. When Sea Woman returns with a piece of land, Raven turns the child over to her and the two of them escape into the waters.

Raven proceeds to walk around on the ground he has gained. He circles around it, again and again, flattening it and pushing it out like a large pancake of mud. Eventually this ever expanding piece of flattened land becomes the earth upon which humans came to dwell and where they live today. Some researchers believe that this form of the Raven creation story refers to the end of the last **glaciation** period, when the ice sheets covering most of the Yukon melted.

Another Raven story, closely linked to that of the creation myth, credits Raven with putting water on the land, which had replaced the water that had covered the earth before Raven created the world. According to this myth, all water was being hoarded by Loon. But Raven managed to break into Loon's hiding place and drink all the water before being confronted by Loon. He then flew away. As Raven flew across the world, he proceeded to release single drops of water which fell to the earth and were transformed into lakes. Into some of the lakes Raven spit fish. Finally, the last water in Raven's mouth turned sour and he spit it away in disgust. This sour water became the world's oceans.

Religion

Yukoners overwhelmingly follow either the Christian faith or have no declared religion. As there was no question regarding religion on the 1996 Census of Canada because this was termed a half-census in which not all questions were asked, the most recent statistics regarding religion derive from the 1991 full census.

According to that census, the predominant Christian religion was Catholic, of which there were 5,535 Roman Catholics and 45 Ukrainian Catholics. The Protestant faith numbered 11,905, largely divided among two churches, with Anglicans numbering 4,090 and United Church adherents 2,400. Significant other Protestant populations counted 885 Baptist, 665 Lutheran, 600 Pentecostal, 360 Presbyterian, 285 Jehovah's Witness, and 160 Latter-day Saints (Mormons).

Those Yukoners who reported having no religion numbered 9,470.

Although **First Nations peoples** are reaffirming their culture in many ways, in 1991 this had not spread to religion in a large way. Only 175 Yukoners reported a North American native religion as their primary religion. Researchers, however, believe this number has probably increased in recent years as First Nations reclaim their traditional spiritual beliefs (*see* **First Nations Spirituality**).

There were also small scatterings of most other major world religions, with 45 Jewish people, 35 Islamic, 40 Sikh, 10 Hindu, and 100 Baha'i. No Yukoners reported being Buddhists.

Richardson Mountains

The Richardson Mountains are a band of mountains stretching from Mackenzie Bay in the extreme northeastern corner of the Yukon to meet the northern tip of the **Selwyn Mountains** in the Peel River region. At their northern extent they merge with the British Mountains, which curve across the top of the territory, fronting the **Beaufort Sea**. The southern mountains in this formation are characterized by smooth, rounded profiles. The northern Richardsons were unglaciated and are rougher and higher, reaching elevations of up to 1,753 metres. Only the eastern slopes of the southern part of this range were glaciated, to about the 1,100-metre level.

Temperatures remain cold here year round. Mean annual temperature is about −9⁰ Celsius. Except for the southern tip, the Richardsons lie entirely within the zone of continuous **permafrost**. **Pingos** are common. There are few trees here, although some stands of black and white spruce are found in protected valleys. The Richardson Mountains contain the highest latitudinal limit of tree growth in Canada (white spruce). For the most part, however, the terrain is characterized by **tundra**. The mountain range is virtually uninhabited.

The Richardson Mountains were named by explorer John Franklin in 1825 after John Richardson, a member of both of Franklin's overland expeditions. He also commanded the Mackenzie River overland portion of the vain search for Franklin undertaken in 1848 and 1849 after Franklin had gone missing in 1845 during an attempt to complete the first voyage through the Northwest Passage.

Rivers. *See* **Yukon River.**

Ross River

Situated on the southeast bank of the Pelly River, the community of Ross River has a **population** of approximately 400, mostly Kaska **First Nations peoples** of the Ross River Indian Band. The village serves as a jumping-off point for hunting and fishing in the nearby wilderness area and the only resupply stop for travellers on the **Canol Road**, as well as one of the few stops on the Campbell Highway. Mineral exploration operations also use this community as a base for launching forays into the mineral-rich east and central regions of the Yukon.

The community derives its name from the river of the same name which joins the Pelly River at this point. Hudson's Bay Company explorer Robert Campbell named the river in 1843 after HBC chief factor Donald Ross.

St. Elias Mountains

The St. Elias Mountains hold the world's most extensive icefields, outside the polar caps. Some of the glaciers in this incredibly rugged range are up to 112 kilometres long and more than 1 kilometre thick. From the ice of these glaciers flow some of the wildest and most remote rivers in North America—the Alsek and Tatshenshini, which drain into the Pacific Ocean, and the Donjak, Duke, Slims, and White rivers, which flow into the **Yukon River**. In 1850, one of these glaciers created a vast ice dam that blocked the Alsek River to create a huge valley lake near **Haines Junction**. The lake was 150 metres deep and reportedly took two days to empty in a massive outpouring when the ice dam finally broke.

The St. Elias Mountains extend southeastward from the Wrangell Mountains in Alaska for about 400 kilometres through the extreme southwesterly corner of the Yukon, across the extreme northwestern corner of British Columbia, and terminating in the Alaskan Panhandle at Cross Sound. A number of the range's peaks exceed 5,000 metres, including **Mount Logan** at 5,959 metres—the highest mountain in Canada and the Yukon.

Most of the St. Elias Mountains contained in the Yukon form the heart of 22,015-square-kilometre **Kluane National Park Reserve**. Within the park are 20 peaks standing higher than 4,200 metres. Most of the terrain here lies above the 1,500-metre level and so is above the treeline, which starts at about 1,050 metres. There are, however, some narrow valleys in which willow and shrub birch occur on the higher slopes, blending with open and stunted white spruce, aspen, balsam poplar, paper birch and, rarely, lodgepole pine at lower elevations. Sedge tussock fields are found in the valley bottoms that have poor drainage, with grassy meadows in other areas. There are no lakes in these valleys because of the angle of the slopes. At the toe of some glaciers, small ponds do occur.

The mountains are composed primarily of intrusive rock, with some metamorphic and volcanic rock also present. The intrusive rock is mainly granite and granodiorite, while the metamorphic and volcanic formations contain andesite, greenstone, quartzite, basalt, marble, argillite, phyllite, and slate.

Because of the harsh weather experienced in the St. Elias Mountains and their isolation, little meteorological data is available. It is known that the high peaks intercept most of the precipitation coming inland off the Pacific Ocean. This renders the southwest side of the mountains very wet and prone to extremely heavy snowfalls in higher elevations. For example, Yakutat, Alaska, on the Pacific side, receives about 3,364 millimetres of precipitation annually, while **Burwash Landing**, along the northeastern flank, receives only about 283 millimetres per year. Winter snowfalls in the mountains themselves average between 150 and 250 centimetres annually. Most of the mountains experience an average of 120 days per year when temperatures are lower than –20° Celsius. This is also the least sunny region of the territory, averaging between 1,200 and 1,400 hours a year, compared to the Yukon annual average of about 1,600 to 1,800 hours.

Selwyn Mountains

Following a north-south line parallelling the more easterly **Mackenzie Mountains**, the Selwyn Mountains contain a chain of glaciated mountain peaks, ridges, plateaus, and U-shaped valleys. The highest mountain in the Selwyns is 2,972-metre Keele Peak. The other peaks in these mountains range from about 2,100 to 2,700 metres. Higher elevations commonly feature bare rock outcrops and deposits of rubble.

Extensively glaciated, the Selwyns are composed of sedimentary strata intruded by granitic stocks. Three major icefields cover Keele Peak, the Itsi Range, and the Ragged Range respectively. The mountains contain several other valley and alpine glaciers. The valleys contain many small lakes, with bog fen common throughout the region.

The Selwyns are home to most of the animals found in the Yukon, including a number of woodland **caribou** herds that include the mountains in their range.

Virtually unexplored and unmapped until after World War II, the Selwyns remain extremely isolated. There are no major permanent settlements anywhere in the Selwyn Mountains and it is estimated that at most 50 people live here.

Northerly portions of the mountain range feature valleys that fall within the territory's **tundra** region, although black and white spruce and paper birch stands are found below 1,200 metres. **Permafrost** is extensive throughout the Selwyns but is discontinuous on western slopes.

The southerly portions of the mountains house the headwaters of such rivers as the Pelly, Ross, Macmillan, Hess, and Rogue, all of which drain into the **Yukon River**. Farther north, the divide between the MacKenzie and Yukon river watersheds occurs. Here, the Snake, Bonnet Plume, and Wind rivers flow into the Peel River, which in turn enters the MacKenzie; while the Beaver, Rackla, and Nadaleen rivers enter the Stewart River to eventually empty into the Yukon River.

The Selwyns were named in 1901 after Dr. Alfred Richard Selwyn, one of the most distinguished geologists of the late 1800s. Selwyn served as director of the Geological Survey of Canada from 1869 to 1895.

Sourdough

The unavailability of yeast in gold-mining camps during the **Klondike Gold Rush** led to this fermented bread dough's popularity with prospectors. The starter dough for the next batch of bread was saved from the previous batch, eliminating the requirement for yeast.

Klondike sourdoughs in front of the Keir brothers' claim. (Ernest F. Keir photo, NAC PA-126210)

Over time, the knowledge of how to bake sourdough bread became viewed as proof that the prospector was an experienced veteran of northern living. Such veterans had met the difficult challenge of surviving a northern winter from freeze-up to spring thaw. As many Klondike stampeders failed to establish a worthwhile claim after arrival in the spring and quit the north in disillusionment before freeze-up closed the region to outside travel, those surviving a winter were termed "sourdoughs" as a mark of respect. The term remains in common usage today.

During the **gold** rush, newcomers to the Yukon were usually called cheechakos, Chinook First Nations jargon for "newcomer." Chinook jargon was a form of language incorporating English, French, Chinook, and words from other **First Nations languages**, and was used throughout the western fur-trading operations during the 19th century.

Originally, prospectors adopted the moniker to differentiate inexperienced goldseekers from the veterans of previous gold rushes. Eventually the term came to denote those who had yet to weather a Klondike winter. Today, it is used throughout the Yukon to label newcomers who may, or may not, be able to endure a winter. Those who do graduate automatically to the status of sourdoughs.

Sour-Toe Cocktail

Since 1973, more than 12,000 people have become members of The Yukon Order of the Sour-Toe Cocktail by partaking of an alcoholic drink containing a pickled toe. The rite of passage can be taken at a **Dawson** hotel where the notorious order was founded by Captain Dick Stevenson in response to a dare.

According to the legend that has grown around this dare, Stevenson—a long-time Yukoner—discovered the petrified remains of a human toe under the floorboards of an abandoned cabin along the Sixtymile River near the Alaska border in 1973. Keeping the toe, Stevenson took to showing it off in Dawson saloons. This led to the suggestion that the toe should be dropped into a drink and as a manly dare Stevenson should swallow it. He apparently did. The act was witnessed by a newspaper reporter and so, not only was a legend born, but undoubtedly one of the most bizarre specialty drinks in the world was created.

Until Stevenson retired from his pickled toe hobby in 1995, he could often be found at the bar with a small wooden box containing severed toes that had been allowed to dry up, then preserved in salt and pickled. Those wishing to take the dare paid a fee, watched the drink prepared, watched the toe popped in, and then had to at least allow the toe to touch the lips. Braver souls, with strong stomachs, were known to follow Stevenson's example and actually swallow the toe. A certificate was awarded to either successful type of sour-toe cocktail drinker.

Since Stevenson's retirement, others have carried on the tradition of supplying the toes, donated by people—mostly Yukoners—who lose a toe to a badly swung axe, frostbite, or other calamity. Successful imbibers still get a certificate.

Special Events

Across the territory various special events are held throughout the year. The following is a selection of some of the most significant and regularly held events presented in a month-by-month fashion.

In January, **Haines Junction** hosts the annual Yukon Native Bonspiel and Alcan 200 International Snowmachine Race. The latter event features Canadian and American racers attempting to complete a 296-kilometre return race from Haines, Alaska to Dezadeash Lake with speeds exceeding 160 kilometres per hour.

February is a busy month across the territory. **Dawson** hosts the Annual Klondyke Centennial Ball, **Watson Lake** holds the Northern Lights Winter Festival, **Whitehorse** is the starting point for the **Yukon Quest** Sled Dog Race and the site of the Yukon Sourdough Rendezvous Festival known as the official cure for "winter cabin fever."

In March, Dawson holds the Percy DeWolfe Memorial Mail Race that follows the historic mail route along the **Yukon River** travelled by this determined mail carrier for 40 years. The route covers 338 kilometres from Dawson to Eagle, Alaska and back. **Mayo** holds its winter carnival in the third week of March.

Burwash Landing is home to the Burwash "27" Ice Races in mid-April, a car race on the ice of Kluane Lake that offers $10,000 in prizes. The Whitehorse Folk Society meanwhile holds concerts during the month as part of the Yukon Alaska International Folk Festival. Reciprocal concerts are held in Skagway, Alaska.

May is most noted for the Dawson City International Gold Show and the Kluane Mountain Festival at Haines Junction, which celebrates the people and geography of the **St. Elias Mountains**.

In June, Dawson is home to the Commissioner's Ball, hosted by the Commissioner of the Yukon Territory, where guests attend dressed in turn-of-the-century style. **Faro** holds an annual summer arts festival, and Haines Junction is the base for the Annual Kluane to Chilkat International Bike Relay, entered by as many as 1,000 cyclists each year. Whitehorse hosts the Yukon International Storytelling Festival, a four-day storytelling event that features First Nations storytellers and others from around the world.

Dawson hits high gear in July with the Yukon Gold Panning Championships, the Dawson City Music Festival, and the Moosehide Gathering. The latter is hosted by **First Nations peoples** from the Han culture sharing traditions and knowledge. It is open to the nations of the world, with all visitors invited to share their knowledge of past and present experiences and traditions, and future hopes. For something entirely different, check out Whitehorse's Great Canadian Yukon River Rubber Duck Race on July 1.

In August, Watson Lake gets into duck racing as well with the Discovery Days Celebrations and Annual Duck Race, while Whitehorse diversifies from ducks to bathtubs with the Annual Gold Rush Bathtub Race.

Come September, Dawson residents host the Great Klondike International Outhouse Race through the streets of the historic community, while residents of Burwash Landing release 800 plastic frogs as part of the Great Burwash Frog Race. In Whitehorse, the Klondike Trail of '98 International Road Relay has more than 100 teams comprising a total of 1,000 runners competing.

October is marked by the Francofete Festival celebration of French culture and heritage in the Yukon.

November is most noted for the more serious Yukon Geoscience Forum in Whitehorse where geoscientists gather annually to exchange scientific information. Some noted Yukon prospectors also participate. In December, Yukoners tend to retreat into their homes for a month to prepare for, and celebrate, Christmas.

SS *Klondike* National Historic Site

The SS *Klondike* National Historic Site located in **Whitehorse** preserves the largest of the Yukon River's **sternwheelers**, but this vessel is the second incarnation—the *Klondike I* having run aground and been wrecked in 1936. SS *Klondike* was constructed in 1929 at the Whitehorse shipping yards by the

British Yukon Navigation Company, a subsidiary of the **White Pass & Yukon Railway** company. It was considered a breakthrough in sternwheeler design because it maintained the traditional shallow draft required for plying the **Yukon River** while increasing cargo capacity by 50 percent. She could handle more than 272 tonnes of cargo in her holds and on deck.

Her short career ended when the *Klondike* ran aground on a section of the river between **Lake Laberge** and the Teslin River. Undaunted, the company immediately set about building the SS *Klondike II*, which was virtually identical to her predecessor. Launched in May 1937, the *Klondike II* was 64 metres long by 12.5 metres wide by 1.5 metres deep. Her registered tonnage was 918.45 tonnes and she could carry a cargo of 270 tonnes, along with 75 paying passengers housed in first- and second-class accommodations. The crew numbered 20 to 25. Power was provided by two 525-horsepower compound jet–condenser engines and a locomotive boiler that had been salvaged from the earlier *Klondike*.

It took the *Klondike II* about 36 hours to travel the 740 kilometres downriver from Whitehorse to **Dawson** and four to five days to steam upriver on the return trip. From 1937 to 1952 the *Klondike II* served primarily as a cargo vessel, carrying merchandise and passengers on the downstream journey and silver-lead ore mined at **Keno** and picked up at **Stewart Crossing** on the return to Whitehorse.

In 1950 an all-weather road was opened between **Mayo** and Whitehorse. The Keno silver-lead ore could then be transported by truck instead of sternwheeler regardless of the season. As the river was only free of ice for four to five months a year, the *Klondike II* could hardly compete and the ship's career looked bleak. A major refurbishment was undertaken in a last-ditch effort to transform the cargo ship into an elegant cruise ship but there was insufficient tourist traffic to finance its continued operation. In August 1957 she steamed into Whitehorse on her last upstream run and was subsequently donated to the federal government, which had the *Klondike II* meticulously restored to the 1937–40 period of her career and declared a national historic site.

Statutory Holidays

The following statutory holidays are celebrated in the Yukon: New Year's Day, January 1; Heritage Day, third Friday of February; Good Friday; Easter Sunday; Easter Monday; Victoria Day, third Monday of May; Canada Day, July 1;

Discovery Day, third Monday of August; Labour Day, first Monday of September; Thanksgiving, second Monday of October; Remembrance Day, November 11; Christmas Day; and Boxing Day.

Heritage Day and Discovery Day are statutory holidays in the Yukon only, while the rest are also celebrated in the rest of Canada.

Steamboats. *See* **Sternwheelers.**

Sternwheelers

Yukon **First Nations peoples** have always relied heavily on the Yukon, Stewart, Porcupine, Pelly, Peel, Alsek, Teslin, and other rivers as a primary means of transportation. When the first Europeans arrived in the territory in the 1840s seeking furs, they followed the First Nations example of moving by river and short portage routes that linked the various streams. In the 1870s, Hudson's Bay Company fur traders switched from using mainly canoes to 10- to 12-metre-long wooden boats known as York boats. Their main route through the territory was to travel from the Mackenzie River up a variety of small rivers that came close to connecting with the Porcupine River watershed, portage into tributaries of the Porcupine, and then follow this large river down to Fort Yukon, located at the Porcupine's junction with the **Yukon River**. Using York boats, the trade goods and supplies were floated down the river. Then, the traders made an arduous return trek, often having to drag the heavily laden boats upriver with ropes and winches.

The turnaround period, from the time a shipment of trade goods started the journey to Fort Yukon from York Factory on the shores of Hudson Bay until the furs finally reached England for sale to fur-manufacturing outlets, averaged seven years. The sheer logistical difficulty meant that, lacking a more efficient and safer route, the Yukon would never be more than a secondary fur source for the Hudson's Bay Company. The Russians trying to conduct a **fur trade** from coastal stations in Alaska were able to do a little better, but relied entirely on First Nations traders to acquire the furs inland and bring them to their stations on the Alaska coast rather than establishing their own presence in the Yukon.

Not until 1869 did a development occur that transformed the Yukon transportation system overnight into one that could be travelled relatively quickly

The sternwheeler Whitehorse *runs Five Finger Rapids.* (NAC C5230)

and inexpensively, in terms of workers needed. That year, the American-owned Parrott and Company launched the sternwheeler steamboat *Yukon* and sailed it from the river's mouth almost to **Five Finger Rapids**, proving that more than 1,600 kilometres of its waterway was navigable.

From that date on, the quickest, but still expensive, route to ship supplies and people into the Yukon was to travel by ocean steamer to St. Michael, Alaska near the river's mouth and then upriver in shallow-draft sternwheelers and other steamboats. Several sternwheelers were soon plying the Yukon River, carrying trade goods to the various posts and hauling out furs. The turnaround for these trips was cut from an average of seven years to about one year.

The early sternwheelers such as the *Yukon*, *New Racket*, and *St. Michael* were relatively basic in design and function. Their average length was only a little over 20 metres compared to an average of 45 metres for sternwheelers on the Mississippi and Missouri rivers in the 1870s. Generally these early sternwheelers made the journey upstream towing three to four barges carrying cargo and traders. Initially the sternwheelers were crewed by First Nations and Inuit men with European or American captains and engineers.

Although the journey upriver by sternwheeler was quicker than any other form of river or land travel, it remained somewhat perilous. Low water levels, constantly shifting channels in the river mouth and Yukon Flats section in Alaska, and submerged sandbars along the whole route all presented hazards.

Storms occurred frequently and the early onset of freeze-up could leave a stern-wheeler locked in the ice hundreds of kilometres from the home port of St. Michael. Then there were rapids at Five Finger Rapids and in the Ramparts that were rife with steep rock outcroppings, ledges, and boulders thrusting up in the channels. Added to these natural hazards were the usual sternwheeler calamities, such as mechanical breakdowns, boiler explosions, and onboard fires. During spring breakup, another challenge for the first captains up the river was to find and chart the main channel, which shifted each year with the breakup of the ice.

The sternwheeler operational season was only four to five months; the rest of the year the Yukon River was locked under ice. Because the entire river froze there were no safe harbours for steamers caught outside safe, well-prepared facilities. A sternwheeler caught in the ice was likely to have its hull crushed to pieces. Steaming up the river during spring runoff was also perilous, as the river contained large chunks of floating ice and tributaries poured flood levels of water out into the Yukon's main channel. Even when the Yukon was free of ice it was usual for the Bering Sea to remain frozen for a month longer, so that the ocean steamers carrying the year's supplies for the forts and prospectors, who were beginning to appear in the territory, could not reach St. Michael.

Despite these difficulties, sternwheelers provided the best means of transportation. With the beginning of the **Klondike Gold Rush**, however, the existing fleet was obviously too small and the craft too primitive to meet the needs of the stampeders flooding into the region. So began the Yukon sternwheelers' boom period. Until the late 1880s the Alaska Commercial Company, which had early on bought out Parrott and Company, held a monopoly on the industry, making the increasing numbers of miners working neighbouring creeks in Alaska and western Yukon dependent on its sternwheeler operation.

In 1889, the Alaska Commercial Company launched its biggest ship to date, the *Arctic*. Thirty-eight metres long and nearly 10 metres wide, it was the fastest ship in the fleet, capable of making four to five trips a season from St. Michael to the creeks at Forty Mile. But, on its maiden voyage, the *Arctic* slammed into a snag or rock and most of its cargo was lost during the desperate effort to keep the vessel afloat. This left many miners to survive on near-starvation rations that winter or to abandon their claims and retreat to St. Michael to escape a winter famine.

In 1892, another company arrived on the scene to provide competition. The North American Transportation and Trading Company launched a ship that was even larger than the *Arctic*. Named after the company's president, the *Portus B. Weare* was 53 metres long. Instead of towing barges behind the ship, Weare established a practice of pushing them forward with the bow. Additionally, the company's sternwheelers were fitted with two boilers, engines, and smokestacks. With more power, the ships could push more weight than the Alaska Commercial Company ships could pull. Weare also abandoned the tradition of hiring First Nations crews, opting to keep his crews all white.

With the start of the Klondike Gold Rush in 1897, the two companies suddenly faced an outbreak of competition that resulted in the greatest transportation boom of the territory's history. More than 30 companies announced intentions to set sternwheelers plying the Yukon River. But many of these failed to gain sufficient capital and never launched a vessel. Others naively purchased sternwheelers from San Francisco shipyards and tried sailing them up the Pacific and Bering Sea coastlines to St. Michael under their own power. Most of these arrived already hopelessly worn out from the difficult, stormy journey. The usual practice was to have the sternwheelers built in San Francisco and then either knocked down for shipping and reassembly at St. Michael or to have the sternwheeler lifted onto the deck of an ocean steamer and shipped intact to St. Michael.

Companies that did succeed in adding ships to the Yukon fleet were the Alaska Exploration Company, the Seattle-Yukon Transportation Company, the Empire Transportation Company, the Canadian Pacific Navigation Company, and the British American Steamship Company. Some of these companies, such as the North British American Trading and Transportation Company, had short life spans due to a lack of entrepreneurial shrewdness and good timing. Owned by former U.S.–frontier marshal Pat Galvin, the company was well financed by London, England banks to purchase two ships, the *Mary Ellen Galvin* and the *Yukoner*. The first was so badly constructed it never left San Francisco's shipyards. The second was purchased from another company already sailing on the Yukon and had the fame of having made the fastest round trip between **Dawson** and St. Michael. Not being organized to sail to Dawson in 1898 until September, the *Yukoner* failed to reach the boomtown before freeze-up but its crew managed to safely overwinter the vessel along the shore of the river in a hastily constructed makeshift harbour. Not until June of 1899 did the *Yukoner* reach Dawson, only to find little market for its supplies, which had largely spoiled. Galvin declared bankruptcy, left the Yukon, and reportedly died of cholera in Manila.

Meanwhile, the spring breakup of 1897 had brought the end of the Yukon's first sternwheeler, the *Arctic*. Reaching Dawson before any of the competition, the *Arctic* had become trapped in an ice jam. A decision was made to blast the ship free. Explosives were laid and a gigantic explosion succeeded in not only breaking up the ice but also largely destroying the sternwheeler.

During the **gold** rush's peak years from 1897 to 1900, about 135 steamers, tugs, barges, and launches worked the Yukon. Three of these rivalled the best ships on the Mississippi. The *Susie, Sarah,* and *Hannah,* all built in 1898, measured 68 metres long by 13 metres wide by almost 2 metres deep and could push three barges upriver at a speed of 24 kilometres per hour. They were also the most elaborately fitted ships on the river. Each had electric lights, steam heat, cold-storage plants, and well-ventilated state rooms for the wealthiest passengers, who dined on fine cuisine in luxurious dining rooms.

Competition between the shipping companies became increasingly fierce, with ships often racing to beat each other into Dawson. This led to wrecks and collisions, but few accidents resulted in injuries to crew or passengers. The worst disaster to befall the sternwheeler fleet occurred on September 25, 1906 when an explosion on the *Columbian* killed six crew (*see* **Columbian Disaster**).

One of the biggest problems facing the sternwheeler operations was the procurement of sufficient wood to fuel the boilers. An average steamer burned 25 cords a day. Coal was used only rarely because of the cost of importing it. Initially, steamer crews paused about every six hours and went ashore to fall trees and chop them into firewood. By the time of the Klondike rush the companies were operating woodyards supplied by contract woodcutters, with wood refuelling stations along the length of the route. By 1903, some companies started to experiment with burning imported crude oil from California, but wood continued to dominate the industry.

In 1903, the decline of the gold rush finally caught up to one of the biggest companies, North American Transportation and Trading Company, which posted a $400,000 loss. The following year the company shut down, but enjoyed a brief resurgence the next year, only to merge with another sternwheeler line in 1906. By 1912, the reorganized company shut its doors for good. World War I brought further mergers aimed at ensuring the survival of some of the fleet. By 1923 only one sternwheeler, the venerable *Yukon*, was sailing from Dawson to Fairbanks.

By this time the **White Pass & Yukon Railway** had largely displaced the sternwheelers as the cheapest and quickest means of transportation into the Yukon. Although steamboats would continue to ply the river until 1955, the combination of new **highways** and railways made them an anachronism long before the last one steamed into Dawson on August 18, 1955 on a final journey upriver. In August 1957, the SS *Klondike* completed its last voyage from **Stewart Crossing** to **Whitehorse** and the sternwheeler age formally closed.

Stewart Crossing

Situated 180 kilometres north of **Whitehorse** on the Klondike Highway, where it intersects the Silver Trail, Stewart Crossing is a small service centre for both **highways**. It has a **population** of about 50. The community is named after James G. Stewart, an assistant of Hudson's Bay Company trader and explorer Robert Campbell.

A fur-trading post was established here in 1868 and the community later served as an important refuelling stop for river steamships during and after the **Klondike Gold Rush**, as well as a port for transferring ore from the mines at **Keno** from shallow-draught steamboats to the larger river **sternwheelers**.

Symbols

The Yukon's coat of arms is composed of a red, blue, gold, and white shield surmounted by a malamute standing atop a mound of snow. Running down the centre of the shield are wavy vertical white and blue stripes to represent the Klondike's **gold**-bearing creeks. Red peaked forms on opposite flanks of the creeks symbolize the mountains, with gold circles inside the peaks standing for the territory's rich mineral resources. The cross of St. George tops the shield in honour of the early English explorers. At the centre of the cross a "roundel in vair" symbolizes the fur trade.

Commissioned by the federal department of Indian Affairs and Northern Development in the early 1950s, the coat of arms was designed by Alan Beddoes, an expert in heraldry. Queen Elizabeth II approved it in February 1956.

The Yukon flag consists of three panels, with the coat of arms appearing in the middle panel, which is white. Framing the coat of arms from below and extending up halfway on each side are sprigs of fireweed—the official flower of the Yukon. The inner panel is green and the outer blue. Green stands for forests, white for snow, and blue for rivers and lakes.

Fireweed derives its name from the fact that it is one of the first plants to appear in burned-over areas. It also grows in profusion along the Yukon's roadsides, streambanks, and lake shores. The entire plant is edible. Fireweed was adopted as Yukon's official flower in 1957, but it was not the legislative council's first choice. Three years earlier the council had selected the crocus only to find that Manitoba had beat them to it.

The Yukon's official gemstone is lazulite, a rare and beautiful phosphorescent stone. Relatively soft and easily scratched, lazulite is valued for its beauty and scarcity rather than its cut stone value.

In 1985, the Yukon's ubiquitous **raven** was adopted as the official bird after much lobbying by local citizens. Many First Nations myths credit Raven with being the creator of the world or of humankind.

The Yukon has no official motto.

Tagish

A tiny community of about 100, Tagish owes its existence primarily to the construction of a road from **Carcross** to Jake's Corner on the **Alaska Highway** in 1942 as part of a project to lay a gas pipeline from Skagway to **Watson Lake**. The major challenge in the 54.7-kilometre road's construction was to build a bridge across the Six Mile River, and present-day Tagish developed there out of a construction camp. It lies on a narrow strip of land between Tagish and Marsh lakes and the Six Mile River.

A little southeast of this point was a traditional Tlingit First Nations settlement known as Tagish, which means "fish trap." It was at this site that the **North-West Mounted Police** built the important post of Fort Sifton in early 1897 to bring some order to the onslaught of **gold** stampeders intending to launch hastily constructed boats on the Six Mile River, a tributary of the **Yukon River**.

All boats passing the police post were required to stop and register, enabling the police to keep track of the number of prospectors entering the region and to ensure the boats met even minimal construction requirements, so they would have some chance of a safe passage down the Yukon River. The post was closed in 1901 when the flood of miners slowed from a torrent to a trickle.

One of the co-discoverers of the gold on Bonanza Creek that started the entire **Klondike Gold Rush** was known to many non–First Nations Yukoners as Tagish Charlie, although the Tagish always knew him as Dawson Charlie. Like his uncle, Skookum Jim, and his aunt, Kate Carmack, who were also involved in the gold discovery, he was Tagish and was born near this community. Dawson Charlie had the distinction of becoming the first Yukon First Nations person to be granted the full right of Canadian citizenship by an act of Parliament because of the fame and wealth he gained from the discovery. He bought a hotel in nearby Carcross and became famous for his love of lavish entertaining. On January 26, 1908, while crossing a railway bridge at Carcross, Dawson Charlie fell into the frigid waters below and drowned.

Tagish today is a popular summer recreation spot with many cabins dotting the shorelines of the two lakes.

Teslin

With a population of about 450, Teslin is located at the 1,294-kilometre point of the **Alaska Highway** on the northeastern shoreline of Teslin Lake. This was historically a summer home for the Tlingit **First Nations peoples** of coastal Alaska and British Columbia. They were mostly nomadic and were the only First Nations people to live in the Yukon who did not speak an Athapaskan language.

In 1903, a permanent community was founded at Teslin with the establishment of a fur-trading post. Teslin's name is a derivation from the First Nations' name for the lake, which meant "long, narrow water." The post operated until about 1955, but the community remained active after its closure.

Today, Teslin is one of the largest First Nations communities in the territory and is home to the George Johnston Museum, which has the Yukon's largest Tlingit artifact collection. Johnston was a Tlingit hunter and trapper, and was also renowned throughout the territory for his skills as a photographer. Many of his black and white stills capturing early Tlingit life are on display in the museum, as is the 1928 Chevrolet car he imported to use on an eight-kilometre road he had constructed for his exclusive use. In winter, he also drove the car over frozen Teslin Lake.

The bridge linking Teslin to the highway is, at 575 metres, the longest span constructed on the Alaska Highway. Although the highway is a boon to the community today, supporting much of its economic health, the arrival of construction crews here in 1942 brought to the community many diseases for which the **population** had no immunity. Mumps, whooping cough, meningitis, and measles afflicted the residents and many died or suffered long-term consequences.

Tintina Trench

Resembling a deep valley cutting through the relatively low Yukon Plateau, the Tintina Trench provides an incredible display of plate tectonics. The trench is part of one of the world's longest topographically distinct features, known as the Tintina–Northern Rocky Mountain Trench Fault. It extends more than 2,600 kilometres from Alaska to Williston Lake in northeastern British Columbia.

The birth of the Tintina Trench dates back about 85 million years to a time when a huge plate, known as the Farallon Plate, which lay under the western Pacific Ocean floor, was converging on the westward-moving mass of ancient North America. At this time, much of present-day Yukon had yet to be created by the mountain-building process of plate tectonics. The Farallon Plate was broken into two parts by a spreading ridge rising between the two sections. One section drifted southeastward toward South America's northwest coast. The northern half, called the Kula Plate, travelled north toward the Aleutian Islands off Alaska.

As the Kula Plate drifted northward it placed enormous frictional stress on the rocks of the North American continent—stretching them apart in a process similar to the way toffee candy stretches when pulled in opposite directions. In the Yukon this effect caused the development of massive faults, many of them hundreds of kilometres in length.

Unlike normal faults, where one block of rock moves downward past another, or thrust faults, where one rises up over another, the faults here, known as transcurrent or strike-slip faults, are formed as blocks move horizontally past each other. In North America, all transcurrent faults trend northwesterly, with the westward side moving north in relation to the eastern block. The greatest of these faults is the Tintina–Northern Rocky Mountain Trench Fault. In the Yukon, the gap created between the two separated blocks is called the Tintina Trench, which extends from south of **Dawson** to the eastern boundary of **McArthur Wildlife Sanctuary**.

Easily recognized, the trench has been described by one geologist as "a gun barrel-straight valley with steep sides and a flat floor some 200 metres deep." Here the floor bedrock is seldom exposed, but there are points where minutely crushed rock, tightly folded strata, and lava flows can be recognized that were all created by the faulting process. That fault movement took place sometime between 85 and 40 million years ago, over many thousands of years. The chunk of rock on the westward side of the fault is believed to have moved at least 750 kilometres northwestward, creating the vast trench valley through which much of the Klondike Highway passes today between **Stewart Crossing** and Dawson.

(*See also* **Ancient Yukon**.)

Tourism

Each year almost 290,000 tourists from the rest of Canada, the United States, Europe, and other parts of the world come to the Yukon. During most of the summer, it is not unusual for the number of tourists in the territory to outnumber total Yukoners by two to three times. Certainly, during the prime tourist season, there are always far more tourists in the Yukon wilderness and on the territory's **highways** than residents.

Tourist numbers in the Yukon have been rising more or less steadily throughout the 1990s by 1 to 3 percent each year. Occasionally, outside influences—such as the cancellation by Air Canada of air service to **Whitehorse** from Edmonton—cause a slight, passing downturn in tourist arrivals. In 1997, tourism suffered after B.C. fishers, angry over Alaska's refusal to agree to catch limits on Pacific salmon, prevented the Alaska ferry from leaving Prince Rupert. The Alaska government responded by cancelling the ferry service for the remainder of the summer season, a move that resulted in the Yukon government condemning the actions of the B.C. fishers.

Tourism is considered to be the Yukon's second-largest industry, after mining, with an estimated boost to the territorial **economy** of more than $100 million per year.

Most tourists coming to the Yukon are from the United States, constituting about 82 percent of all visitors. More European travellers visit the territory annually than do Canadians. In 1996, for example, some 23,000 Europeans vacationed in the Yukon compared to only about 17,000 Canadians. Of the European tourists, about 75 percent are German-speaking and from either Germany, Austria, or Switzerland. These German-speaking Europeans are primarily responsible for the continuing increase in the numbers of Europeans visiting the territory. There has also been an increase in the numbers of South Pacific tourists, although this number remains low at fewer than 5,000 a year. The rise in South Pacific visitors is mainly due to the number of Australian tourists, which increased in 1996, for example, by 21 percent over 1995.

Tourists are drawn to visit the Yukon for two main reasons: to see the great wilderness expanses and related national parks and to visit the **Klondike Gold Rush** region around **Dawson**. Eco-tourist activities such as hiking, cycling, whitewater rafting, and various other guided recreational pursuits are increasingly important tourist draws. Traditional sport hunting and fishing outfitters also continue to constitute an important part of the Yukon tourism industry.

Despite efforts to enhance the Yukon's attractiveness to tourists as a winter destination, most travellers come in the summer. Most years fewer than 35,000 travellers pass through Canada Customs points of entry from January to April, with about the same numbers entering the territory from October to December. But in July the number of travellers peaks each year at between 83,000 and 85,000, with all summer months posting numbers only marginally lower.

Trails of '98

In mid-July of 1897 word of the **gold** discovery near **Dawson** reached the outside world and the **Klondike Gold Rush** began in earnest. By the fall and winter of 1897 as many as 100,000 people from all parts of North America and elsewhere in the world were trying to reach the Klondike. The majority of these people would only reach the various northern gateways to the Klondike in early 1898—hence the trails into the Yukon that were followed by the hopeful miners are commonly referred to as the Trails of '98.

Most famous of all the trails was the Chilkoot Trail—a 53-kilometre route over the coastal mountain range from Dyea, Alaska to Bennett Lake in British Columbia. Gold stampeders referred to it as the "cussedest trail this side of hell" because of the torturous climb over its 1,067-metre summit. About 30,000 stampeders travelled this route. The greatest challenge on this trail was the 6.4-kilometre ascent up the mountain that culminated in the 1,500 "Golden Stairs" hacked by entrepreneurs out of the 35-degree pitched slope of virtually solid ice and snow that covered the slope during winter months. As difficult as the winter ascent was, it was easier than scaling the boulder-strewn slope of other seasons.

Had the stampeders only been faced with one ascent of the Chilkoot, the pass would have been less cursed. But the **North-West Mounted Police**, fearing the influx of goldseekers would cause a famine in the territory if each prospector was not self-sufficient, required everyone entering Canadian territory from the Alaskan starting points to be equipped with a year's worth of provisions, about 521 kilograms of food and other supplies. In one ascent each prospector could carry a pack weighing about 22 kilograms. Unless the stampeder could afford to hire packers, who charged an average of $2.50 for each kilogram carried, the transfer of supplies over the Chilkoot required about 25 trips up and down the staircase.

The pitch of the trail at the staircase was so precipitous that no horses or other pack animals could be used. Within weeks of the stampeders arriving at the Chilkoot, however, entrepreneurs were erecting various types of tramways to mechanically move supplies from the base to the summit for a steep price. The most ambitious of these was the aerial tramway built by the Chilkoot Railroad and Transportation Company. Running 22 kilometres from **Canyon City** on the Dyea River to the summit, the steam-powered tramway boasted the world's longest single span—670.5 metres between supports—and could move nine standard-measure tons of supplies an hour.

Without doubt the Chilkoot was the most popular of the routes to the gold fields. In the winter of 1897–98 alone, some 21,000 were checked through the Canadian border station on the summit. The route was so popular primarily because it provided a relatively quick and—as the tramways began operation—direct route to the interior beyond the coastal and **St. Elias Mountains**. From Bennett Lake, the stampeders could travel by water from the headwaters of the **Yukon River** to Dawson—805 kilometres away by boat. In the spring of 1898 some 30,000 gathered on the lakes forming the headwaters of the river. Within 48 hours of the ice melting, 7,124 hand-constructed boats carrying almost 14,000 kilograms of supplies sailed for Dawson in a mass flotilla.

In 1897 a steady stream of goldrushers ascended the Golden Stairs of the Chilkoot Trail to reach Dawson and the gold fields. (R. Laroche photo, NAC C28652)

Not all the hopeful prospectors reached the interior by the Chilkoot Trail. The majority of those stampeders not using the Chilkoot Trail travelled the neighbouring 67.5-kilometre White Pass Trail—also known as the Skagway Trail. The White Pass had the advantage of more gradual grades than the Chilkoot, so could be crossed by pack animals. Appearances were, however, deceptive as the trail switchbacked through a terrain of bogs, boulder-strewn hillsides, seemingly endless river crossings, and numerous low mountain cross-ings before reaching Bennett Lake. In the fall of 1897, some 5,000 men and women set out on this trail. Only a handful reached the lake in time to travel down the Yukon River before freeze-up. About 3,000 horses were used by these goldseekers and almost all the animals perished en route because of the trail's terrible conditions and the frequent brutality of the people driving them. This event led to the trail earning a third ignominious name—Dead Horse Trail. Ultimately the White Pass would be the route taken by the **White Pass & Yukon Railway**.

A series of interconnected routes that led to the Yukon River via Teslin Lake and the Teslin River were known as the Ashcroft and Stikine Trails. One route extended from Ashcroft in the British Columbia interior up the Overland Route used by miners during the 1860–62 Cariboo Gold Rush, across 1,600 kilometres of rugged terrain. About 1,500 men and 3,000 horses are believed to have set out on this route, but only a few ever reached Dawson. Most turned around and fled back to Ashcroft long before reaching the Skeena River, where they would have been able to continue much of the trip by boat. Others, avoiding the difficult wilderness between Ashcroft and the Skeena River, used canoes and other boats to paddle up the Skeena River from its mouth on the British Columbia coast. The few who succeeded in defying the Skeena's strong currents still faced an overland trek to the Stikine River and another long trek through wilderness to Teslin Lake.

The Stikine Trail, which followed the Stikine River from its mouth to Telegraph Creek and then overland to Teslin Lake, was promoted by outfitters in Vancouver and Victoria as the best route to the Klondike. Thousands of the stampeders who took this route purchased tickets for, and expected to find, a railway spanning the 240 kilometres between Telegraph Creek and Teslin Lake. On arriving at Telegraph Creek, however, they discovered that only 19 kilometres of track had been finished and their only way to Teslin Lake was to tackle a narrow, rutted trail that offered virtually no forage for horses. Hundreds of stampeders fought their way across country by this route. Among them were the members of the **Yukon Field Force**.

Another all-Canadian route was the Edmonton Trail. This was really a series of inadequately explored and mapped trails leading from Edmonton via a circuitous network of rivers and overland crossings spanning more than 4,000 kilometres. About 1,600 people set off from Edmonton on a trek that took an average of two years to complete. Estimates vary, but it is doubtful that more than 150 actually reached the Klondike by this route. The remainder turned around or gave up along the way and settled in the vicinity of Peace River, Alberta. About 50 died en route, mostly from scurvy.

Those using the Edmonton Trail fared better than the several thousand who tackled Alaska from the south in an attempt to reach Dawson via the all-American route. On a map it appeared that the quickest route to the Klondike was to get dropped by boat at the head of either Yakutat Bay, Prince William Sound, or Cook Inlet. From here it was 600 kilometres across the icefields and treacherous passes of either the St. Elias or Wrangell mountain ranges. Fronting Prince William Sound was the 46-kilometre expanse of the Valdez Glacier, which some 3,500 men and women sought to cross in the winter of 1897–98. Only about 200 managed to successfully reach the Copper River, which promoters said would provide easy access to the Yukon's tributary, Tanana River. In reality, Copper River's swift currents were virtually impassable and less than 20 of the 3,500 are believed to have reached the Klondike. Many died in avalanches and blizzards encountered on the glacier, hundreds were permanently blinded by the glare off the ice, and the majority abandoned the trip long before reaching the other side of the Valdez Glacier. Of those who set off from Yakutat Bay or Cook Inlet, few if any succeeded.

If these all-American routes were notorious for their hardship, there was one American route that provided the easiest access to the Klondike. This was the "Rich Man's Route," so named because it involved travelling from start to end by commercial shipping. This route was, however, very expensive and well beyond the resources of most stampeders. There was one other drawback. The Yukon River was only ice-free for a short season and in the winter of 1897 and 1898— when most stampeders were trying desperately to reach the Klondike before the best claims were snapped up—the river was closed by ice. Eighteen hundred stampeders had set out on the river in the fall of 1897, but only 43 reached Dawson before freeze-up. The rest were stranded at various points along the river and many nearly starved. In the spring most had to retreat back to the river's mouth to resupply.

No matter which trail the stampeders took in 1898 most were disappointed on their arrival at the Klondike gold fields. After suffering terrible trials, crossing hundreds or thousands of kilometres of wilderness, and usually spending their life savings, the majority of the goldseekers found that the best claims had already been staked and the largest share of the gold to be found by **placer mining** had already been taken.

Tundra

The largest treeless area in Canada, as well as in the Yukon, the tundra accounts for 24 percent of the nation's land mass. Most of the 197,940 square kilometres of the Yukon total land area of 478,970 square kilometres that is unforested is considered tundra or transitional tundra range. The majority of the territory north of a line running from **Dawson** to where the Bonnet Plume Range fronts the **Mackenzie Mountains** falls inside the territory's tundra zone.

Plant growth in tundra regions is limited to short summer periods. Sedges, grasses, mosses, lichens, dwarf willows, and wildflowers are common tundra **vegetation**. Only a small, relatively thin biomass of vegetation develops in tundra zones because of the cold **climate** and extensive **permafrost** close to the surface. Rock outcroppings are common throughout.

Low annual precipitation levels throughout the tundra lead to striking similarities with desert climates despite the much colder temperatures, including the presence of stretches of drifting sand. In most areas of tundra the snow pack during winter is moderately thin, dry, and often piled in drifts by almost continual winds and occasional blizzards. Much of the wildlife found in the Yukon's tundra regions is migrational—returning to the tundra in the short, bright summer months and travelling south during the winter seasons.

Few Yukoners live in the tundra. The only permanent settlement of any size is **Old Crow**, which is inaccessible by road and home to a largely First Nations **population**. The **Dempster Highway** is the only highway route in the territory that provides direct access to the tundra's heartland.

Vegetation

Yukon vegetation consists primarily of boreal forest and **tundra** growth. In the southern Yukon, trees cover most plateaus and valleys, with the greatest tree variety found in the southeast Yukon. Here, white and black spruce, lodgepole pine, aspen, and balsam are common species. At higher elevations, alpine fir dominates in the south, central, and eastern Yukon, while white spruce occurs more often in subalpine forests in western and northern areas. Willow and shrub birch become increasingly prevalent toward the northern boundary where the boreal forest merges into the tundra region. Small grasslands occur in south and central Yukon on well-drained south-facing slopes.

Tussock fields of sedges or cottongrass, mixed with forbs, lichens, and mosses, constitute the main Arctic tundra vegetation. Also present are many dwarf shrubs and willows.

It is estimated that more than 1,300 plant species grow in the Yukon. In 1981, a National Museum of Canada project listed 313 of these plants as being rare. Although some are widely distributed throughout the territory, other rare plants occur only in a small area or within certain types of terrain.

Some plants occurring only in the Yukon date back to before the last ice age when these species would have been eliminated from other northern latitudes in Canada by **glaciation**. Much of central and northern Yukon escaped glaciation, along with an adjacent portion of Alaska. Although the southern Yukon was ice covered, many peaks protruded above the icefields. These peaks are known as nunatuks and provided unique biological refuges in which ancient plants were able to survive.

More than 30 distinct plant species survived on these islands amid the ice of the southern Yukon. Among these are *Carex sabulosa*, a type of sedge. It was first discovered in the **Carcross** Desert sand dunes in 1914 and has since been found on sand dunes at three other Yukon locations. In the larger Yukon/Alaska refugium (as the northern and central region which was never glaciated is sometimes known) the purple many-headed anemone has survived to the present day. It is now found on Arctic and alpine tundra regions in parts of northern Yukon and northern Alaska.

Vuntut National Park

Described by some naturalists as the "crown jewel of northwestern Canadian wildlife habitat," Vuntut National Park encompasses 4,400 square kilometres of the **Old Crow Flats**. This huge plain is riddled with more than 2,000 lakes and has a maximum elevation of 300 metres above sea level, providing a stark contrast to the surrounding Richardson, British, and Davidson mountains, and the Old Crow range that rise as high as 1,500 metres on all sides of the flats.

The national park protects this highly productive wetlands, which provides a nesting habitat for thousands of ducks and other water **birds**. It is also a vital staging and feeding ground for more than one million migrating waterfowl during the late summer and early fall. Both the wetlands and waterfowl habitat have been listed by several international habitat-preservation conventions as being of international importance to the survival and propagation of waterfowl species.

Vuntut National Park is equally important to mammalian species, especially grizzly **bears**, moose, and muskrats. The foothills and mountains surrounding the flats form part of the range of the 160,000-strong Porcupine barren-ground **caribou** herd.

The Old Crow Flats is a well-known archaeological site, providing the richest palaeontological and archaeological ice age mammal finds in the nation. During the Pleistocene Epoch, this unglaciated region was a haven for such species as **woolly mammoths**, mastodons, giant horses, lions, giant beavers, and camels—all of which eventually became extinct.

Vuntut is a Gwitchin word for Crow Flats. The use of a First Nations word for the park reflects the importance of the region to the First Nations who still dwell here, primarily residing in the nearby village of **Old Crow**. Settlement of the First Nations land claim by the Vuntut Gwitchin First Nations resulted in the park's creation in 1995. Under this agreement the park is cooperatively managed by the federal government and Vuntut Gwitchin First Nations council. For this purpose, the park is designated part of the Old Crow Flats Special Management Area. Under the land claim agreement, the current and traditional use of Vuntut by **First Nations peoples** is recognized and they are included as full partners in the management and preservation of wildlife and wildlife habitat within the park's boundaries.

Specific principles have been set out under the agreement that include: maintaining the area's integrity as one ecological unit; protecting and conserving **fish**, wildlife, and wildlife habitats considered of local, national, and international significance; and protecting the diversity of fish and wildlife populations and their habitats from activities that might reduce the land's capability to support animal species.

Vuntut National Park is, like the community of Old Crow itself, inaccessible by road. The nearest road is the **Dempster Highway**, which lies about 175 kilometres to the southeast. Air service is available to Old Crow from **Whitehorse**, **Dawson**, and Inuvik in the Northwest Territory.

Anyone visiting the park must be entirely self-sufficient. There are no services and no visitor information centre. Wilderness camping, hiking, and fishing are all possible. Limited accommodation is available in Old Crow and some outfitters conduct guided trips into the park from the village.

Water

The Yukon is a land of many rivers and comparatively few lakes. The lakes tend to be small and narrow, trending along valley floors that follow a north-south direction.

While lakes contribute very little to the hydrology of the territory, rivers exert a great influence on the ecology, **economy**, and social organization of the Yukon. The five primary rivers—Yukon, Porcupine, Peel, Liard, and Alsek—drain an area, within the Yukon alone, of 418,000 square kilometres. The **Yukon River** drains 264,000 square kilometres of the territory, about 14 percent more land than is drained by British Columbia's Fraser River.

The Fraser, however, has a much greater flow rate than the Yukon. The Yukon River has an average discharge rate of 8.4 cubic metres per 1,000 square kilometres of area drained, while the Fraser's rate of discharge is 14.7 cubic metres per 1,000 square kilometres. The Yukon's low flow is influenced by five major factors:

- Yukon Territory is climatically a semi-arid region with snowfall varying from 250 centimetres in the southwest to less than 100 centimetres in the Arctic. Annual rainfall varies from 200 millimetres in the south to 100 millimetres in the Arctic;
- Long winters result in low flows in late winter and peak flows in the early spring when the snow melts;
- Storage of snow in winter results in between 6 and 10 months of precipitation being released in one rapid early-spring melt;
- The territory's large southern lakes are capable of storing a significant amount of the water volume produced by the higher southern precipitation levels. This moderates the effect of seasonal flows and sporadic flows caused by storms. In the north, there are few lakes for storing water. Here, the

streams tend to experience high spring runoff and some flash flooding. Also, in the north, **permafrost** limits groundwater storage ability. This increases the runoff for northern rivers;

Glaciers dominate the **St. Elias Mountains** in the southwest, forming vast icefields. Alpine glaciers are also common throughout the Yukon in higher elevations. Glaciers tend to attract more water to them than they distribute over the surrounding lowlands. So the bulk of water provided to many Yukon rivers derives from glacial melt, which occurs later in the season. The peak runoff period for rivers fed by glacial melting is often late summer. In high snowfall years, glaciers melt less, and the volume of water reaching the rivers is reduced. Conversely, in low snowfall years, river flow increases due to greater rates of glacial melt.

None of this means that the Yukon is a water-poor part of Canada. Given its small population and the thousands of creeks and streams feeding into the major Yukon rivers, water is seldom hard for either wildlife or humans to find. It does mean, however, that there are limitations to the territory's ability to utilize rivers for hydroelectric projects, which remain the Yukon's main source of energy and are vital to most of its large mining projects. There are four hydroelectric dams in the Yukon located at **Whitehorse**, Aishihik Lake, **Mayo**, and Fish Lake west of Whitehorse. Collectively, they account for 76.3 megawatts of the territory's entire electrical capacity of 134 megawatts. Except for a small wind plant that produces 0.2 megawatts, the rest of the Yukon's electricity is generated by a community-based network of diesel plants.

Watson Lake

The third most populous community of the Yukon, Watson Lake has only about 1,800 permanent residents. It is also the territory's most southerly community and, because of its location as the first community encountered on the **Alaska Highway** north of the British Columbia border, is billed as the gateway to the Yukon. The town is situated at the highway's 1,051-kilometre point.

As is true of so many communities along the highway, Watson Lake boomed during the World War II–era construction period, serving as a major Canadian government–operated air force base. The airport was required as a stopover and refuelling station for American military planes en route from the U.S. to Russia to provide the Soviet military with supplies and equipment vitally needed to turn back the German invasion forces. In 1941, General Construction Ltd. started building an airport here for the federal government. Two runways, approximately 1,525 metres long, were constructed, a Royal Canadian Air Force squadron was brought in, and administration and staff quarters were erected for both air force and federal transport department personnel. U.S. army engineers also used Watson Lake as a major camp during the Alaska Highway construction.

The airport was built well in advance of the Alaska Highway so it was necessary to bring in building materials and personnel by an alternate route. This involved shipping supplies and equipment by boat from Vancouver, B.C. to Wrangell, Alaska, shifting loads onto river barges to travel 257 kilometres up the Stikine River to Telegraph Creek, and then trucking everything 122 kilometres over a virtually impassable road to Dease Lake. From here supplies and people were again loaded on barges and transported down the Dease River to its junction with the Liard River at Lower Post. From this point, it was another 42 kilometres by road to the airport construction site.

In early 1942, a homesick U.S. GI, Carl L. Lindley, painted the name of his hometown of Denville, Illinois and its distance away on a board and nailed it to a post so the arrow pointed in roughly the right southerly direction. It is doubtful Lindley intended to found a tradition but today more than 30,000 signposts erected by travellers passing through Watson Lake make up the Signpost Forest and point every which way, including directly up to the stars or down toward the Earth's core.

Watson Lake serves as a vital community centre for southeastern Yukon and is one of the larger service centres along the Yukon to Alaska section of the Alaska Highway. The Watson Lake Visitor Reception Centre has a display on the highway project's history that includes a multi-projector slide presentation. Nearby, the **Northern Lights Centre** planetarium explains the phenomenon of the **northern lights** through one of the world's most sophisticated multimedia facilities.

The name Watson Lake is derived from Yorkshireman Frank Watson, who wandered into the region in spring 1898 after departing Edmonton in early 1897 to travel the Edmonton Trail to the Klondike **gold** fields near **Dawson** (*see* **Trails of '98**). Like many other goldseekers using the Edmonton route, Watson spent more than a year battling his way through dense, unmapped tracts of wilderness. By the time he reached the upper Liard River, Watson was completely dispirited and realized that, if he continued the journey, his chances of living to see the Klondike were slim. The surrounding country, however, struck him as promising for both prospecting and trapping, so he stayed, married a First Nations woman from Lower Post, and built a cabin on the shores of a lake that soon became known by his last name, rather than the ubiquitous Fish Lake.

Still alive when the airport and highway construction crews arrived in the early 1940s, Watson found the influx of strangers and the noise of the work crews too disruptive. He moved his family a few kilometres north to Windid Lake and never moved back.

Whitehorse

With a **population** of approximately 24,000 of the Yukon's 33,580 people, Whitehorse is a vital cornerstone of the economic, political, social, and cultural life of the Yukon Territory. Its role as home to about 70 percent of the territory's population and as the undisputed service centre to the entire region was guaranteed when the territorial capital shifted here from **Dawson** in 1953. The addition of the majority of the Yukon's federal and territory **government** employees to the community secured its future. At the time, however, Whitehorse had a total population of about 2,300.

Whitehorse is located at the 1,455-kilometre point of the **Alaska Highway**. Most of the city lies on the west side of the **Yukon River** on a 600-metre-wide river plain walled by 60-metre-high escarpments. The escarpments serve to shelter much of the community in a valley-like setting that gives Whitehorse, by northern standards, a relatively mild **climate**. July temperatures average 14° Celsius, while in January the average temperature is −18.7° Celsius. Total precipitation averages 268.8 millimetres, with 59.4 percent occurring as rain and the rest as snow. In an average year, precipitation occurs on only 122 days.

Whitehorse came into existence as a stopover point for **gold** seekers heading to the **Klondike Gold Rush** who had just passed through three major hazards—**Miles Canyon**, Squaw Rapids, and Whitehorse Rapids. Unlike nearby **Canyon City**, Whitehorse enjoyed the advantage of being the final upstream point on the Yukon River accessible to **sternwheelers** and other larger river vessels. This resulted in Canyon City ultimately being abandoned in favour of Whitehorse.

In 1900, with completion of the **White Pass & Yukon Railway** (WPYR) between Whitehorse and Skagway, Alaska, the community's future centred on its role as a transportation and service hub for the territory. The town's core was focused at the junction of the railway with the small river port. The railway company played an essential role in Whitehorse's development, providing services and employment. Through its sister company—the British Yukon Navigation Company—it used Whitehorse as a riverboat-construction facility and operated a sternwheeler fleet between the community and Dawson until 1954. Throughout the 1920s and 1930s, the rail company also promoted Whitehorse as a **tourism** base for hunting and fishing expeditions into the surrounding wilderness. An air wing was added to the company's transportation operation in 1935, which flew out of Whitehorse.

Had WPYR not placed such emphasis for its various operations on Whitehorse, the community might well have faded away. By 1941, its population had declined to only about 750 people—most dependent in some way on the WPYR for their livelihood.

Whitehorse's fortunes, however, took a turn for the better with the outbreak of World War II and the decision to make the community the headquarters for the construction of the Alaska Highway. More than 3,000 U.S. army troops were housed in a tent city overlooking Whitehorse from a plateau atop the escarpments. A year after construction began, Whitehorse's population exceeded 10,000—the majority American military personnel. With the soldiers came the construction of new retail businesses, numerous warehouses, and houses that would remain when the army left at the war's end. As the highway passed the town on the west side, the orientation of the community permanently shifted away from the waterfront. By 1942 it was divided into two distinct sections—one bordering the river, the other atop the escarpment overlooking the one below. This geographical fragmentation of Whitehorse continues to affect local planning and development issues.

In the 1950s, Whitehorse became the territorial capital and emerged as the central hub for mineral exportation from the territory to outside markets. It continues in this role today. Whitehorse's population growth has continued to be relatively steady since the 1950s—growing incrementally from about 2,300 in 1951 to approximately 18,000 in 1981. In 1961 and 1971, Whitehorse's boundaries were expanded to encompass surrounding communities. It now covers about 413.5 square kilometres and has a population density of only about 57 people per kilometre.

Today, Whitehorse is a vibrant community with a diverse commercial core, a healthy arts and cultural sector, and a college. There are also several museums, including the **SS _Klondike_ National Historic Site** and the **Yukon Beringia Interpretive Centre**. The MacBride Museum offers 465 square metres of exhibits from prehistory to modern times. The Old Log Cabin Church Museum is a heritage church built in 1900. The Yukon Transportation Museum presents the history of northern travel, including **dog sledding**, early river travel, bush-plane aviation, railroad history, and displays about the Chilkoot Trail and other **Trails of '98**.

The name Whitehorse derives from the Klondike Gold Rush period, when miners en route to the gold fields at Dawson imagined that the whitecaps on the rapids downstream from Miles Canyon looked like charging white stallions. The town's name was originally separated into two words—White Horse. But in 1957, the Geographic Board of Canada joined them together.

Whitehorse Fishway

Built in 1959 and located on the outskirts of **Whitehorse**, the Whitehorse Fishway is the world's longest wooden **fish** ladder. It is 366 metres in length and 2 metres wide by 2 metres deep. The fishway was constructed to enable migrating chinook—known in the U.S. as king—salmon to pass by the first phase of the Whitehorse Dam, constructed by the Northern Canada Power Commission in 1957–58.

The fishway enables hundreds of chinook salmon to reach spawning creeks and beds on the **Yukon River** that are as much as 3,000 kilometres upstream from the river's mouth in Alaska. This migration takes the salmon an average of three months to complete and leaves them incredibly battered. The migration is only undertaken by Yukon River–spawned fish six or seven years after birth, and on average only 150 to 1,500 fish per year make the journey. These low numbers render the Yukon River chinook salmon among the world's most resilient but fragile spawning populations.

Attracted to the fish ladder by water discharging from it, so that the fishway mimics the Whitehorse Rapids which the dam replaced, the salmon migrate up the ladder by jumping over partitions separating its many steps or by swimming through underwater doorways constructed in each partition. At the halfway point there is a large chamber where the salmons' size and gender can be recorded by observers. Some of the salmon are captured here and taken to the Whitehorse Rapids Fish Hatchery, the most northerly salmon hatchery in Canada.

Not all the migrating salmon use the ladder; some try to negotiate the dam turbines and spillway. About 20 percent of the salmon attempting these routes through the dam die in the process. To replace the numbers lost in traversing the obstacle of the dam, the Whitehorse Rapids Fish Hatchery, located one kilometre downstream, draws on captured salmon to breed 350,000 to 400,000 fry each year for release in late spring as a supplement to the natural spawning process. When salmon migration success rates are average to better than average, the fry are produced by collecting sperm and eggs from about 75 captured female and 60 captured male salmon, fertilizing the eggs, and incubating them over winter. It is estimated that about 80 percent of eggs, fertilized and incubated in the hatchery survive to the fry stage, compared to only about 10 percent in the wild. The fry are released at two main spawning sites: Michie and Wolf creeks.

The Whitehorse Dam originally had two turbines generating 11.6 megawatts of power. In 1969, a third turbine boosted capacity to 20 megawatts, followed by the addition in 1984 of a fourth turbine, bringing total capacity to 40 megawatts. The Whitehorse Dam generates more than half of the territory's entire hydroelectric production of 76.3 megawatts. Seasonal variations in river flow, however, greatly affect the power generation capability of the dam. During winter freeze-up, power production generally declines to only 24 megawatts, precisely the season when Whitehorse heating requirements require the most energy.

Whitehorse Rapids. *See* **Canyon City; Miles Canyon; Whitehorse Fishway.**

White Pass & Yukon Railway

Shortly after the discovery of **gold** in the Klondike in 1896, stampeders started using the White Pass as a route from the Pacific coast to the headwaters of the **Yukon River** (*see* **Trails of '98**). From the headwaters, they then travelled down the river by boat to **Dawson** and its adjacent gold fields.

On February 20, 1899 the first passenger train over the White Pass paused at the summit for this photo of the passengers and train crew. (Yukon Archives, Macbride Museum Collection, #4120)

With an elevation of 889 metres, the White Pass straddles the Alaska and British Columbia border, providing the most gradual climb from the coast to the interior of the Yukon. For this reason, it was selected as the optimal route for a railway from Skagway, Alaska to **Whitehorse** by a group of entrepreneurs in 1898, led by the Church brothers of London, England. Initial fieldwork into the feasibility of the railroad yielded the opinion that the project was beyond the capability of contemporary engineering expertise. Canadian contractor Michael J. Heney, however, convinced company officials that he could successfully construct the railway.

Work began in 1898 to construct what was to be the steepest-pitched railway in Canada. It was a daunting project. Virtually every kilometre of trackbed had to be blasted out with dynamite and the grade required extensive rock support work. Local timber proved too small and weak for ties, stringers, or bridges and timber had to be imported from the south. Heney's railroad crews worked around the clock during the summer months, but were often driven out of the pass by winter snows and blizzards.

On February 20, 1899, however, the summit was reached by crews working eastward from Skagway. From the summit, the Skagway crew continued down from the pass and linked up with a crew working westward from Whitehorse at **Carcross** on July 29, 1900. The 177-kilometre railway had cost $10 million and had a maximum gradient in the pass of 3.9 percent. As the last spike was driven at Carcross, however, the gold fields in the Klondike were already largely exhausted and goldseekers were either leaving the north or rushing off to a strike at Nome, Alaska.

The primary reason for the railway's construction had been to service the gold fields. Undaunted, the owners of the railway struggled to keep it alive during the early 1900s by carrying small amounts of passengers and freight. The company also added a riverboat component to its operations so that it could control the movement of goods from Skagway to Whitehorse by rail and then by **sternwheelers** down the Yukon River to Dawson and communities in eastern Alaska. During construction of the **Alaska Highway** in 1942, the U.S. army breathed new life into the struggling railway by leasing its operations to move construction supplies and workers into the territory.

The mining boom in the 1960s again revived the failing railway, especially the development of a lead and zinc mine at **Faro**. When this boom ground to a halt in 1982, the little railway finally closed and Whitehorse lost its sea-rail link.

Throughout its history, the railway never received a government subsidy, not even for the track's initial construction. With the problems the railway faced economically and in trying to maintain the track over difficult terrain, the trains often ran behind schedule. This led to the company's initials often being touted as standing for "Wait Patiently and You'll Ride."

Today the railway has been partially revived with an excursion train running tourists from Skagway to the summit on a regular basis and providing limited charter service from Skagway to Whitehorse and back.

Wolves

The vast, relatively unpopulated Yukon provides good habitat for many species that are threatened or vulnerable elsewhere in Canada and the world. The grey, or timber, wolf is one such species. Although viewed as being at risk internationally by the Convention for International Trade in Endangered Species (CITES), wolves have established a presence throughout all 23 of the territory's **ecosystems**.

There are an estimated 4,500 wolves in the Yukon, based on population density surveys that have been conducted over about one-third of the territory. Wolf densities are highest in areas where there is relative abundance of the wolf's prey species, primarily moose, **caribou**, and mountain sheep. The highest densities are in the Teslin Burn area in south central Yukon. The lowest densities are found in the Carmacks-Nisling area in west central Yukon and in northern Yukon. Elsewhere in the territory, wolf population density averages about 8 to 10 wolves per 1,000 square kilometres.

The wolf's significance to First Nations culture and spirituality renders it an important Yukon species. The matrilineal clan system of many Yukon **First Nations peoples** means that a person is a member of one of two clans—wolf or crow.

Concern about the impact of wolf predation on declining woodland caribou populations has prompted two short-term controversial wolf kill programs in the Finlayson and Aishihik areas during the 1990s. Under the programs, wolf numbers were reduced over five to seven years in combination with caribou-hunting closures to boost the calf survival rates in these threatened herds. In the Finlayson area, long-term research from 1983 to 1995 has recorded increases in both the wolf population and the population of woodland caribou and other prey species.

Wolf control programs are highly controversial. In the Yukon, the program is guided by the Yukon Wolf Conservation and Management Plan, which was written by a public panel and adopted by the **government** in 1993. It calls for regular review and close monitoring of wolf, caribou, and moose populations. It also sets out guidelines for the way in which the wolf kill is conducted. Although the plan is strongly condemned by many environmental groups, it has also shown recognition in the territory that wolves have a right to exist rather than to be killed indiscriminately.

Each year about 100 wolves are killed annually by trappers for their fur and by hunters for sport.

Male wolves weigh between 35 and 60 kilograms, while females are slightly smaller and lighter. There is great colour variation, ranging from black to white, with most being a dull brown or grey. They have broad faces and their eyes are always shaded a tinge of yellow.

Wolves are pack animals, living in packs composed of a mating pair, pups, and close relatives. Pack numbers average 4 to 7 but can reach 14. Each pack has a set territory that varies from 130 to 1,500 square kilometres. Their tireless gait can carry them over 30 to 40 kilometres a day.

Their senses of smell and hearing are extremely keen, while their eyesight is also good. A wolf howl is best described as "a long, guttural, quavering wail," a sound humans find thrilling or threatening, although there has never been a documented case of a wolf killing a human in North America.

Wolves primarily hunt big game, which accounts for about 80 percent of their total diet, including moose, caribou, elk, deer, mountain sheep, and bison. They also eat rabbits, marmots, mice, and other small **mammals**.

Hampering their hunting effectiveness is the fact that, over short distances, wolves are slower than many of their regular prey. They make up for this by being stealthy and cunning hunters that work well as a team. Wolves have been known to split into units, with one driving the prey directly into an ambush set by the rest.

Wood Bison

The North American wood bison once roamed most of the boreal forest of north-western Canada, including parts of southern Yukon. Although wood bison are generally believed to have disappeared from the Yukon as long as 1,000 years ago, the population thrived further south and to the east. The cause of the disappearance from the Yukon is unknown, but some theories attribute their disappearance to overhunting, climatic change in the form of harsher winters reducing grazing area, and diseases to which wood bison are prone, such as anthrax.

In the early 1800s, the entire species population numbered about 168,000. But with the introduction of firearms to **First Nations peoples** and the arrival of Europeans, wood bison populations—like those of the related plains bison—were quickly decimated. Hunted for fur, meat, sport, and to remove this natural competitor to cattle and other domestic livestock, by 1891 only about 300 wood bison remained anywhere in the world.

Since then, the federal, territorial, and relevant provincial governments have all endeavoured to bring the species back from looming extinction. The efforts have started to pay off.

By 1975, the species had stabilized sufficiently in two reserves in Alberta and the Northwest Territory to begin a program to re-establish the species in other areas. Seven captive breeding herds and three free-roaming herds now exist in western Canada. The Yukon herd was started in 1986 when 34 adult wood bison were transplanted from Elk Island National Park in Alberta to the Nisling Valley west of **Carmacks**. For two years the bison were kept in a 6-square-kilometre enclosure to enable them to adjust to the new **climate** and feed. A first group of 18 bison was released into the wild in 1988. By 1992 another 60 had been released.

The health and distribution of the animals is monitored by radio collars attached to some of the animals and through aerial surveys. The re-establishment program aims to nurture the free-roaming herd until its population reaches 200 adults, at which time it will be considered a success and the herd should be self-perpetuating.

The wood bison remains listed by the Committee on the Status of Endangered Wildlife in Canada (COSEWIC) as threatened in the Yukon and is also covered by special protection legislation through the Yukon Wildlife Act (*see* **Endangered Species**).

Wood bison have larger horn cores and denser fur than plains bison. They are longer from nose to tail, more elongated in front, and darker in colour. They weigh an average of 840 kilograms. Unlike plains bison, wood bison bulls do not assemble female harems. Rather they defend one female until she is ready to mate. They do not usually undertake the long migrations that are characteristic of plains bison.

Healthy adult bison have no natural enemies other than humans. Calves, however, are vulnerable to predation by **bears**, **wolves**, and coyotes. Congregating in herds provides the adult bison with an ideal environment for protecting the young until they can fend for themselves. It also meets the need of these highly gregarious animals for the company of their own species.

Woolly Mammoths

Once these hairy elephants roamed throughout the Yukon before becoming extinct about 11,000 years ago. The mammoths grew to approximately three metres high at the shoulder, or about the size of today's Asian elephants. They also had a similar dental structure, with massive cheek teeth.

The woolly mammoth's coat was similar to that of the modern-day muskox, consisting of up to 90-centimetre-long dark guard hairs and fine underwool underlain by an insulating fat layer that could be up to 90 millimetres thick. Mammoths probably shed their coats in summer, as do muskox.

Their trunk was shorter than those of present-day African or Asian elephants, their head was high and peaked, and their tusks were up to 4.2 metres in length and elaborately curved. Males' tusks were larger than those of females. Tusk remains often show signs of wear, suggesting that the mammoths scraped them against the ground while rubbing snow and ice off **vegetation**. The woolly mammoth's habitat was cold, where tundralike conditions prevailed. It preferred grasslands where food was plentiful.

Remains of woolly mammoths have been found in northern parts of Eurasia and North America. The species is believed to have originated in north central Eurasia about 150,000 years ago from steppe mammoths. Over time they spread west throughout Europe and east via **Beringia** into northern North America. During the last **glaciation**, most of Canada was sheathed in ice and the mammoth was isolated in refuges north and south of the ice sheets.

One of the best mammoth remains found in Canada was a skeleton discovered on the Yukon's Whitestone River. It was radiocarbon dated as having died about 30,000 years ago.

Woolly mammoths are believed to have been a favoured food source for the early humans who crossed the Bering Strait land bridge into North America and lived in Beringia, the ice-free corridor that encompassed a large portion of the Yukon. Archaeological finds of mammoth bones in the **Old Crow Flats** show indications of breakage caused by humans. Their fur was probably prized for warm clothing. There is evidence that the bones were used by Paleolithic humans as structural supports for huts, and as needles, awls, harpoons, boomerangs, cleavers, shaft wrenches, musical instruments—primarily flutes—figurines, dolls, bracelets, beads, pendants, and combs.

When the ice age ended about 10,000 years ago, major climatic changes destroyed the grass ranges and this is generally believed to have led to the mammoth's extinction, although another theory credits its disappearance to human overhunting.

Today, mammoth ivory tusks are often uncovered by **placer mining** operations throughout the territory. As a consequence, ivory is a welcome byproduct for miners, who are often able to get prices ranging from $1 to $500 a kilogram depending on the condition of the tusks. Whole tusks are particularly valuable, fetching good prices from museums and collectors. Mammoth tusks usually survive in such excellent condition only in northern climates where **permafrost** is present. In the Yukon, mammoth tusks were further protected from the ravages of time because the region remained relatively ice free during periods of glaciation. Elsewhere, glacial ice often crushed and splintered the tusks into pieces.

Because all mammoth tusks are at least 10,000 years old and can be more than 100,000 years of age, Yukon artists and jewellers have to use special techniques to work the ivory, which is always in poor condition compared to modern ivory. Usually this entails cutting the ivory into pieces and allowing it to dry for several years in a cool, dark place. Once cured, the ivory is sufficiently stable that it can be easily worked. The colour of mammoth ivory ranges from white to grey to brown, ensuring great variety in the jewellery pieces created from it. Often jewellery made from ivory tusks is inlaid with semiprecious stones and **gold**.

Yukon Archives

Situated in **Whitehorse**, adjacent to Yukon College, the Yukon Archives provides an extensive resource for researching the territory's history, culture, and social and economic development. The archives contain **government** records, photographs, corporate records, private manuscripts, films, sound recordings, a Yukon-focused library, maps and plans, and newspaper collections. Almost everything contained in this collection pertains to the archives mandate to acquire, preserve, and make available documentary sources related to Yukon history, cultures, and development. The collection is stored in a fireproof security vault equipped with temperature and humidity control systems.

The government records stored at the archives contain documents dating back to 1896. Subjects covered in these records include **education**, elections, wildlife, transportation, legislation, and land issues. Territorial records also contain the Territorial and Gold Commissioner's Court records and the Public Administrator estate files. There are records of the **North-West Mounted Police**, Yukon Telegraph Service, and microfilm copies of the United States Army and Northwest Service Command records relevant to construction of the **Alaska Highway** and the **Canol Road** and pipeline.

More than 57,000 photographs portraying miners and mining activity, **gold dredges**, **sternwheelers** and river travel, pack trains, stagelines, aviation, the Alaska Highway, **White Pass & Yukon Railway**, **First Nations peoples**, North-West Mounted Police, scenes of the **Klondike Gold Rush**, and stampeders on the **Trails of '98** are held.

Corporate records include those of the 1899 to 1960 operation of the White Pass & Yukon Railway, correspondence and dredging records of the Yukon Gold Company from 1907 to 1920, Yukon Order of Pioneer records from 1886 to 1980, and many other collections that provide economic and social history information on the territory.

The private manuscript collection includes diaries, correspondence, scrapbooks, account books, and other papers of individuals associated with the Yukon as financial agents, lawyers, politicians, naturalists, miners, doctors, clergy, writers, and researchers. Klondike Gold Rush material is particularly well represented, including the Henderson family papers from 1892 to 1947, some of the papers maintained by Martha Louise Black, and Klondike Kate Rockwell's correspondence between 1922 and 1955.

Martha Black was a Chicago-raised socialite who came to the Yukon in 1898 after divorcing her husband en route. She stayed for the rest of her life. In 1904, Martha married lawyer George Black, who became a territorial commissioner in 1912. After World War I, he represented the Yukon in the House of Commons for four terms. In 1935, illness forced Black to retire. Martha, then in her sixties, ran for election in his place. She won, becoming the second woman ever elected to the Canadian parliament. For her part, Kathleen Eloisa Rockwell arrived in **Dawson** in 1900. Already a veteran of southern dance halls and theatres, she quickly established herself as Klondike Kate. Through an impressive campaign of self-promotion, Klondike Kate emerged as the undisputed queen of the Dawson dance halls, helping establish the stereotype of Klondike women being mostly dance hall girls and prostitutes.

Film footage contains scenes from the construction of the Alaska Highway and Canol project, gold rush scenes, sternwheelers, railway travel, and early aviation. In the sound recording collection are tapes with interviews about First Nations history and traditions, and pioneer life.

The library has more than 14,500 volumes in its collection. Primarily Yukon in emphasis, this collection includes monographs and series concerning history, ethnography, northern development, northern pipelines, community surveys, and scientific, social, and economic studies. Its map collection consists of 8,500 maps, plans, and atlases relating to the Yukon and northwest Canada. Included are exploration maps, gold rush route maps, townsite and lot plans, river survey maps, numerous sketches of creeks and tributaries in the Klondike gold fields, and route maps for the White Pass & Yukon Railway and the Klondike Mines Railway.

One of the archival treasures is its holding of more than 50 individual newspaper collections. These include the 1898 to 1903 editions of the *Klondike Nugget*, 1899 to 1904 issues of the *Yukon Sun*, and the *Dawson News* from 1899 to 1953.

Yukon Beringia Interpretive Centre

Opened in 1997, the Yukon Beringia Interpretive Centre tells the story of **Beringia**. This multimedia exposition features life-sized exhibits of animals of the last ice age, interactive CD-ROM kiosks, and dioramas depicting the unique landscape, flora, and fauna that characterized the ice-free portion of the Yukon between 25,000 and 15,000 years ago. Highlights of the centre include a full-sized cast of the largest **woolly mammoth** ever discovered and a reconstruction of the 24,000-year-old Bluefish Caves archaeological site near **Old Crow**.

Operated by the Heritage Branch of Tourism Yukon, the centre is located beside the Yukon Transportation Museum near the **Whitehorse** airport. It is open daily from mid-May to mid-September, with reduced hours the rest of the year.

Yukon Field Force

By the fall of 1897 the federal government realized that the following year would see a minimum of 30,000 prospectors in the Yukon. News of the **Klondike Gold Rush** was spreading rapidly throughout the world. But nowhere was the news generating more excitement and causing greater numbers of prospective

The Yukon Field Force musters for a drill parade, 1900. (Larrs and Duclos photo, NAC C1339)

stampeders to head for the territory than in the depression-struck United States. Additionally, most of the prospectors to arrive first at the **gold** fields were Americans from Alaska. By early 1898 U.S. citizens accounted for more than 80 percent of the Yukon's total **population**.

The predominance of Americans in the Yukon sparked fears that Canadian sovereignty might be threatened. Not that the government was seriously concerned that the U.S. might try to forcibly annex the Yukon to Alaska. Rather, the fear was that the Americans in the territory might take matters in their own hands and stage a coup. If they seized the tenuous symbols of Canadian sovereignty, such as the district mine licensing office, and disarmed the 232 members of the **North-West Mounted Police** (NWMP) who were in the territory, there was no certainty that the United States would not choose to recognize the prospectors' claims that they wanted to be protected under the American flag. Virtually every American miner in the territory carried at least one personal firearm so, if it came to a contest between the Mounties and the miners over national issues, there was little doubt that the police would lose the fight.

The newly appointed Commissioner for the Yukon Territory, Major James Morrow Walsh, himself a former Mountie, worried about "how thoroughly this district is in the hands of a foreign element. It would be the easiest thing in the world for a few bold men to take possession. If such a thing did happen, not another Canadian Policeman or soldier would be permitted to cross the United States territory to reach this district." Access to the Yukon was another critical issue. There was, at the time, no viable route into the Yukon that did not pass through some part of Alaska.

Neither was the likelihood of the United States accepting the outcome of a localized coup that far-fetched. Both Oregon and California had been brought under the American flag through similar scenarios.

The federal government's initial response was to open negotiations with civil engineering firms to construct a narrow-gauge railway into the territory from the navigable head of the Stikine River in British Columbia to Teslin Lake in the Yukon, some 232 kilometres away. The Yukon Railway Bill called for House of Commons ratification of a contract the Liberal government had signed with the civil engineering firm of Mackenzie and Mann. This deal called for the company to receive a grant of 10,000 hectares of land and a border on the right-of-way for every 1.6 kilometres of track laid. When the bill to ratify the contract came before Parliament it was immediately condemned by the opposition as an overly generous sop to the railway company. It was during this acrimonious debate, however, that the idea of sending a Canadian military force to the Yukon was first floated. The idea was that of North York MP N. C. Wallace, who actually argued that the Mounties could easily maintain law and order in the territory. But, he added, "I think it quite a proper safeguard to send a force to the Yukon Territory, a moderate force."

Minister of the Interior Clifford Sifton, fearing the railway bill would become hopelessly mired in the pro-Conservative Senate, agreed that the danger posed to Canadian sovereignty was real. The Mounties, he said, would find themselves in the coming winter surrounded "by starving thousands of armed men, of alien men, not citizens of Canada, but citizens of foreign countries, and these men would have possession of the Yukon district instead of the Government of Canada." He continued, "We have before us the great danger of the authority of this government being over-ridden, being destroyed, and the Government of that district being, theoretically, if not actually, taken out of our hands."

On March 10, Prime Minister Sir Wilfred Laurier advised that "a small corps is being prepared at the present time to be sent out at the earliest moment." Eleven days later an Order-in-Council directed that "a Field Force composed of volunteers from the permanent troops of the Dominion should be dispatched to

Fort Selkirk." On May 4, Minister of Militia and Defence Dr. F. W. Borden defended the decision before the House of Commons. A permanent military force in the Yukon, he said, "would have a decided moral effect upon the scattered population throughout the district." The force, he said, would make the trip via the Stikine River and overland to Teslin Lake and then by boat to Fort Selkirk. Armed with Lee-Enfield rifles, two Maxim machine-guns, and two seven-pound guns, Borden was confident the force would make the appropriate statement of sovereignty to the Americans.

It was not really surprising that the federal government decided that such a gesture of armed might was a necessary and appropriate response to the presence of so many Americans within Canadian territory. This situation had existed before in 1873 and had given birth to the very NWMP that the Field Force was now being dispatched to reinforce. In present-day southern Alberta, American whiskey traders had erected a number of forts on Canadian land and were considered a threat to national sovereignty. To close the forts and secure the authority of the federal government over these lands, Ottawa sent out a force of some 275 officers and men, nicknamed the Thin Red Line, and officially designated the North-West Mounted Police. The show of force had the desired effect. The forts closed without a shot being fired and there were no further threats to Canada's jurisdiction over any lands north of the 49th parallel.

This time, rather than creating a scratch force from militia members and volunteers, the government decided to cobble a unit together from existing troops, despite the fact that it would strip the regular army of roughly a quarter of its full-time strength. Placed in command was Major Thomas B. D. Evans, who was given a promotion to acting lieutenant-colonel. Having risen from the ranks, Evans was a highly qualified soldier competent in commanding infantry, artillery, and cavalry. On May 6, 1898, Evans departed Ottawa by train with a command of about 190 officers and men. Two days later, the force picked up another 16 men in Winnipeg. The Yukon Field Force, as it was formally identified, was joined by six women, four of whom were members of the Victorian Order of Nurses, and 11 employees of the Department of the Interior en route to **Dawson** for administrative duties.

Never before in Canadian history had a military force been deployed to such a northern location. Further complicating matters, the only way the force could reach the territory was to pass through the sovereign lands of the very nation it was concerned might annex the Yukon.

This potentially difficult diplomatic circumstance led the Yukon Field Force to take a route that was less direct than it might have been. The simplest route would have been to sail through Alaska on the **Yukon River** to Fort Selkirk. Although the 1871 Treaty of Washington granted Canada the right of free navigation on the Yukon, Porcupine, and Stikine rivers in exchange for U.S. rights of navigation on the St. Lawrence, it was felt that sailing a heavily armed contingent of Canadian troops up the Yukon could cause an international incident. The Chilkoot and White Pass routes to the territory were also ruled out because the force would have to get permission from Washington to drag its machine-guns, artillery, and other military supplies over American territory. Considering these problems, it was decided that the Field Force would travel the so-called "all-Canadian route," which, because it started at Wrangell, Alaska, was not really all-Canadian at all. This route, however, did allow the force to move through Alaska by an all-water route up the Stikine through only a little-populated and isolated corner of the Alaskan Panhandle.

On May 19, 1898, the Yukon Field Force sailed from Wrangell aboard two river steamers en route to the Yukon. A few hours later the ships passed into Canadian territory. What followed was a harrowing and gruelling journey over land that was unmapped and in many cases unexplored. It would not be until September 11, 1898 that the troops arrived aboard a small flotilla of handbuilt boats and scows at Fort Selkirk. More than four months after leaving Ottawa, the Yukon Field Force established its presence in the territory.

By this time, however, **government** officials in the Yukon were already having second thoughts about the need for the force's deployment. On November 12, 1898, the new Yukon Commissioner, William Ogilvie, wrote Ottawa to advise that there was no more need for "the presence of the militia in the country." Ogilvie added that: "As for a rebellion, the time for that is past and gone."

In July 1899, the government ordered the Field Force reduced to half its strength. On September 8, 92 men left Fort Selkirk for southern Canada. On October 11, the Boer War broke out in South Africa and Canada committed itself on the same day to raising a 1,000-strong contingent for service in the war. Most of the Field Force soldiers coming out of the territory joined this force, as did their commander.

The remaining element of the Field Force shifted headquarters to **Dawson** and was renamed the Yukon Garrison. It continued to provide a military presence that was widely considered unnecessary for another seven months. Fort

Selkirk was entirely abandoned in May 1900 and on June 25, 1900 the rest of the force, save one man, was ordered home. The man who remained behind was a prisoner of the Mounties who had been arrested, and ultimately convicted of murder. He was hanged on August 23, 1901 at the Dawson Police Barracks. Four other members of the Field Force died while serving in the Yukon. Each, as well as Lieutenant-Colonel Evans, would have a minor Yukon mountain peak named in his honour. This was even true of Jerry Corcoran, who succumbed to alcohol poisoning at Fort Selkirk.

Did the Field Force serve any useful purpose at all during its short time in the Yukon? This is a question that is seldom debated because, unlike the NWMP force that established the Canadian presence in southern Alberta, the force has been largely forgotten. Certainly its presence did reinforce the fact that the Yukon was a Canadian jurisdiction and might have helped the NWMP to enforce law and order.

Yukon Quest

Considered the world's toughest dog sled race, the Yukon Quest is a 1,600-kilometre journey between **Whitehorse** and Fairbanks, Alaska. Run in early February, temperatures vary from $-62°$ to $0°$ Celsius. The race follows a trail through some of North America's most sparsely populated and wilderness regions. It takes between 10 and 14 days to complete, depending on trail and weather conditions.

The trail roughly encompasses the historic routes that two distinct groups of goldseekers followed en route to the **Klondike Gold Rush**, with the midpoint at the stampeders' destination of **Dawson**. The Whitehorse to Dawson leg reflects the route followed by those who reached the Yukon **gold** fields via the Chilkoot Trail or White Pass, while the Dawson to Fairbanks portion follows the "rich man's route" of the **Trails of '98** from the **Yukon River** mouth to Dawson.

On even-numbered years, the race starts in Fairbanks. Odd-numbered years, it begins in Whitehorse. An exception, however, was made in 1998 to allow the race to begin in Whitehorse as part of the ceremonies commemorating the 100th anniversary of the 1898 Klondike Gold Rush.

Limited to 50 teams, mushers come from around the world to compete for a cash pool of $125,000 U.S., with a first prize of $30,000. The first 15 finishers all get a graduated share of the pot. Besides teams from Canada and the

A Yukon Quest musher follows a low ridgeline during the world's toughest dog sled race.
(Erik Simanis photo)

United States, each year's entrants usually include teams from France, Switzerland, Germany, Finland, Scotland, and Japan.

While the mushers come from all walks of life—ranging from trappers to dentists—all competitors share a dedication to **dog sledding**. Each musher has a team numbering 14 dogs that are expensive to keep and require rigorous year-round daily training. Most teams begin training in earnest in August, using wheeled versions of sleds until they can begin training with sleds on snow. The majority of dogs used in the race are malamutes, Siberians, or husky/shepherd crosses.

Compared to other races, including the famous 1,707-kilometre Iditarod race from Anchorage to Nome, Alaska, the Yukon Quest presents challenges that have earned it the reputation as the hardest race of all. This is primarily because of the terrain covered, the variable weather conditions, and the lack of support and assistance available because of the isolation over most of the route. The other factor is the limited number of dogs that are allowed to participate on each team. While this enables smaller kennel owners to compete, it also ensures that each dog entered has to have a high degree of stamina and be in peak health to complete the race.

Teams are allowed to start the race with no more than 14 dogs and a minimum of 8 dogs. Whatever number they start with, they cannot add dogs along the way and must complete the race with no fewer than 6 dogs. All dogs starting with a team must be on the towline or in the sled; none are allowed to be led behind the sled. This strictly limits the ability of the musher to alternate dogs to let the animals have a rest. Only one musher is permitted and no substitutions are allowed once the race is underway.

The race begins as teams cross the start line at two-minute intervals. The team with the fastest time clocked between starting and crossing the finishing line wins. Each team is required to take a 36-hour mandatory layover in Dawson to rest the dogs and the musher. This time is not included in the timing of the race.

Every team must carry cold-weather camping and survival gear. Food caches are left at designated checkpoints and picked up en route. The race generally passes through only seven communities along the way: **Carmacks**, **Pelly Crossing**, Dawson, and, in Alaska, Eagle, Circle City, Central, and Angel Creek.

Before the beginning of the race the trail is broken and set. Weather conditions, however, often result in long sections of the trail being covered in deep snow by the time the racers reach it. In some years, sections may experience melting and occasionally teams have had to drag their sleds over stretches of gravel, slowing the race to a crawl. On average, teams complete the race in about 12 days. In 1998, for example, the winner crossed the finish line with a time of 11 days, 11 hours, and 27 minutes.

Yukon River

The fifth-longest river in North America, the Yukon River runs for 3,185 kilometres from its headwaters in Tagish Lake on the British Columbia–Yukon border north and northwest across the territory to follow a great westward arc through Alaska to its mouth in Norton Sound on the Bering Sea. In the Yukon it drains 264,000 square kilometres of land, but overall the river's drainage areas is 800,000 square kilometres. Of its entire length, 1,149 kilometres lie within

Canada, with all but the immediate headwaters portion at Tagish Lake falling inside the Yukon.

Five major Yukon tributaries, draining the majority of the territory, feed the river. Rising in Teslin Lake and joining the Yukon north of **Lake Laberge** after a 393-kilometre run, Teslin River is the closest major river to the Yukon's headwaters. Next comes the 608-kilometre-long Pelly River, with its headwaters in the **Selwyn Mountains** to the east. Pelly River joins the Yukon at **Fort Selkirk** due west of **Pelly Crossing** on the **Alaska Highway**. The 320-kilometre-long White River drains the great glacial icefields of the **St. Elias Mountains** in the southwest corner of the territory and flows into the Yukon along the eastern flank of the Dawson Range not far from the historic site of Stewart. Finally, the Yukon's flow within the territory is increased by waters running out of 644-kilometre-long Stewart River, which has its headwaters in the mountainous country beyond the mining region of **Mayo** and **Keno**. In Alaska, the Yukon picks up the waters of the Porcupine River. With headwaters in Yukon's **Richardson Mountains**, the Porcupine is 721 kilometres long and drains a large portion of northern Yukon, including **Eagle Plain** and most of the **Ogilvie Mountains**. The only major rivers in the territory that fail to drain into the Yukon River are the Peel and Liard rivers. The Peel River drains a plateau region in northeastern Yukon and flows eastward to join the Mackenzie River in the Northwest Territory. Liard River catches the water found in a lower-lying plain in the southeast and then also runs east to the Mackenzie. In all, about 75 percent of Yukon Territory is ultimately drained into the Yukon River.

For most of its northwestward journey through the Yukon, the river is confined to a single dominant channel funnelled effectively by a bottom of hard, glacially carved metamorphic rock. It is a slow-moving river and, except during spring runoff, is relatively shallow. The gradient is quite even throughout, meaning that rapids are few and far between. The worst rapids at **Miles Canyon**, which posed a life-threatening risk to **gold** stampeders en route to the **Klondike Gold Rush** have been drowned by the Whitehorse Dam hydroelectric project (*see* **Whitehorse Fishway**). When the river is joined by the White River, it takes on a muddy colour and picks up a heavy load of silt due to the glacial flow. From this point to **Dawson**, the river is sprinkled with wooded islands and is bordered by mountains. This is the most scenic stretch of the river's Yukon run and is popular with canoeists and other boaters seeking an easy, almost lazy river drift. Beyond Dawson, the valley narrows before entering Alaska and widening

This view of the Yukon River just below Dawson captures the essential placidness and wilderness setting of North America's fifth-longest river. (Yukon Archives, Vogee Collection, #271)

into a broad interior plateau known as the Yukon Flats. On the flats, the river breaks into a maze of channels that meander through a vast area of swamps and small lakes. It is in the Yukon Flats that the Porcupine joins up with the Yukon River. Swollen by the Porcupine's additional waters, the Yukon finally enters a steep-sided valley, known as the Ramparts, which is never more than five kilometres wide, and runs until it picks up its largest tributary—the 645-kilometre-long Tanana River—in another broad lowland. From here, the Yukon divides into several channels before finally entering a delta area and flowing into the Bering Sea.

The Yukon River provided a primary migration route for North America's first humans travelling through **Beringia**. Later, **First Nations peoples**, mostly Athapaskans, maintained migratory hunting and subsistence lives focused on the river and its tributaries. The name Yukon derives from the Kutchin Athapaskan peoples, who knew the river as *Yu-kun-ah,* or "great river." When

Hudson's Bay Company (HBC) trader John Bell descended the Porcupine River to its junction in 1846 he bastardized the Kutchin name to Youcon.

Bell was not the first European to assign a First Nations' phrase for "great river" to this major waterway. Russian Navy first mate Andrei Glazunov opened the Alaskan portion of the Yukon River to the **fur trade** in a 104-day trip along the river in 1833–34 and named it *Kwikhpak,* which was Aleut Inuit for great river. The First Nations of the Tanana had always known it as *Niga-to,* which had the same meaning.

The Russians maintained fur-trading operations on the lower reaches of the Yukon from the early 1830s to about 1845 before abandoning the Yukon River trading post. An epidemic of smallpox that devastated local First Nations proved the Russians' undoing. Blamed with deliberately introducing the disease, several Russian traders were killed.

Meanwhile, far to the east, the Hudson's Bay Company was making forays into the Yukon region in an attempt to establish a trading foothold and to reach the Pacific Ocean by an inland route. HBC governor Sir George Simpson was convinced the Pelly River flowed into the Pacific at Cook's Inlet and ordered trader and explorer Robert Campbell to verify his belief. In 1848, Campbell descended the Pelly to its junction with the Yukon. He decided to name the upper portion of this new river Lewes and to consider that the lower portion was a continuation of the less mighty Pelly River (perhaps to continue humouring Simpson in his belief that the Pelly was the key to reaching the Pacific). The decision was a curious one because Campbell was already convinced that he had happened across the upper reaches of the Yukon River.

In 1847, Alexander Hunter Murray had established the first HBC trading post on the river. This was named Fort Yukon and was built in present-day Alaska where the Porcupine joins the Yukon. The HBC traders remained uncertain whether the lower reaches of what Campbell called the Pelly and the upper reaches of what Bell had named the Yukon were actually the same river. Campbell was increasingly certain they were. Murray, drawing on reports from First Nations peoples trading at his fort, also believed both rivers were one and the same. Simpson, meanwhile, remained unconvinced that the "lower Pelly" was in reality the Yukon. He believed this river was too far south to be the Yukon, which he maintained must drain into the Arctic rather than the Pacific. To resolve the issue, however, Simpson ordered Campbell to explore as much of this mysterious river as he could. On June 4, 1851, Campbell set out in a canoe from **Fort Selkirk**. He soon passed the White and Stewart rivers and named them after HBC colleagues. Only four days into his journey, Campbell reached Fort Yukon and settled the question.

HBC traders continued to explore the Yukon from one end to the other. The Yukon was the last major North American river to be explored by Europeans. With the discovery of gold at Bonanza Creek in 1896 and the beginning of the Klondike Gold Rush, the river became a vital conduit for thousands of prospectors. Because all of the river from **Whitehorse** to its mouth is navigable, the Yukon soon was heavily travelled by **sternwheelers** carrying freight and passengers to the gold fields. During the peak years from 1897 to 1900, some 135 steamers, tugs, barges, and launches operated on the river. Without the presence of the Yukon River it is doubtful that the gold rush at Dawson would have been as big or as rapidly developed.

For the next 50 years, the river would remain an important communication and supply route through the heart of the territory. But with construction of the Alaska Highway during World War II, motor vehicle traffic began displacing the riverboats. The last one sailed with freight and passengers in 1957.

Since then, the Yukon River has returned to a more wild state. Except in the immediate vicinity of Whitehorse and Dawson, few roads access the river's shores and many sternwheeler refuelling stations and former HBC trading post sites have been abandoned because their only access was by boat.

Yukon's Name

The Yukon derives its territorial name from the great river that flows through its heart, draining more than 75 percent of its landscape. Until recently, when various highways superseded the river's importance, for as long as humans have dwelled in the region, this river provided the primary transportation route.

The Kutchin (sometimes grouped with and referred to as Loucheux) Athapaskan peoples called it *Yu-kun-ah*, which meant "great river." Hudson's Bay Company trader John Bell bastardized the name to Youcon in 1846 and this was later changed to the present spelling. The name was first applied to a trading fort at the junction of the Yukon and Porcupine rivers, then to all of the **Yukon River**, and soon after to the territorial land itself.

For many years a small debate has gone on in the Yukon over whether Yukon should be preceded by "the." There seems to be no definitive answer to this conundrum and both "Yukon Territory" and "the Yukon Territory" are often used interchangeably, although some Yukoners are passionately in favour of one usage over the other. The territorial and federal governments mostly use "the Yukon Territory," but even here there is inconsistency. Some Yukon sourdoughs maintain that only cheechakos would put "the" before Yukon, but no set pattern of use based on time spent in the north has emerged. The debate, however, is certain to continue.

Other Books by Mark Zuehlke

For Adults

The Alberta Fact Book

The B.C. Fact Book

The Gallant Cause: Canadians in the Spanish Civil War,
1936–1939

Scoundrels, Dreamers & Second Sons: British Remittance Men
in the Canadian West

The Vancouver Island South Explorer: The Outdoor Guide

Magazine Writing from the Boonies (co-author Louise Donnelly)

For Children

Fun B.C. Facts For Kids

About the Author

Frances Backhouse

Mark Zuehlke is the author of numerous books. *The Yukon Fact Book* is the fourth in a series including *The B.C. Fact Book*, *The Alberta Fact Book*, and *Fun B.C. Facts for Kids*. Two of his books, *The Gallant Cause: Canadians in the Spanish Civil War, 1936–1939* and *Scoundrels, Dreamers & Second Sons: British Remittance Men in the Canadian West*, were Book-of-the-Month Club selections. Mark is particularly interested in making historical subjects accessible to readers. He lives in Victoria, B.C.